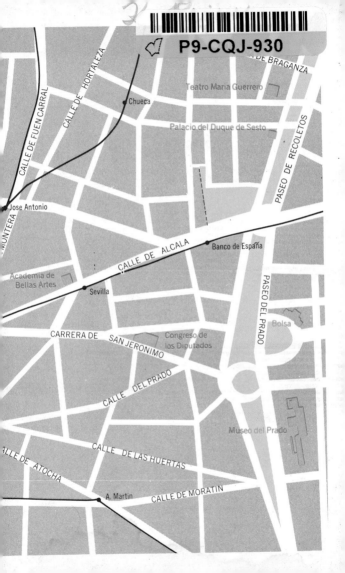

SPANISH
AT A GLANCE

PHRASE BOOK & DICTIONARY FOR TRAVELERS

SPANISH
AT A GLANCE

PHRASE BOOK & DICTIONARY FOR TRAVELERS

BY HEYWOOD WALD, Ph.D.
Chairman, Department of Foreign Languages
Martin Van Buren High School
New York

BARRON'S

BARRON'S EDUCATIONAL SERIES, INC.
New York ■ London ■ Toronto ■ Sydney

Cover and Book Design   Milton Glaser, Inc.
Illustrations   Juan Suarez

© Copyright 1984 by Barron's Educational Series, Inc.

All inquiries should be addressed to:
Barron's Educational Series, Inc.
250 Wireless Boulevard
Hauppauge, New York 11788

Library of Congress Catalog Card No. 84-2782

Paper Edition
International Standard Book No. 0-8120-2711-6

Library of Congress Cataloging in Publication Data
Wald, Heywood.
   Spanish at a glance.
   Includes index.
   1. Spanish language — Conversation and phrase
books — English. I. Title.
PC4121.W28   1984   468.3*421   84-2782
ISBN 0-8120-2711-6 (pbk.)

PRINTED IN UNITED STATES OF AMERICA
90   880   17 16 15 14 13

CONTENTS

PREFACE

So you're taking a trip to one of the many fascinating countries of the world. That's exciting! In more ways than one, this new phrase book will prove an invaluable companion that will make your stay more interesting and truly unforgettable.

This phrase book is part of a new series being launched by Barron's Educational Series, Inc. In these books we present the phrases and words that a traveler most often needs for a brief visit to a foreign country, where the customs and language are often different. Each of the phrase books highlights the terms particular to that country, in situations that the tourist is most likely to encounter. With a specially developed key to pronunciation, this book will enable you to communicate quickly and confidently in colloquial terms. It is intended not only for beginners with no knowledge of the language, but also for those who have already studied it and have some familiarity with it.

Some of the unique features and highlights of the Barron's series are:

Easy-to-follow *pronunciation keys* and complete phonetic transcriptions for all words and phrases in the book.

Compact *dictionary* of commonly used words and phrases—built right into this phrase book so there's no need to carry a separate dictionary.

Useful phrases for the *tourist*, grouped together by subject matter in a logical way so that the appropriate phrase is easy to locate when you need it.

Special phrases for the *business traveler*, including banking terms, trade and contract negotiations, and secretarial services.

Thorough section on *food and drink*, with comprehensive food terms you will find on menus; these terms are often difficult or impossible to locate in dictionaries, but our section gives you a description of the preparation as well as a definition of what it is.

Emergency phrases and terms you hope you won't need: legal complications, medical problems, theft or loss of valuables, replacement or repair of watches, camera, and the like.

■ *Sightseeing itineraries*, shopping tips, practical travel tips, and regional food specialties to help you get off the beaten path and into the countryside, to the small towns and cities, and to the neighboring areas.

■ A *reference section* providing: important signs, conversion tables, holidays, abbreviations, telling time, days of week and months of year.

■ A brief *grammar section*, with the basic elements of the language quickly explained.

Enjoy your vacation and travel with confidence. You have a friend by your side.

ACKNOWLEDGMENTS

We would like to thank the following individuals and organizations for their assistance on this project: Patricia Brooks, author, *Fisher's Guide to Spain and Portugal*; René Campos, Director, Spanish Institute, New York, New York; Mercedes Garcia-Rodriguez, Spanish Institute, New York, New York; George Lang, George Lang, Inc., New York, New York; Professor Robert Piluso, SUC New Paltz, New York; Professor Henry Urbanski, chairman, Department of Foreign Languages, SUC New Paltz, New York; Pilar Vico, Spanish National Tourist Office, New York, New York; Professor Lynn Winget, Wichita State University, Kansas; Herta Erville; Fernando Pfannl; Alfonso Hernández.

Also the Association of American Travel Writers, New York *Times*, *Signature* magazine, the Spanish Institute, the Spanish National Tourist Office, *Travel-Holiday* magazine, *Travel and Leisure* magazine, U.S. Tour Operators, and the U.S. Travel Data Center.

QUICK PRONUNCIATION GUIDE

Although all the phrases in this book are presented with an easy-to-use key to pronunciation, you will find speaking Spanish quite a bit easier if you learn a few simple rules. Many letters in Spanish are pronounced approximately as they would be in English. There are some differences, however, which are given below. Since these sounds rarely vary, you can follow these guidelines in pronouncing all Spanish words.

Spanish contains three additional letters not found in English: *ch, ll,* and *ñ.* All letters are pronounced, with the exception of *h;* the letters *v* and *b* are most often both pronounced like the English *b.* Words ending in a vowel, an *n,* or an *s* are stressed on the next-to-last syllable—**casa** *(KAH-sah).* Words ending in a consonant (other than *n* or *s*) are stressed on the last syllable—**general** *(hehn-eh-RAHL).* A written accent is required on any words which break either of these rules—**lápiz** *(LAH-pees).*

NOTE: When pronouncing the words in the following examples, stress the vowels that appear in CAPITAL letters.

SPANISH LETTER(S)	SOUND IN ENGLISH	EXAMPLES
	VOWELS	
a	ah (y<u>a</u>cht)	taco *(TAH-koh)*
e	ay (d<u>a</u>y)	mesa *(MAY-sah)*
	eh (p<u>e</u>t)	perro *(PEH-roh)*
i	ee (m<u>ee</u>t)	libro *(LEE-broh)*
o	oh (<u>o</u>pen)	foto *(FOH-toh)*
u	oo (t<u>oo</u>th)	mucho *(MOO-choh)*
	COMMON VOWEL COMBINATIONS (DIPHTHONGS)	
au	ow (c<u>ow</u>)	causa *(COW-sah)*
		auto *(OW-toh)*

SPANISH LETTER(S)	SOUND IN ENGLISH	EXAMPLES
ei	ay (d<u>ay</u>)	aceite *(ah-SAY-tay)*
ai	y (t<u>y</u>pe)	baile *(BY-lay)*
ie	yeh (y<u>e</u>t)	abierto *(ah-BYEHR-toh)*
ue	weh (w<u>e</u>t)	bueno *(BWEH-noh)*

CONSONANTS

c (before *a, o, u*)	hard k sound (<u>c</u>at)	campo *(KAHM-poh)* cosa *(KOH-sah)* Cuba *(KOO-bah)*
c (before *e, i*)	soft s sound (<u>c</u>ent)	central *(sehn-TRAHL)* cinco *(SEEN-koh)*
cc	hard and soft cc (ks sound) (a<u>cc</u>ept)	acción *(ahk-see-OHN)*
ch	hard ch sound (<u>ch</u>air)	muchacho *(moo-CHAH-choh)*
g (before *a, o, u*)	hard g (<u>g</u>o)	gafas *(GAH-fahs)* goma *(GOH-mah)*
g (before *e, i*)	breathy h (<u>h</u>ot)	general *(hehn-eh-RAHL)*
h	always silent	hasta *(AHS-tah)*
j	breathy as in h sound (<u>h</u>ot)	José *(ho-SAY)*
l	English l sound (<u>l</u>amp)	lámpara *(LAHM-pahr-ah)*
ll	as in English y (<u>y</u>es)	pollo *(POH-yoh)*
n	English n (<u>n</u>o)	naranja *(nah-RAHN-ha)*
ñ	English ny (can-<u>y</u>on)	señorita *(seh-nyoh-REE-tah)*
qu	English k (<u>k</u>eep)	que *(kay)*
r	trilled once	caro *(KAH-roh)*
rr (or r at beginning of word)	trilled strongly (operator saying three)	rico *(RREE-koh)* perro *(PEH-rroh)*
s	English s (<u>s</u>ee)	rosa *(ROH-sah)*

SPANISH LETTER(S)	SOUND IN ENGLISH	EXAMPLES
v	Approximately as in English b (<u>b</u>ook)	primavera (pree-mah-BEHR-ah)
x	English s, ks (<u>s</u>ign, so<u>cks</u>)	extra (ES-trah) examinar (ek-sah-mee-NAHR)
y	English y (<u>y</u>es) (by itself y = i)	yo (yoh) y (ee)
z	English s	zapato (sah-PAH-toh)

The above pronunciations apply to the Spanish that is spoken in Central and South America, and that is also spoken in parts of southern Spain. The remaining areas of Spain use the Castilian pronunciation, which differs mostly in the sound of the letters *ll* and of the *z* and the *c* before *e* and *i*. For example, the Castilian pronunciations are as follows:

SPANISH LETTER(S)	SOUND IN ENGLISH	EXAMPLES
ll	ly sound as in million	llamo (LYAH-moh)
c (before *e* or *i*) ⎱ z ⎰	a <u>th</u> sound instead of an <u>s</u> sound	gracias (GRAH-thee-ahs) lápiz (LAH-peeth)

THE BASICS FOR GETTING BY

MOST FREQUENTLY USED EXPRESSIONS

The following are expressions you'll use over and over—the fundamentals of polite conversation, the way to express what you want or need, and some simple question tags which you can use to construct all sorts of questions. We suggest you become very familiar with these phrases.

Hello!	**¡Hola!**	*OH-lah*
Yes	**Sí**	*see*
No	**No**	*noh*
Maybe	**Quizás**	*kee-SAHS*
Please	**Por favor**	*pohr-fah-BOHR*
Thank you (very much)	**(Muchas) gracias**	*(MOO-chahs) GRAH-see-ahs*
You're welcome	**De nada**	*day-NAH-dah*
Excuse me		
(having disturbed or bumped into someone)	**Perdón**	*pehr-DOHN*
(leaving a group or walking in front of a person)	**con permiso**	*kohn pehr-MEE-soh*
(getting one's attention)	**por favor**	*pohr fah-BOHR*
I'm sorry	**Lo siento**	*loh see-EHN-toh*
Just a second	**Un momento**	*oon moh-MEN-toh*
That's all right, okay	**Está bien**	*eh-STAH bee-ehn*

It doesn't matter	**No importa**	*noh eem-PORT-ah*
Good morning	**Buenos días**	*bway-nohs DEE-ahs*
Good afternoon	**Buenas tardes**	*bway-nahs TAHR-dehs*
Good evening (night)	**Buenas noches**	*bway-nahs NOH-chehs*
Sir	**Señor**	*seh-NYOHR*
Madame	**Señora**	*seh-NYOHR-ah*
Miss	**Señorita**	*seh-nyohr-EE-tah*
Good-bye	**Adiós**	*ah-DYOHS*
See you later (so long)	**Hasta la vista (hasta luego)**	*AH-stah lah BEE-stah (AH-stah loo-AY-goh)*
See you tomorrow	**Hasta mañana**	*AH-stah mah-NYAH-nah*

COMMUNICATIONS

Do you speak English?	**¿Habla usted inglés?** *ah-blah oos-TEHD een-GLAYS*
I speak (a little) Spanish.	**Hablo español (un poco).** *AH-bloh ehs-pah-NYOHL (oon POH-koh)*
I don't speak Spanish.	**No hablo español.** *noh AH-bloh ehs-pah-NYOHL*
Is there anyone here who speaks English?	**¿Hay alguien aquí que hable inglés?** *AH-ee AHL-ghee-EHN ah-KEE kay AH-blay een-GLAYS*
Do you understand?	**¿Comprende usted?** *kohm-PREHN-day oos-tehd*
I understand.	**Yo comprendo.** *yoh kohm-PREHN-doh*
I don't understand.	**No comprendo.** *noh kohm-PREHN-doh*

What does this mean?	**¿Qué quiere decir ésto?** *kay kee-YEH-ray day-SEER ehs-toh*
What? What did you say?	**¿Cómo?** *KOH-moh*
How do you say ____ in Spanish?	**¿Cómo se dice ____ en español?** *KOH-moh say DEE-say ____ ehn ehs-pah-NYOHL*
What do you call this (that) in Spanish?	**¿Cómo se llama esto (eso) en español?** *KOH-moh say YAH-mah EHS-toh (EHS-oh) ehn ehs-pahn-YOHL*
Please speak slowly.	**Hable despacio, por favor.** *AH-blay dehs-PAH-see-oh pohr fah-BOHR*
Please repeat.	**Repita, por favor.** *ray-PEE-tah pohr fah-BOHR*

INTRODUCTIONS

I'm American (English) (Australian) (Canadian).	**Soy norteamericano(a), (inglés, inglesa), (australiano, australiana), (canadiense).** *soy nohr-tay-ah-mehr-ee-KAH-noh (nah), (een-GLAYS, een-GLAY-sah), (ow-strahl-YAH- noh, nah), (kah-nah-DYEHN-say)*
My name is ____.	**Me llamo ____.** *may YAH-moh*
What's your name?	**¿Cómo se llama usted?** *KOH-moh say YAH-mah oos-TEHD*
How are you?	**¿Cómo está usted?** *KOH-moh ehs-TAH oos-TEHD*
How's everything?	**¿Qué tal?** *kay tahl*
Very well, thanks. And you?	**Muy bien, gracias. ¿Y usted?** *mwee bee-EHN GRAH-see-ahs ee oos-TEHD*

GETTING AROUND

Where is ____?	**¿Dónde está ____?** *DOHN-day ehs-TAH*

the bathroom	**el baño** *ehl BAH-nyoh*
▪ the dining room	**el comedor** *ehl koh-meh-DOHR*
▪ the entrance	**la entrada** *lah ehn-TRAH-dah*
▪ the exit	**la salida** *lah sahl-EE-dah*
▪ the telephone	**el teléfono** *ehl tehl-EHF-oh-noh*
I'm lost.	**Me he perdido.** *may heh pehr-DEE-doh*
We're lost.	**Nos hemos perdido.** *nohs HEH-mohs pehr-DEE-doh*
Where are ____?	**¿Dónde están ____?** *dohn-day ehs-TAHN*
I am looking for ____.	**Busco ____.** *BOOS-koh*
▪ to the left	**a la izquierda** *ah lah ees-kee-EHR-dah*
▪ to the right	**a la derecha** *ah lah dehr-EH-chah*
▪ straight ahead	**derecho** *deh-REH-choh*

SHOPPING

How much is it?	**¿Cuánto es?** *KWAHN-toh ehs*
	¿Cuánto vale? *KWAHN-toh BAH-lay*
I'd like ____.	**Quisiera ____.** *kee-see-YEHR-ah*
Please bring me ____.	**Tráigame, por favor ____.** *TRAH-ee-gah-may pohr fah-BOHR*
Please show me ____.	**Muéstreme, por favor ____.** *MWEHS-treh-may pohr fah-BOHR*
Here it is.	**Aquí está.** *ah-KEE eh-STAH*

MISCELLANEOUS

I'm hungry.	**Tengo hambre.** *TEHN-goh-AHM-bray*
I'm thirsty.	**Tengo sed.** *tehn-goh SEHD*

I'm tired.	**Estoy cansado (m.) Estoy cansada (f.)** *eh-stoy kahn-SAH-doh (dah)*
What's that?	**¿Qué es eso?** *kay ehs EHS-oh*
What's up?	**¿Qué hay?** *kay AH-ee*
I (don't) know.	**Yo (no) sé.** *yoh (noh) say*

QUESTIONS

Where is (are) _____?	**¿Dónde está (están) _____?**	*DOHN-day eh-STAH (STAHN)*
When?	**¿Cuándo?**	*KWAHN-doh*
How?	**¿Cómo?**	*KOH-moh*
How much?	**¿Cuánto?**	*KWAHN-toh*
Who?	**¿Quién?**	*key-EN*
Why?	**¿Por qué?**	*pohr-KAY*
Which?	**¿Cuál?**	*kwal*
What?	**¿Qué?**	*kay*

EXCLAMATIONS, SLANG, COLLOQUIALISMS

Ouch!	**¡Ay!**	*AH-ee*
Wow! Gosh! (expressing surprise) or Darn it! (expressing annoyance)	**¡Caramba! ¡Caray!**	*kah-RAHM-bah kah-RAH-ee*
How pretty!	**¡Qué bonito! (m.)**	*kay boh-NEE-toh*
	¡Qué bonita! (f.)	*kay boh-NEE-tah*
Ugh!	**¡Uf!**	*oof*
Phew!	**¡Huy!**	*OO-ee*

That's awful!	¡Es horrible!	*ehs ohr-EE-blay*
Great! Wonderful!	¡Estupendo! ¡Magnífico! ¡Fenomenal!	*ehs-too-PEHN-doh* *mahg-NEE-fee-koh;* *feh-noh-meh-NAHL*
That's it!	¡Eso es!	*ehs-oh EHS*
My goodness!	¡Dios mío!	*dyohs MEE-oh*
Good Heavens!	¡Cielos!	*see-YEH-lohs*
Bottoms up, cheers.	¡Salud!	*sah-LOOD*
Quiet!	¡Silencio!	*see-LEHN-see-oh*
Shut up!	¡Cállese!	*KAH-yeh-say*
That's enough!	¡Basta!	*BAHS-tah*
Never mind!	¡No importa!	*noh eem-POHR-tah*
Of course!	¡Claro!	*KLAH-roh*
With pleasure.	¡Con mucho gus-to!	*kohn MOO-choh GOOS-toh*
Let's go!	¡Vamos!	*BAH-mohs*
What a shame (pity)!	¡Que lástima!	*kay LAH-stee-mah*
What a nuisance! (showing annoyance)	¡Qué lata!	*kay LAH-tah*
Nonsense! No way!	¡Qué va!	*kay bah*
Don't be stupid!	¡No sea tonto!	*noh say-ah TOHN-toh*
Are you crazy?	¡Está loco?	*eh-stah LOH-koh*
What a fool!	¡Qué idiota!	*kay ee-dee-OH-tah*
Good luck!	¡(Buena) suerte!	*bweh-nah SWEHR-tay*

PROBLEMS, PROBLEMS, PROBLEMS
(EMERGENCIES)

Watch out!	**¡Cuidado!**	*kwee-DAH-doh*
Hurry up!	**¡Dése prisa!**	*day-say PREE-sah*
Look!	**¡Mire!**	*MEE-reh*
Listen!	**¡Escuche!**	*ehs-KOO-cheh*
Wait!	**¡Espere!**	*ehs-PEHR-eh*
Fire!	**¡Fuego!**	*FWAY-goh*

ANNOYANCES

What's the matter with you?	**¿Qué le pasa?**	*kay lay PAH-sah*
What (the devil) do you want?	**¿Qué (diablos) quiere usted?**	*kay (dee-AH-blohs) kee-EHR-eh oos-TEHD*
Stop bothering me!	**¡No me moleste más!**	*noh meh moh-LEHS-tay mahs*
Go away!	**¡Váyase!**	*BAH-yah-say*
Scram! Beat it!	**¡Lárguese!**	*LAHR-gay-say*
Leave me alone!	**¡Déjeme en paz!**	*DAY-heh-meh ehn PAHS*
Help, police!	**¡Socorro, policía!**	*soh-KOH-roh poh-lee-SEE-yah*
I'm going to call a cop!	**¡Voy a llamar a un policía!**	*boy ah yah-MAHR ah oon pohl-ee-SEE-yah*
Get out!	**¡Fuera!**	*FWEHR-ah*
That guy is a thief!	**¡Ese tipo es un ladrón!**	*ehs-eh tee-poh ehs oon lah-DROHN*
He has stolen ____.	**Me ha robado ____.**	*may ah roh-BAH-doh*
I have lost ____.	**He perdido ____.**	*ay pehr-DEE-doh*

■ my car	**el coche** *ehl KOH-chay*
■ my passport	**el pasaporte** *ehl pah-sah-POHR-tay*
■ my purse	**la bolsa** *lah BOHL-sah*
■ my suitcase	**la maleta** *lah mahl-EH-tah*
■ my wallet	**la cartera** *lah kahr-TEHR-ah*
■ my watch	**el reloj** *ehl ray-LOH*
This young man is annoying me.	**Este joven me está molestando.** *ehs-teh HOH-behn may ehs-TAH moh-lehs-TAHN-doh*
He keeps following me.	**Me está siguiendo.** *may ehs-TAH see-ghee-YEHN-doh*
Stop that boy!	**¡Paren a ese muchacho!** *PAH-rehn ah ehs-eh moo-CHAH-choh*

COMPLICATIONS

I haven't done anything.	**Yo no he hecho nada.** *yoh noh eh EH-choh NAH-dah*

It's a lie!	**¡Es mentira!** *ehs mehn-TEE-rah*
It's not true.	**No es verdad.** *noh ehs behr-DAHD*
I'm innocent.	**Soy inocente.** *soy een-oh-SEHN-teh*
I want a lawyer.	**Quiero un abogado.** *kee-YEHR-oh oon ah-boh-GAH-doh*
I want to go _____.	**Quiero ir _____.** *kee-YEHR-oh eer*
■ to the American (British) (Australian) (Canadian) Consulate	**al consulado norteamericano, inglés, australiano, canadiense** *ahl kohn-soo-LAH-doh nohr-tay-ah-mehr-ee-KAH-noh, een-GLAYS, ow-strahl-YAH-noh. kah-nah-DYEHN-say*
■ to the police station	**al cuartel de policía** *ahl kwahr-TEHL day poh-lee-SEE-ah*
I need help, quick.	**Necesito ayuda, pronto.** *nehs-ehs-EE-toh ah-YOO-dah PROHN-toh*
Can you help me, please?	**¿Puede usted ayudarme, por favor?** *pweh-day oos-TEHD ah-yoo-DAHR-may pohr fah-BOHR*

Does anyone here speak English?	**¿Hay alguien aquí que hable inglés?** *AH-ee AHL-ghee-yehn ah-KEE kay AH-blay een-GLEHS*	
I need an interpreter.	**Necesito un intérprete.** *neh-seh-SEE-toh oon een-TEHR-preh-tay*	

NUMBERS

You will use numbers the moment you land, whether it be to exchange money at the airport, purchase a bus ticket for a ride into town, or describe the length of your stay to a customs official. We list here first the cardinal numbers, then follow with ordinal numbers, fractions, and other useful numbers.

CARDINAL NUMBERS

0	**cero**	*SEHR-oh*
1	**uno**	*OO-noh*
2	**dos**	*dohs*
3	**tres**	*trehs*
4	**cuatro**	*KWAH-troh*
5	**cinco**	*SEEN-koh*
6	**seis**	*sayss*
7	**siete**	*SYEH-tay*
8	**ocho**	*OH-choh*
9	**nueve**	*NWEH-bay*
10	**diez**	*dyess*
11	**once**	*OHN-say*
12	**doce**	*DOH-say*
13	**trece**	*TREH-say*
14	**catorce**	*kah-TOHR-say*
15	**quince**	*KEEN-say*

16	**diez y seis (die-cipéis)**	*dyeh-see-SAYSS*
17	**diez y siete (die-cisiete)**	*dyeh-see-SYEH-tay*
18	**diez y ocho (di-eciocho)**	*dyeh-see-OH-choh*
19	**diez y nueve (diecinueve)**	*dyeh-see-NWEH-bay*
20	**veinte**	*BAYN-tay*
21	**veintiuno**	*bayn-tee-OO-noh*
22	**veintidós**	*bayn-tee-DOHS*
23	**veintitrés**	*bayn-tee-TREHS*
24	**veinticuatro**	*bayn-tee-KWAH-troh*
25	**veinticinco**	*bayn-tee-SEEN-koh*
26	**veintiséis**	*bayn-tee-SAYSS*
27	**veintisiete**	*bayn-tee-SYEH-tay*
28	**veintiocho**	*bayn-tee-OH-choh*
29	**veintinueve**	*bayn-tee-NWEH-bay*
30	**treinta**	*TRAYN-tah*
40	**cuarenta**	*kwahr-EHN-tah*
50	**cincuenta**	*seen-KWEHN-tah*
60	**sesenta**	*seh-SEHN-tah*
70	**setenta**	*seh-TEHN-tah*
80	**ochenta**	*oh-CHEHN-tah*
90	**noventa**	*noh-BEHN-tah*
100	**cien(to)**	*syehn(toh)*
101	**ciento uno**	*SYEHN-toh OO-noh*

102	**ciento dos**	*SYEHN-toh DOHS*
200	**doscientos (as)**	*dohs-SYEHN-tohs (tahs)*
300	**trescientos (as)**	*trehs-SYEHN-tohs (tahs)*
400	**cuatrocientos (as)**	*kwah-troh-SYEHN-tohs (tahs)*
500	**quinientos (as)**	*kee-NYEHN-tohs (tahs)*
600	**seiscientos (as)**	*sayss-SYEHN-tohs (tahs)*
700	**setecientos (as)**	*seh-teh-SYEHN-tohs (tahs)*
800	**ochocientos (as)**	*oh-choh-SYEHN-tohs (tahs)*
900	**novecientos (as)**	*noh-beh-SYEHN-tohs (tahs)*
1.000	**mil**	*meel*
2.000	**dos mil**	*dohs meel*
1.000.000	**un millón**	*oon mee-YOHN*
2.000.000	**dos millones**	*dohs mee-YOHN-ays*

ORDINAL NUMBERS

1°	**primero (primer, -a)**	*pree-MEH-roh (rah)*
2°	**segundo (a)**	*seh-GOON-doh (dah)*
3°	**tercero (tercer, -a)**	*tehr-SEH-roh (rah)*
4°	**cuarto (a)**	*KWAHR-toh (tah)*
5°	**quinto (a)**	*KEEN-toh (tah)*
6°	**sexto (a)**	*SEHS-toh (tah)*
7°	**séptimo (a)**	*SEHT-tee-moh (mah)*
8°	**octavo (a)**	*ohk-TAH-boh (bah)*

9°	**noveno (a)**	*noh-BAY-noh (nah)*
10°	**décimo (a)**	*DEH-see-moh (mah)*
last	**último (a)**	*OOL-tee-moh (mah)*
once	**una vez**	*OO-nah-behs*
twice	**dos veces**	*dohs BEH-sehs*
three times	**tres veces**	*trehs BEH-sehs*

FRACTIONS

half of ____.	**la mitad de ____.**	*lah mee-TAHD day*
half (of) the money	**la mitad del dinero**	*lah mee-TAHD del dee-NEH-row*
half a ____.	**medio ____.**	*MEH-dyoh*
half a kilo	**medio kilo**	*MEH-dyoh KEE-loh*
a fourth (quarter)	**un cuarto**	*oon KWAHR-toh*
a dozen ____.	**una docena de ____.**	*OO-nah doh-SAY-nah day*
a dozen oranges	**una docena de naranjas**	*OO-nah doh-SAY-nah day nah-RAHN-hahs*
100 grams	**cien gramos**	*syehn GRAH-mohs*
200 grams	**doscientos gramos**	*dohs SYEHN-tohs GRAH-mos*
350 grams	**trescientos cincuenta gramos**	*trey SYEHN-tohs seen-KWEHN-tah GRAH-mos*
a pair (of) ____	**un par de____**	*oon pahr day*
a pair of shoes	**un par de zapatos**	*oon pahr day sah-PAH-tohs*

WHEN YOU ARRIVE

PASSPORT AND CUSTOMS

Customs is usually a routine procedure in Spain. Items that can be brought in duty-free include: clothing, jewelry, and personal effects needed for a visit; 200 cigarettes or 50 cigars; 2 liters of wine or 1 liter of spirits (above 22 percent alcohol); ¼ liter of cologne.

For personal use, you may bring in: 2 still cameras and up to 10 rolls of film per camera; 1 16 mm or smaller camera with 10 rolls of film; a portable radio; typewriter; binoculars; bicycle; musical instrument; record player; pocket calculator; tape recorder; cassette player; unlimited foreign currency or travelers checks, but only 50,000 Spanish pesetas.

Customs in other Spanish-speaking countries vary greatly, although crossing the border into Mexico is usually a very casual affair. We suggest you check ahead, should you be entering any country in Central or South America.

My name is ____.	**Me llamo ____.**	*may YAH-moh*
I'm American (British) (Australian) (Canadian).	**Soy norteamericano (a) (inglés, a) (australiano, a) (canadiense).**	*soy nohr-tay-ah-mehr-ee-KAH-noh (nah) (een-GLAYS, ah) (ow-strahl-YAH-noh, nah) (kah-nah-DYEHN-say)*
My address is ____.	**Mi dirección es ____.**	*mee dee-rehk-SYOHN ehs*
I'm staying at ____.	**Estoy en el hotel ____.**	*ehs-TOY ehn ehl oh-TEHL*
Here is (are) ____.	**Aquí tiene ____.**	*ah-KEE TYEHN-ay*
▪ my documents	**mis documentos**	*mees doh-koo-MEHN-tohs*
▪ my passport	**mi pasaporte**	*mee pah-sah-POHR-tay*

my tourist card	**mi tarjeta de turista** *mee tahr-HAY-tah day toor-EES-tah*
I'm _____.	**Estoy _____.** *ehs-TOY*
on a business trip	**en un viaje de negocios** *ehn oon bee-AH-hay day neh-GOH-see-ohs*
on vacation	**de vacaciones** *day bah-kah-SYOHN-ays*
visiting relatives	**visitando a mis familiares** *bee-see-TAHN-doh ah mees fah-meel-YAHR-ays*
just passing through	**solamente de paso** *soh-loh-MEHN-tay day PAH-soh*
I'll be staying here _____.	**Me quedaré aquí _____.** *may kay-dahr-AY ah-KEE*
a few days	**unos días** *OON-ohs DEE-ahs*
a few weeks	**unas semanas** *OON-ahs seh-MAH-nahs*
a week	**una semana** *OON-ah seh-MAH-nah*
a month	**un mes** *oon mehs*
I'm traveling _____.	**Viajo _____.** *bee-AH-hoh*
alone	**solo (a)** *SOH-loh (lah)*
with my husband	**con mi marido** *kohn mee mah-REE-doh*
with my wife	**con mi mujer** *kohn mee moo-HAIR*
with my family	**con mi familia** *kohn mee fah-MEEL-yah*
with my friend	**con mi amigo (a)** *kohn mee ah-MEE-go*

    Customs in the major ports of entry is a simple affair. As you pass through the gates, you'll see signs dividing the path in two directions: Follow the green arrow if you have nothing to declare (**nada que declarar**), or head for the red arrow if you have items to declare (**artículos para declarar**).

NADA QUE DECLARAR	ARTICULOS PARA DECLARAR

These are my bags.	**Estas son mis maletas.**	*EHS-tahs sohn mees mah-LAY-tahs*
I have nothing to declare.	**No tengo nada que declarar.**	*noh tehn-goh NAH-dah kay day-klahr-AHR*
I only have ____.	**Sólo tengo ____.**	*SOH-loh tehn-goh*
▪ a carton of cigarettes	**un cartón de cigarrillos**	*oon kahr-TOHN day see-gahr-EE-yohs*
▪ a bottle of whisky	**una botella de whisky**	*OON-nah boh-TEH-yah day WEE-skee*
What's the problem?	**¿Hay algún problema?**	*AH-ee ahl-GOON proh-BLAY-mah*
They're gifts (for my personal use).	**Son regalos (para mi uso personal).**	*sohn ray-GAH-lohs (pah-rah mee OO-soh pehr-sohn-AHL)*
Do I have to pay duty?	**¿Tengo que pagar impuestos?**	*ten-goh kay pah-GAHR eem-PWEHS-tohs*
May I close my bag now?	**¿Puedo cerrar la maleta ahora?**	*pweh-doh sehr-AHR lah mah-LEH-tah ah-OHR-ah*

IDENTITY CARD (TARJETA DE IDENTIDAD)

Upon entering the country (or on your flight into the country), you will be required to complete an identity card, usually with the following information.

Apellidos: (Surname) _____

Nombre: (First Name) _____

Nacionalidad: (Nationality) _____

Fecha de nacimiento: (Date of Birth) _____
Profesión: (Profession) _____
Dirección: (Address) _____
Pasaporte expedido en: (Passport Issued in) _____

BAGGAGE AND PORTERS

You will find carts for your baggage in the Madrid airport. After you have retrieved your bags, push your cart through the "Nothing to Declare" doors. After customs, you can carry your bags to the taxi or bus stand—or ask a porter for help. Porters are readily available. In Spain, the rate should be approximately 50 pesetas per bag, unless you have something unusually heavy; in other, Spanish-speaking countries, expect the equivalent of 50¢ a bag. If you are charged a higher figure, ask to see the posted rate card.

Where can I find a baggage cart?	**¿Dónde está un carrito para maletas?** *DOHN-day eh-STAH oon kahr-REE-toh pah-rah mah-LET-tahs*
I need a porter!	**¡Necesito un maletero!** *neh-seh-SEE-toh oon mah-leh-TEH-roh*

These are our (my) bags.	**Estas son nuestras (mis) maletas.** *EHS-tahs sohn NWEHS-trahs (mees) mah-LEH-tahs*
▪that big (little) one	**esa grande (pequeña)** *eh-sah GRAHN-day (peh-KAYN-yah)*
▪these two black (green) ones	**estas dos negras (verdes)** *EHS-tahs dos NEH-grahs (BEHR-days)*
Put them here (there).	**Póngalas aquí (allí).** *POHN-gah-lahs ah-KEE (ah-YEE)*
Be careful with that one!	**!Cuidado con ésa!** *kwee-DAH-doh kohn EH-sah*
I'll carry this one myself.	**Yo me llevo ésta.** *yoh may YEH-boh EHS-tah*
I'm missing a suitcase.	**Me falta una maleta.** *may FAHL-tah oo-nah mah-LEH-tah*
How much do I owe you?	**¿Cuánto le debo?** *KWAHN-toh lay DEHB-oh*
Thank you (very much). This is for you.	**(Muchas) gracias. Esto es para usted.** *(moo-chahs) GRAHS-yahs EHS-toh ehs pah-rah oos-TEHD*
Are you sure that amount is correct?	**¿Está seguro de que ése es el precio?** *ehs-TAH seh-GOOR-oh day kay EH-say ehs ehl PRAY-see-oh*

TRAVEL TIP

If you have had to change your plans and cannot use your airline ticket, you can apply for a complete refund. Treat your ticket as if it were cash, and return it to your travel agent or to the airline for your money back. Note, however, that some charter tickets are nonrefundable. If you do not use the ticket, you have lost the money, but if you take out special flight insurance, you can collect your refund for that charter ticket from the insuring company.

BANKING AND MONEY MATTERS

The **peseta** is the currency of Spain, with 100 **céntimos** in each **peseta**. Best exchange rates are usually offered at banks, of which there are dozens. Banco Exterior has an office at the airport in Madrid.

In Mexico and many countries in Central and South America, the **peso** is the currency, with 100 **centavos** equaling one peso. In recent years, devaluations and value fluctuations have had profound effects on the peso's exchange value. You will get a very favorable exchange for pounds or dollars.

Credit cards are widely accepted, as are all major travelers checks.

Banking hours are generally from 9 a.m. to 3 p.m., Monday through Friday, plus Saturday morning. Business hours are usually from 9 a.m. to 1:30 p.m., then 4:30 p.m. to 8 p.m., Monday through Friday. Many businesses keep Saturday morning hours too. "Morning" in Spain or Mexico generally means until it is time for the lunch break—i.e., 1 or 1:30 p.m.

CURRENCIES OF SPANISH SPEAKING COUNTRIES

Argentina	**peso**	*PEH-soh*
Bolivia	**boliviano**	*boh-lee-VYAH-noh*
Chile	**peso**	*PEH-soh*
Colombia	**peso**	*PEH-soh*
Costa Rica	**colón**	*koh-LOHN*
Cuba	**peso**	*PEH-soh*
Ecuador	**sucre**	*SOO-kray*
Guatemala	**quetzal**	*kayt-SAHL*
Honduras	**lempira**	*lem-PEER-ah*

México	**peso**	*PEH-soh*
Nicaragua	**córdoba**	*KOHR-doh-bah*
Panama	**balboa**	*bahl-BOH-ah*
Paraguay	**guaraní**	*gwahr-ah-NEE*
Peru	**sol**	*sohl*
República Domini-cana	**peso**	*PEH-soh*
Salvador	**colón**	*koh-LOHN*
Spain (España)	**peseta**	*peh-SEH-tah*
Uruguay	**peso**	*PEH-soh*
Venezuela	**bolívar**	*boh-LEE-bahr*

EXCHANGING MONEY

Where is the currency exchange (bank)?	**¿Dónde hay un banco para cambiar moneda extranjera?** *DOHN-day AH-ee oon BAHN-koh pah-rah kahm-bee-AHR moh-NAY-dah ehs-trahn-HEHR-ah*
I wish to change ____.	**Quiero cambiar ____.** *kee-YEHR-oh kahm-bee-YAHR*
▪ money	**dinero** *dee-NEHR-oh*
▪ dollars (pounds)	**dólares (libras)** *DOH-lahr-ays (LEE-brahs)*
▪ travelers checks	**cheques de viajero** *CHEH-kays day bee-ah-HAIR-oh*

Can I cash a personal check?

¿Puedo cambiar un cheque personal?
PWEH-doh kahm-bee-YAHR oon CHEH-kay pehr-sohn-AHL

At what time do they open (close)?

¿A qué hora abren (cierran)? *ah kay ohra AH-brehn (SYEHR-ahn)*

Where is the cashier's window?

¿Dónde está la caja, por favor?
DOHN-day eh-STAH lah KAH-hah pohr fah-BOHR

The current exchange rates are posted in banks which exchange money and are also published daily in the city newspapers. Since the rates fluctuate from day to day, it may be useful to convert the common amounts here for your quick reference.

PESETA	YOUR OWN CURRENCY	PESO	YOUR OWN CURRENCY
100		10	
500		20	
1000		50	
5000		100	

What's the current exchange rate for dollars (pounds)?

¿A cóme está el cambio hoy del dólar (de la libra)? *ah KOH-moh ehs-TAH ehl KAHM-bee-oh oy del DOH-lahr (day lah LEE-brah)*

What commission do you charge?

¿Cuál es el interés que Vds. cobran? *kwahl ehs ehl een-tehr-AYS kay oos-TEHD-ays KOH-brahn*

I'd like to cash this check.

Quisiera cobrar este cheque. *kee-SYEHR-ah koh-BRAHR EHS-teh CHEH-kay*

Where do I sign?	**¿Dónde debo firmar?** *DOHN-day DEH-boh feer-MAHR*
I'd like the money _____.	**Quisiera el dinero _____.** *kee-SYEHR-ah ehl dee-NEHR-oh*
in (large) bills	**en billetes (grandes)** *ehn bee-YEH-tehs (GRAHN-days)*
in small change	**en suelto** *ehn SWEHL-toh*
Give me two twenty-peso bills.	**Déme dos billetes de a veinte pesos.** *DEH-may dohs bee-YEH-tays day ah BAYN-tay PAY-sohs*
fifty-peso bills	**cincuenta** *seen-KWEHN-tah*
one hundred-peseta bills	**cien** *see-YEHN*
Do you accept credit cards?	**¿Acepta usted tarjetas de crédito?** *a-SEHP-tah oo-STEHD tahr-HAY-tahs day KREHD-ee-toh*

BUSINESS BANKING TERMS

bad check	**un cheque sin fondos** *oon CHEH-kay seen FOHN-dohs*
banker	**el banquero** *ehl bahn-KEH-roh*
borrow (to)	**pedir prestado** *peh-DEER prehs-TAH-doh*
cashier	**el (la) cajero(a)** *ehl (lah) kah-HEHR-oh (ah)*
capital	**la capital** *lah kah-pee-TAHL*
cashier's office	**la caja** *lah KAH-hah*
checkbook	**el librete de cheques** *ehl lee-BREH-tay day CHEH-kays*
endorse (to)	**endosar** *ehn-doh-SAHR*
income	**el ingreso** *ehl een-GREHS-oh*
interest rate	**el tipo de interés** *ehl TEE-poh day een-tehr-AYS*
investment	**la inversión** *lah een-behr-SYOHN*
loss	**la pérdida** *lah PEHR-dee-dah*
make change (to)	**dar (el) cambio** *dahr (ehl) KAHM-bee-oh*
mortgage	**la hipoteca** *lah eep-oh-TEH-kah*
open an account (to)	**abrir una cuenta** *ah-BREER oo-nah KWEHN-tah*
poster	**el cartel** *ehl kahr-TEHL*
premium	**el premio** *ehl PRAY-mee-oh*
profit	**la ganancia** *la gah-NAHN-see-ah*
secretary	**el (la) secretario(a)** *ehl sehk-reh-TAHR-ee-oh (ah)*
safe	**la caja fuerte** *lah KAH-ha FWEHR-tay*

| signature | **la firma** *lah FEER-mah* |
| window | **la ventanilla** *lah ben-tah-NEE-yah* |

TIPPING

In many areas, service charges are often included in the price of the service rendered. These usually come to about 10 to 15% and should be indicated on the bill.

Usually a customer will leave some small change in addition to any charge that has been included if the service has been satisfactory. At times, a set amount should be given.

The following table is merely a suggested guide. Tips will vary from country to country and from time to time due to inflation and other factors. It is therefore advisable to ask some knowledgeable person (hotel manager, tour director, etc.) once you get to the country, or to check the current rate of exchange.

	TIP	
SERVICE	SPAIN	MEXICO
Waiter	15% plus small change	15% plus small change
Bellboy, porter	50 pestas per suitcase	20 pesos per suitcase
Chambermaid	40–50 pesetas per day	25 pesos per day
Usher	10–15 pesetas	5–10 pesos
Taxi driver	10%	optional; small change

	TIP	
SERVICE	SPAIN	MEXICO
Guide	$3 per day	full day: $5 for 2 persons
Barber, hair-dresser	25–50 pesetas	30–50 pesos
Shoeshine	small change	small change
Bathroom attendant	10–15 pestas	———

TRAVEL TIP

Touring on the cheap? You'll find that keeping travel costs under control is a lot easier if you watch your daily expenses on such items as breakfast. Just how important is it for you to have that scrambled egg every morning? If you have the more native "continental breakfast," you'll have the money leftover to enjoy a theater performance or buy that special gift you saw in the shop window. Another way to save money and have more fun is to take public transportation. Sure, taxis are easier, but you'll get to the heart of the country a lot faster when you take the bus or metro. You'll observe how everyday people get around town, and you're likely to have some interesting adventures too. Exercise caution, however, and do not travel crowded trains or buses with valuables easily within view. Pick-pockets are everywhere and, as a tourist, you are usually paying more attention to the sights than to riders nearby. Women should keep a firm grasp on their purses.

AT THE HOTEL

If you are unfamiliar with the city to which you are going, you'll probably find it best to make a hotel reservation in advance from home. It is possible that you would do better on prices for a room in some Mexican hotels, however, if you bargain for your room once you get there.

You can buy a *Guía de Hoteles* at a Spanish National Tourist Office, which gives official government listings of hotels in Spain by category. Ratings run from 5-star deluxe to plain 1-star. Every hotel has a plaque outside with an "H" (for hotel) on it and the star rating it has been allocated. "HS" on the plaque stands for Hostal; "HR" signifies Hotel-residencia, which means the hotel serves breakfast only. "P" stands for Pensión.

The following is a listing of the types of hotels you will encounter in Spain.

Hoteles	hotels
Hostales	small hotels or inns with no restaurant
Pensiones	guesthouses providing full board only
Paradores	first-class hotels run by the state located in places of historical interest and attractive surroundings. Many are converted castles, palaces, or monasteries
Refugios	retreats or rustic lodges, which are located in scenic mountain areas and are popular with hunters, hikers, and fishermen
Albergues Nacionales de Carretera	state-run roadside inns (period of stay is restricted). They also provide gas station and car repair services
Albergues juveniles	youth hostels provide cheap accommodations for young people who are members of the international Youth Hostels Association; maximum length of stay at any one hostel is 3 nights

NOTE: Paradors are extremely popular with tourists. There are more than 80 located throughout Spain, but because they have relatively few rooms and prices are modest (for value received), they are often booked far in advance. Arrangements to stay at a parador can be made by writing directly or by contacting their U.S. representative, Marketing Ahead, 515 Madison Avenue, New York, NY 10022. Brochures on paradors, albergues, and refugios are available free from the Spanish National Tourist Office.

Hotels include a service charge in the bill. It is customary, though, to tip the porter carrying your luggage 25–50 pesetas per bag, maids approximately 50 pesetas a day at 4- or 5-star hotels, room service 50–100 pesetas, and the doorman who summons your cab 10–50 pesetas. A helpful concierge might receive a tip of 100 pesetas or so for doing special favors, such as securing theater tickets or making phone calls and reservations.

GETTING TO YOUR HOTEL

I'd like to go to the ____ Hotel.	**Quisiera ir al Hotel ____.** *kee-SYEH-rah eer ahl oh-TEL*
Is it near (far)?	**¿Está cerca (lejos) de aquí?** *ehs-TAH SEHR-kah (LAY-hohs) day ah-KEE*
Where can I get a taxi?	**¿Dónde puedo coger un taxi?** *DOHN-day PWEH-doh koh-HEHR oon TAHK-see*
What buses go into town?	**¿Qué autobuses van al centro?** *kay ow-toh-BOOS-ays bahn ahl SEHN-troh*
Where is the bus stop?	**¿Dónde está la parada?** *DOHN-day ehs-TAH lah pah-RAH-dah*
How much is the fare?	**¿Cuánto cuesta el billete?** *KWAHN-toh KWEHS-tah ehl bee-YEH-tay*

CHECKING IN

Most first-class or deluxe hotels will have personnel who speak English. If you are checking in to a smaller hotel, you might find these phrases useful in getting what you want. In Spain, all visitors are required to fill out a registration form *(una ficha de identidad)* requiring certain information.

Apellido _____
(Surname)

Nombre _____
(First name)

Fecha de Nacimiento _____
(Date of birth)

Nacionalidad _____
(Nationality)

Lugar de Nacimiento _____
(Place of birth)

Dirección _____
(Address)

No. de Pasaporte _____
(Passport number)

exp. en _____
(Issued at)

Firma del viajero _____
(Signature)

I'd like a single (double) room for tonight.

Quisiera una habitación con una sola cama (con dos camas) para esta noche. *kee-SYEHR-ah OO-nah ah-bee-tah-SYOHN kohn OO-nah SOH-lah KAH-mah (kohn dohs KAH-mahs) pah-rah EHS-tah NOH-chay*

How much is the room _____?

¿Cuánto cuesta el cuarto _____? *KWAHN-toh KWEHS-tah ehl KWAHR-toh*

■ with a shower

con ducha *kohn DOO-chah*

■ with a private bath

con baño privado *kohn BAHN-yoh pree-BAH-doh*

■ with a balcony

con balcón *kohn bahl-KOHN*

■ facing the ocean

con vista al mar *kohn bees-tah ahl mahr*

■ facing (away from) the street

que dé a la calle *kay day ah lah KAH-yeh*

▪ facing the court-yard	**que dé al patio** *kay day ahl PAH-tee-oh*
▪ in the back	**al fondo** *ahl FOHN-doh*
Does it have ____?	**¿Tiene ____?** *tee-YEH-neh*
▪ air-conditioning	**aire acondicionado** *AH-ee-ray ah-kohn-dee-syohn-AH-doh*
▪ hot water	**agua caliente** *ah-guah kahl-YEN-tay*
▪ television	**televisión** *teh-lay-bee-SYOHN*
I (don't) have a reservation.	**(No) tengo reserva.** *(noh) ten-goh reh-SEHR-bah*
Could you call another hotel to see if they have something?	**¿Podría llamar a otro hotel para ver si tienen algo?** *poh-DREE-ah yah-MAHR ah OH-troh o-TEL pah-rah behr see tee-yen-ehn AHL-goh*
May I see the room?	**¿Podría ver la habitación?** *poh-DREE-ah behr lah ah-bee-tah-SYOHN*
I (don't) like it.	**(No) me gusta.** *(noh) may GOOS-tah*
Do you have something ____?	**¿Hay algo ____?** *AH-ee ahl-goh*
▪ better	**mejor** *may-HOHR*
▪ larger	**más grande** *mahs GRAHN-day*
▪ smaller	**más pequeño** *mahs peh-KAYN-yo*
▪ cheaper	**más barato** *mahs bah-RAH-toh*
▪ quieter	**donde no se oigan ruidos** *DOHN-day noh say OY-gahn RWEE-dohs*
What floor is it on?	**¿En qué piso está?** *ehn kay PEE-soh ehs-TAH*
Is there an elevator (lift)?	**¿Hay ascensor?** *AH-ee ah-sen-SOHR*
Is everything included?	**¿Está todo incluído?** *eh-STAH toh-doh een-kloo-EE-doh*

How much is the room with ____?	**¿Cuánto cobra usted por la habitación con ____?** *KWAHN-toh KOH-brah oos-TEHD pohr lah ah-bee-tah-SYOHN kohn*
▪ the American plan (2 meals a day)	**con media pensión** *kohn MEH-dee-yah pen-SYOHN*
▪ bed and breakfast	**con desayuno** *kohn dehs-ah-YOO-noh*
▪ no meals	**sin la comida** *seen lah koh-MEE-dah*
The room is very nice. I'll take it.	**La habitación es muy bonita. Me quedo con ella.** *lah ah-bee-tah-SYOHN ehs mwee boh-NEE-tah may KAY-doh kohn EH-ya*
We'll be staying ____.	**Nos quedamos ____.** *nohs kay-DAH-mohs*
▪ one night	**una noche** *OO-nah NOH-chay*
▪ a few nights	**unas noches** *OO-nahs NOH-chayes*
▪ one week	**una semana** *OO-nah seh-MAH-nah*
How much do you charge for children?	**¿Cuánto cobra por los niños?** *kwahn-toh KOH-brah pohr lohs NEEN-yohs*
Could you put another bed in the room?	**¿Podría poner otra cama en la habitación?** *poh-DREE-ah poh-NEHR oh-trah KAH-mah ehn lah ah-bee-tah-SYOHN*
Is there a charge? How much?	**¿Hay que pagar más? ¿Cuánto?** *AH-ee kay pah-GAHR mahs? KWAHN-toh*

OTHER ACCOMMODATIONS

I'm looking for ____.	**Busco ____.** *BOOS-koh*
▪ a boardinghouse	**una pensión (una casa de huéspedes)** *OO-nah pen-SYOHN (oo-nah kah-sah day WES-pehd-ays)*

■a private house	**una casa particular** *OO-na kah-sah pahr-teek-oo-LAHR*
I want to rent an apartment.	**Quiero alquilar un apartamento.** *kee-YEHR-oh ahl-kee-LAHR oon ah-pahr-tah-MEHN-toh*
I need a living room, bedroom, and kitchen.	**Necesito un salón, un dormitorio, y una cocina.** *neh-seh-SEE-toh oon sah-LOHN, oon dohr-mee-TOHR-ee-oh ee oo-nah koh-SEE-nah*
Do you have a furnished room?	**¿Tiene un cuarto amueblado?** *tee-YEN-ay oon KWAHR-toh ah-mway-BLAH-doh*
How much is the rent?	**¿Cuánto es el alquiler?** *KWAHN-toh ehs ehl ahl-kee-LEHR*
I'll be staying here for ____.	**Me quedaré aquí ____.** *may kay-dahr-AY ah-KEE*
■two weeks	**dos semanas** *dohs seh-MAH-nahs*
■one month	**un mes** *oon mehs*
■the whole summer	**todo el verano** *toh-doh ehl behr-AH-noh*
I want a place that's ____.	**Quiero un sitio ____.** *kee-yehr-oh oon SEE- tee-yo*
■centrally located	**en el centro de la ciudad** *ehn ehl SEHN-troh day lah syoo-DAHD*
■near public transportation	**cerca del transporte público** *SEHR-kah del trahns-POHR-tay POOB-lee-koh*
Is there a youth hostel around here?	**¿Hay un albergue juvenil por aquí?** *AH-ee oon ahl-BEHR-gay hoo-ben-EEL pohr ah-KEE*

ORDERING BREAKFAST

Larger hotels will offer breakfast. The Spanish breakfast is a simple one—**café con leche** (hot coffee mixed half and half with steaming milk), with a sweet roll or **churro** (fried pastry). Mexican breakfasts tend to be a little more elaborate, usually **café con leche** and perhaps a tortilla topped with fried eggs, tomatoes and spices or toasted **bollitos** (small boat-shaped yeast rolls). At hotels that cater to American and British tourists, you will also be able to order an English breakfast (juice, eggs, bacon, and toast). Larger hotels will have a dining room where you can eat breakfast, but the usual procedure is to have breakfast sent up to your room or to go out to a café or chocolatería (the hot chocolate in Spain is marvelous) or, in Mexico, to a street vendor who fries up your breakfast at her curbside stand.

We'll have breakfast in the room.	**Queremos desayunarnos en nuestra habitación.** *keh-RAY-mohs dehs-ah-yoo-NAHR-nohs ehn NWEHS-trah ah-bee-tah-SYOHN*
Please send up _____.	**Haga el favor de mandarnos _____.** *AH-gah ehl fah-BOHR day mahn-DAHR-nohs*
▧ one (two) coffee(s)	**una taza (dos tazas) de café** *oo-nah TAH-sah (dohs TAH-sahs) day kah-FAY*
▧ tea	**una taza de té** *oo-nah TAH-sah day tay*
▧ hot chocolate	**una taza de chocolate** *oo-nah TAH-sah day cho-koh-LAH-tay*
▧ a sweet roll	**un pan dulce** *oon pahn DOOL-say*
▧ fruit (juice)	**un jugo (de fruta)** *oon HOO-goh day FROO-tah*
I'll eat breakfast downstairs.	**Voy a desayunarme abajo.** *boy ah dehs-ah-yoo-NAHR-may ah-BAH-ho*

We'd both like _____.	**Quisieramos _____.** *kee-SYEHR-ah-mohs*
bacon and eggs	**huevos con tocino** *WEH-bohs kohn toh-SEE-noh*
scrambled (fried, boiled) eggs	**huevos revueltos (fritos, pasados por agua)** *WEH-bohs ray-BWEHL-tohs (FREE-tohs, pah-SAH-dohs pohr AH-gwah)*
toast	**pan tostado** *pahn tohs-TAH-doh*
jam (marmalade)	**mermelada** *mehr-may-LAH-dah*
Please don't make it too spicy.	**No lo haga muy picante.** *noh loh AH-gah mwee pee-KAHN-tay*

NOTE: See the food section (pages 84–88) for more phrases dealing with ordering meals.

HOTEL SERVICES

Where is _____?	**¿Dónde está _____?** *dohn-day ehs-TAH*
the dining room	**el comedor** *ehl koh-meh-DOHR*
the bathroom	**el baño** *ehl BAHN-yo*
the elevator (lift)	**el ascensor** *ehl ah-sen-SOHR*
the phone	**el teléfono** *ehl tel-EF-oh-no*
What is my room number?	**¿Cuál es el número de mi cuarto?** *kwahl ehs ehl NOO-mehr-oh day mee KWAHR-toh*
May I please have my key?	**Mi llave, por favor.** *mee YAH-bay pohr fah-BOHR*
I've lost my key.	**He perdido mi llave.** *eh pehr-DEE-doh mee YAH-bay*

I need _____.	**Necesito _____.** *neh-seh-SEE-toh*
■ a bellhop	**un botones** *oon boh-TOH-nays*
■ a chambermaid	**una camarera** *oo-nah kah-mah-REHR-ah*
Please send _____ to my room.	**Haga el favor de mandar _____ a mi habitación.** *AH-gah ehl fah-BOHR day mah-DAHR _____ ah mee ah-bee-tah-SYOHN*
■ a towel	**una toalla** *oo-nah toh-AH-yah*
■ a bar of soap	**una pastilla de jabón** *oo-nah pahs-TEE-yah day hah-BOHN*
■ some hangers	**unas perchas** *oo-nahs PEHR-chahs*
■ a pillow	**una almohada** *oo-nah ahl-moh-AH-dah*
■ a blanket	**una manta** *oo-nah MAHN-tah*
■ some ice cubes	**cubitos de hielo** *koo-BEE-tohs day YEH-loh*
■ some ice water	**agua helada** *ah-guah eh-LAH-dah*
■ a bottle of mineral water	**una botella de agua mineral** *oo-nah boh-TEH-yah day AH-guah mee-nehr-AHL*
■ an ashtray	**un cenicero** *oon sen-ee-SEHR-oh*
■ toilet paper	**papel higiénico** *pah-PEHL ee-HYEHN-ee-koh*
■ a reading lamp	**una lámpara para leer** *oo-nah LAHM-pahr-ah pah-rah lay-EHR*
■ an electric adaptor	**un adaptador eléctrico** *oon ah-dahp-tah-DOHR eh-LEK-tree-koh*

NOTE: If you bring electric appliances with you from the U.S. (electric shaver, for example), in Spain you may need to have an adaptor so that the voltage corresponds with that in the hotel. Newer hotels have 110-volt systems and an adaptor isn't necessary.

AT THE DOOR

Who is it? **¿Quién es?** *kee-EHN ehs*

Just a minute. **Un momento.** *oon moh-MEN-toh*

Come in. **Adelante.** *ah-del-AHN-tay*

Put it on the table. **Póngalo en la mesa.** *POHN-gah-loh ehn lah MAY-sah*

Please wake me tomorrow at ____. **¿Puede despertarme mañana a ____?** *PWEH-day dehs-pehr-TAHR-may mahn-YAH-nah ah*

COMPLAINTS

There is no ____. **No hay ____.** *noh AH-ee*

◾ running water **agua corriente** *AH-gwah kohr-YEN-tay*

◾ hot water **agua caliente** *AH-gwah kahl-YEN-tay*

◾ electricity **electricidad** *eh-lek-tree-see-DAHD*

The ____ doesn't work. **No funciona ____.** *noh foon-SYOHN-ah*

◾ air-conditioning **el aire acondicionado** *ehl AH-ee-ray ah-kohn-dees-yohn-AH-doh*

◾ fan **el ventilador** *ehl ben-tee-lah-DOHR*

◾ faucet **el grifo** *ehl GREE-foh*

◾ lamp **la lámpara** *lah LAHM-pah-rah*

◾ light **la luz** *lah loos*

◾ radio **la radio** *lah RAH-dee-oh*

◾ electric socket **el enchufe** *ehl ehn-CHOO-fay*

◾ light switch **el interruptor** *ehl een-tehr-oop-TOHR*

◾ television **el televisor** *ehl tel-eh-bee-SOHR*

Can you fix it ____? **¿Puede arreglarlo ____?** *PWEH-day ah-ray-GLAHR-loh*

■now   **ahora** *ah-OH-rah*

■as soon as possible   **lo más pronto posible** *loh mahs PROHN-toh poh-SEE-blay*

AT THE DESK

Are there any _____ for me?   **¿Hay _____ para mí?** *AH-ee _____ pah-rah MEE*

■letters   **cartas** *KAHR-tahs*

■messages   **recados** *ray-KAH-dohs*

■packages   **paquetes** *pah-KEH-tays*

■post cards   **postales** *pohs-TAH-lays*

Did anyone call for me?   **¿Preguntó alguien por mí?** *preh-goon-TOH AHL-ghee-ehn pohr MEE*

I'd like to leave this in your safe.   **Quisiera dejar esto en su caja fuerte.** *kee-SYEHR-ah day-HAHR EHS-toh ehn soo KAH-ha FWEHR-tay*

Will you make this call for me?   **¿Podría usted hacerme esta llamada?** *poh-DREE-ah oos-TEHD ah-SEHR-may EHS-tah yah-MAH-dah*

CHECKING OUT

I'd like the bill, please.   **Quisiera la cuenta, por favor.** *kee-SYEHR-ah lah KWEHN-tah pohr fah-BOHR*

I'll be checking out today (tomorrow).   **Pienso marcharme hoy (mañana).** *PYEHN-soh mahr-CHAR-may oy (mahn-YA-nah)*

Please send someone up for our baggage.   **Haga el favor de mandar a alguien para recoger nuestro equipaje.** *AH-gah ehl fah-BOHR day mahn-DAHR ah AHL-ghy-ehn pah-rah ray-koh-HEHR NWEHS-troh AY-kee-PAH-hay*

GETTING AROUND TOWN

In most cities, you will find that getting around town to sightsee is an easy affair. You'll get more of the flavor of a city if you use public transportation, but oftentimes a taxi will be the quicker way to go somewhere, and usually they are not too expensive. For information on train or plane travel, see pages 58–62.

THE BUS

Public transportation in Madrid is cheap, efficient, and frequent. Bus stops are clearly marked by number, and each number's stops are clearly delineated. Be sure to signal when you want the bus to stop, as the driver doesn't stop automatically at every stop on the route. Free bus maps, or **Plano de la Red,** are available at designated kiosks, such as the one at Paseo del Prado, in front of the Palace Hotel. Most bus routes run from 6 a.m. to midnight, though some have 24-hour service. There are no free transfers, but the fare is cheap—about 40 pesetas.

In Mexico City, an unusually large urban area, there are bus routes that crisscross the entire town. Bus routes are at times confusing, so you are best obtaining the specific instructions from your hotel concierge. Buses are more expensive than the subway (underground), but since both are so cheap in comparison to other cities' systems, the difference is negligible (bus is about 3¢; subway (underground) is 1¢).

Where is the bus stop (terminal)?	**¿Dónde está la parada (la terminal) de autobús?** *DOHN-day ehs-TAH lah pah-RAH-dah (lah tehr-mee-NAHL) day AH-oo-toh-BOOS*
Which bus do I take to get to ___?	**¿Qué autobús hay que tomar para ir a ___?** *kay AH-oo-toh-BOOS AH-ee kay toh-MAHR PAH-rah eer ah ___?*

Do I need exact change?	**¿Necesito tener cambio exacto?** *neh-seh-SEE-toh ten-EHR KAHM-bee-oh ehk-SAHK-toh*
In which direction do I have to go?	**¿Qué rumbo tengo que tomar?** *kay ROOM-boh ten-goh kay toh-MAHR*
How often do the buses run?	**¿Con qué frecuencia salen los autobuses?** *kohn kay freh-KWEHN-see-ah sah-lehn lohs AH-oo-toh-BOOS-ehs*
Do you go to ____?	**¿Va usted a ____?** *bah oos-TEHD ah*
Is it far from here?	**¿Está lejos de aquí?** *eh-STAH LAY-hos day ah-KEE*
How many stops are there?	**¿Cuántas paradas hay?** *KWAHN-tahs pah-RAH-dahs AH-ee*
Do I have to change?	**¿Tengo que cambiar?** *TEN-goh kay kahm-bee-AHR*
How much is the fare?	**¿Cuánto es el billete?** *KWAHN-toh ehs ehl bee-YEH-tay*
Where do I have to get off?	**¿Dónde tengo que bajarme?** *DOHN-day ten-goh kay bah-HAHR-may*
Please tell me where to get off.	**¿Dígame, por favor, dónde debo bajarme?** *DEE-gah-may, pohr fa-BOHR DOHN-day deh-boh bah-HAHR-may*

THE SUBWAY (UNDERGROUND)

The subways (metros) in Madrid and Barcelona are clean, cheap, safe, and comfortable. And graffiti-free. There are nine lines in Madrid with interchange points.

The subway (metro) in Mexico City is a very busy one and often too crowded for most tourists, although the system itself is clean and efficient. Best to avoid it during peak hours. There is also a subway (metro) in Buenos Aires, which is also modern and well run.

Is there a subway (underground) in this city?	**¿Hay un metro en esta ciudad?** *AH-ee oon MEHT-roh ehn EHS-tah syoo-DAHD*
Where is the closest subway (underground) station?	**¿Dónde hay la estación más cercana?** *DOHN-day AH-ee lah ehs-tah-SYOHN mahs sehr-KAH-nah*
How much is the fare?	**¿Cuánto es la tarifa?** *KWAHN-toh ehs lah tah-REE-fah*
Where can I buy a token (a ticket)?	**¿Dónde puedo comprar una ficha (un billete)?** *DOHN-day PWEH-doh kohm-PRAHR oo-nah FEE-chah (oon bee-YEH-teh)*
Which is the line that goes to ____?	**¿Cuál es la línea que va a ____?** *kwahl ehs lah LEEN-eh-ah kay bah ah*
Does this train go to ____?	**¿Va este tren a ____?** *bah ehs-teh trehn ah*
Do you have a map showing the stops?	**¿Tiene un mapa que indique las paradas?** *TYEH-nay oon MAH-pah kay een-DEE-kay lahs pahr-AH-dahs*
How many more stops?	**¿Cuántas paradas más?** *KWAHN-tahs pah-RAH-dahs mahs?*
What's the next station?	**¿Cuál es la próxima estación?** *kwahl ehs lah PROHK-see-mah ehs-tah-SYOHN*
Where should I get off?	**¿Dónde debo bajarme?** *DOHN-day deh-boh bah-HAHR-may*
Do I have to change?	**¿Tengo que hacer trasbordo?** *ten-goh kay ah-SEHR trahs-BOHRD-oh*
Please tell me when we get there.	**Haga el favor de avisarme cuando lleguemos.** *AH-gah ehl fah-BOHR day ah-bee-SAHR-may kwahn-doh yeh-GAY-mohs*

TAXIS

Taxis are plentiful, metered, and, generally speaking, cheap. There are legitimate surcharges for baggage, night fares, holiday fares, and extras on certain other occasions. These are legitimate "extras," as the printed surcharge chart in each cab verifies. It is customary on entering a taxi to greet the driver with "Good morning," "Good day," or "Good evening." It is a politeness that is appreciated—and expected.

Is there a taxi stand near here?	**¿Hay una parada de taxis por aquí?** *AH-ee oo-nah pah-RAH-dah day TAHK-sees pohr ah-KEE*
Please get me a taxi.	**Puede usted conseguirme un taxi, por favor.** *PWEH-day oos-TEHD kohn-say-GHEER-may oon TAHK-si pohr fah-BOHR*
Where can I get a taxi?	**¿Dónde puedo coger un taxi?** *DOHN-day PWEH-doh koh-HAIR oon TAHK-see*
Taxi! Are you free (available)?	**¡Taxi! ¿Está libre?** *TAHK-see ehs-TAH LEE-bray*

Take me (I want to go) ____.	**Lléveme (Quiero ir) ____.** *YEHV-eh-may (kee-EHR-oh eer)*
▢ to the airport	**al aeropuerto** *ahl ah-ehr-oh-PWEHR-toh*
▢ to this address	**a esta dirección** *ah ehs-tah dee-rehk-SYOHN*
▢ to the hotel	**al hotel** *ahl o-TEL*
▢ to the station	**a la estación** *ah lah ehs-tah-SYOHN*
▢ to ____ street	**a la calle ____** *ah lah KAH-yeh*
Do you know where it is?	**¿Sabe dónde está?** *sah-bay DOHN-day ehs-TAH*
How much is it to ____?	**¿Cuánto cuesta hasta ____?** *KWAHN-toh KWEHS-tah AHS-tah*
Faster! I'm in a hurry.	**!Más rápido, tengo prisa!** *mahs RAH-pee-doh ten-goh PREE-sah*
Please drive slower.	**Por favor, conduzca más despacio.** *pohr fah-BOHR kohn-DOOS-kah mahs dehs-PAH-see-oh*
Stop here ____.	**Pare aquí ____.** *PAH-ray ah-KEE*
▢ at the corner	**en la esquina** *ehn lah ehs-KEE-nah*
▢ at the next block	**en la otra calle** *ehn lah OH-trah KAH-yeh*
Wait for me. I'll be right back.	**Espéreme. Vuelvo pronto.** *ehs-PEHR-eh-may BWEHL-boh PROHN-toh*
I think you are going the wrong way.	**Creo que me está llevando por una dirección equivocada.** *KRAY-oh kay may ehs-TAH yeh-BAHN-doh pohr oo-nah dee-rek-SYOHN eh-kee-boh-KAH-dah*
How much do I owe you?	**¿Cuánto le debo?** *KWAHN-toh lay DEHB-oh*

This is for you.	**Esto es para usted.** *ehs-toh ehs PAH-rah oos-TEHD*

SIGHTSEEING AND TOURS

You'll want to visit a variety of sights—cathedrals, plazas, shopping streets, parks, and museums—and we give you here some phrases to help you locate the English-language tours, when available.

Where is the Tourist Information Office?	**¿Dónde está la oficina de turismo?** *DOHN-day ehs-TAH lah of-ee-SEEN-ah day toor-EES-moh*
I need a(n) (English-speaking) guide.	**Necesito un guía (de habla inglesa).** *neh-seh-SEE-toh oon GHEE-ah (day AH-blah een-GLAY-sah)*
How much does he charge ____?	**¿Cuánto cobra ____?** *KWAHN-toh KOH-brah*
per hour	**por hora** *pohr OHR-ah*
per day	**por día** *pohr DEE-ah*
There are two (four, six) of us.	**Somos dos (cuatro, seis).** *soh-mohs dohs (KWAHT-roh, sayss)*
Where can I buy a guide book (map)?	**¿Dónde puedo comprar una guía (un mapa)?** *DOHN-day PWEH-doh kohm-PRAHR oo-nah GHEE-ah (oon MAH-pah)*
What are the main attractions?	**¿Cuáles son los puntos principales de interés?** *KWAHL-ehs sohn lohs poon-tohs preen-see-PAHL-ays day een-tehr-AYS*
What are things of interest here?	**¿Qué cosas interesantes hay aquí?** *kay KOH-sahs een-tehr-ehs-AHN-tays AH-ee ah-KEE*
Are there trips through the city?	**¿Hay excursiones por la ciudad?** *AH-ee ehs-koor-SYOHN-ehs pohr lah see-oo-DAHD*

BOOKING A TOUR

When does the tour begin?	**¿Cuando empieza la excursión?** *KWAHN-doh ehm-PYEH-sah lah ehs-koor-SOYHN*
How long is the tour?	**¿Cuánto tiempo dura?** *KWAHN-toh TYEHM-poh DOOR-ah*
Where do they leave from?	**¿De dónde salen?** *day DOHN-day SAHL-ehn*
We want to see ____.	**Queremos ver ____.** *kehr-EHM-ohs behr*
the botanical garden	**el jardín botánico** *ehl har-DEEN boh-TAHN-ee-koh*
the bullring	**la plaza de toros** *lah plah-sah day TOHR-ohs*
the business center	**el centro comercial** *ehl SEN-troh koh-mehr-SYAHL*
the castle	**el castillo** *ehl kahs-TEE-yoh*
the cathedral	**la catedral** *lah kah-tay-DRAHL*
the church	**la iglesia** *lah eeg-LEHS-ee-ah*
the concert hall	**la sala de conciertos** *lah SAH-lah day kohn-see-EHR-tohs*
the downtown area	**el centro de la ciudad** *ehl SEN-troh day lah see-oo-DAHD*
the fountains	**las fuentes** *lahs FWEHN-tays*
the library	**la biblioteca** *lah beeb-lee-oh-TAY-kah*
the main park	**el parque central** *ehl pahr-kay sen-TRAHL*
the main square	**la plaza mayor** *lah plah-sah my-YOR*
the market	**el mercado** *ehl mehr-KAH-doh*
the mosque	**la mezquita** *lah mehs-KEE-tah*

the museum (of fine arts)	**el museo (de bellas artes)** *ehl moo-SAY-oh (day bel-yahs AHR-tays)*
a nightclub	**una sala de fiestas** *oo-nah SAHL-ah day fee-ES-tahs*
the old part of town	**la ciudad vieja** *lah see-oo-DAHD BYEH-ha*
the opera	**la ópera** *lah OH-pehr-ah*
the palace	**el palacio** *ehl pah-LAH-see-oh*
the stadium	**el estadio** *ehl ehs-TAHD-ee-oh*
the synagogue	**la sinagoga** *lah seen-ah-GOH-gah*
the university	**la universidad** *lah oon-ee-behr-see-DAHD*
the zoo	**el parque zoológico** *ehl pahr-kay soh-oh-LOH-hee-koh*

ADMISSIONS

Is it all right to go in now?	**¿Se puede entrar ahora?** *say PWEH-day ehn-TRAHR ah-OHR-ah*
Is it open (closed)?	**¿Está abierto (cerrado)?** *ehs-TAH ah-bee-YEHR-toh (sehr-AH-doh)*
At what time does it open (close)?	**¿A qué hora se abre (cierra)?** *ah kay OHR-ah say AH-bray (see-YEHR-ah)*
What's the admission price?	**¿Cuánto es la entrada?** *KWAHN-toh ehs lah ehn-TRAH-dah*
How much do children pay?	**¿Cuánto pagan los niños?** *KWAHN-toh pah-GAHN lohs NEEN-yohs*
Can they go in free? Until what age?	**¿Pueden entrar gratis? ¿Hasta qué edad?** *PWEH-dehn ehn-TRAHR GRAH-tees ah-stah kay eh-DAHD?*

Is it all right to take pictures?	**¿Se puede sacar fotos?** *say PWEH-deh sah-KAHR FOH-tohs*
How much extra does it cost to take pictures?	**¿Hay que pagar para poder sacar fotos?** *AH-ee kay pah-GAHR pah-rah poh-DEHR sah-KAHR FOH-tohs*
I do (not) use a flash attachment.	**(No) uso flash (luz instantánea).** *(noh) oo-soh flahsh (loos een-stahn-TAHN-ay-ah*

Prohibido Tomar Fotografías	(no picture-taking allowed)

A SIGHTSEEING ITINERARY—SPAIN

Spain is one of the great tourist destinations in the world today, and deservedly so. Many visitors from northern Europe view the country primarily as a place where they can escape the rigors of the cold by relaxing on the beaches of the Costa del Sol while soaking up the hot sun and swimming in the warm, clear-blue waters of the southern Mediterranean.

Spain does offer this, but also much more. Spain is a land of startling contrasts, offering the traveler large modern cities with urban amenities: department stores, museums, theaters, restaurants, high-fashion boutiques, and nightlife. In addition, the country is full of charming tiny villages with ancient churches, palaces, and looming castles that recall other eras.

Here are some of the highlights:

MADRID

The capital and largest city (3.7 million inhabitants), Madrid offers a vast variety of things to see and do.

1. *The Prado Museum* Houses one of the most magnificent art collections in the world, particularly strong in Spanish, Flemish, and Italian art.

2. *La Puerta del Sol* Considered the center of the city. It is a major transportation hub.

3. *La Plaza Mayor* A beautiful 17th-century square lined with shops and a couple of outdoor cafés. One of the entrances to the plaza is the Arco de Cuchilleros, which leads into Old Madrid, one of the most intriguing tourist areas of the city. Crowds throng the narrow streets with their many bars or *tascas* to sample *tapas* (snacks), drink wine, and listen to music.

4. *Retiro Park* A former palace grounds, this popular park near the Prado has tree-shaded paths, fountains, rose gardens, an enormous artificial lake for boating, two nightclubs, and over a dozen outdoor cafés.

5. *Calle Serrano* Madrid's best shopping street—blocks and blocks of chic shops and small restaurants.

6. *Museum of Lázaro Galdiano* A superb art collection displayed in the home of the collector, a writer and scholar.

7. *Museum of Decorative Arts* Five floors of an old mansion filled with ceramics, tiles, silver, crystal.

8. *Botanical Gardens (El Jardín Botánico)* Has a huge number of species of trees and plants from throughout the world.

9. *La Calle de Alcalá* and *La Gran Vía (Avenida de San José)* Wide boulevards which are two of Madrid's main thoroughfares.

10. *El Palacio Real* (Royal Palace) Used nowadays for important state functions. You can visit the luxurious throne room and see the collections of tapestries, porcelain, crystal, clocks, and fine art. The Royal Armory and Carriage Museum are also well worth a visit.

11. *El Rastro* (flea market) Located on Ribera de Curtidores Street, this fascinating open-air market is a place where on Sunday morning one can buy anything from antiques, junk, old clothes, toys and trinkets to furniture and art work. The rest of the week you can visit antique shops in the area. Bargaining is expected here.

12. *Teatro de la Zarzuela* Located behind the Spanish Parliament building (Las Cortes), this theater offers operas, ballets, and authentic Spanish Zarzuelas (light operas).

13. *Museum of the Americas* Has a collection of dolls, toys, masks, and other Indian items brought back from pre-Columbian America.

14. *Archeological Museum* Features a reconstruction of the thirty-thousand-year-old pre-historic Altamira cave, paintings of Altamira, more than 2,000 archaeological objects, and the rare statues called *Dama de Elche* and *Dama de Baza*.

15. *Casa de Campo* The largest park in Madrid, with a zoo, a wooded area, a lake, and an amusement park which can be reached by cable car from Paseo del Pintor Rosales. The car passes over the Manzanares River and affords a spectacular view of the city.

16. *Museo del Pueblo Español* This unusual museum contains dress and household items from the different regions of Spain.

17. *Plaza de España* A spacious plaza with two skyscrapers. (El Edificio España—the tallest building in Spain—and the Torre de Madrid). Note the small park with statues of Miguel Cervantes, Don Quixote, and Sancho Panza.

18. *Temple of Debod* An Egyptian temple of the 4th century, transported from Aswan to rescue it from the flooded dam area.

PLACES NEAR MADRID

1. *El Escorial* An enormous monastery, mausoleum, and palace constructed by King Felipe II.

2. *El Valle de los Caídos* (Valley of the Fallen) General Francisco Franco's tomb and monument dedicated to the memory of those who fell in the Spanish Civil War.

CITIES THAT ARE EASY DAY TRIPS FROM MADRID

1. *Segovia* Known for its first-century Roman aqueduct and its fairytalelike *Alcázar* on a hilltop overlooking the medieval town.

2. *Ávila* A medieval city of churches, with the oldest, best-preserved city walls in Spain, possibly in all Europe.

3. *Aranjuez* With its 18th-century Royal Palace and fabulous gardens.

4. *Toledo* A jewel of a city, still medieval in feeling, famous for its many El Greco paintings and for its mix of Moorish, Jewish, and Christian legacies. Don't miss: the cathedral; El Greco's house and museum; Church of Santo Tomé with one of El Greco's masterpieces; and the Museum of Santa Cruz.

BARCELONA

Spain's principal seaport and industrial heart has a population of approximately two million people. Among its many attractions are:

1. *The Ramblas* A wide, tree-lined boulevard that goes from the center of the city to the waterfront, where one can stroll past flower stalls, caged birds, newspaper and magazine stands, and book shops.

2. *The Pueblo Español* Located on top of Montjuich (reachable by cable railway), is a model village featuring buildings from the various regions of the country. In the village the visitors can see pottery making, glass blowing, and other arts and crafts.

3. *The Plaza de Cataluña* A beautiful and spacious plaza located in the center of the city.

4. *The Catedral* A Gothic monument located in the *barrio gótico* (the Gothic quarter), the old part of the city; this is the site of Sardana dancing on weekends.

5. *The Picasso Museum* Contains one of the world's largest collections of the famous modern Spanish artist, installed in a 13th-century palace.

6. *Museum of Catalonian Art* A rare collection of 11th- and 12th-century Romanesque art, as well as works by El Greco, Tintoretto, and others.

7. *Museum of Federico Marés* An unusual and rare sculpture collection located in a palace near the Cathedral.

8. *The Church of the Sagrada Familia* (Holy Family) The spectacular unfinished work of the architect Antonio Gaudí.

9. *Parque Güell* The whimsical park designed by Gaudí.

SEVILLA

One of the most picturesque and romantic of all Spanish cities. In Sevilla, you can see:

1. *Museo Provincial de Bellas Artes* A collection of Spanish painting, lodged in an old convent.

2. *La Catedral* The largest cathedral in all of Spain.

3. *La Giralda* The bell tower of the cathedral which was constructed originally as the minaret of a mosque. City views from the top are extraordinary.

4. *El Alcázar* A Christian and Moorish fortress with beautiful gardens.

5. *Barrio Santa Cruz* Onetime Jewish quarter of narrow, winding streets.

6. *La Calle de las Sierpes* (Snake Street) The principal business thoroughfare of the city, lined with sidewalk cafés, restaurants, and shops.

7. *Itálica* Remains of a Roman city just outside Sevilla.

GRANADA

When in Granada, don't miss the following:

1. *The Alhambra* Exquisitely beautiful Moorish palace, one of the major sights of Spain.

2. *The Albaicín* The gypsy quarter whose inhabitants dwell in furnished caves with electricity.

3. *The Generalife* Summer palace of the Moorish kings, famous for its beautiful gardens.

CÓRDOBA

One can visit the imposing Mezquita (the Great Mosque), with its beautiful marble columns and intricate mosaics and its superimposed Christian church inside. Also visit *Judería,* the old Jewish quarter of Cordova with a tiny synagogue, the only one left in town.

MARBELLA AND TORREMOLINOS

Fashionable resort areas on the Costa del Sol, with its Mediterranean beaches, luxurious hotels, and fine restaurants.

SIGHTSEEING IN THE NEW WORLD

These lands are so vast, it would be impossible to cover anything but a fraction of what can be seen by the traveler. Here are but a few of the highlights.

MÉXICO CITY

In this large country, don't miss these, all in Mexico City and its vicinity:

1. *Chapultepec Castle and Park* A magnificent park containing a zoo, museums, lakes, and concert halls. One of the largest parks in the world.

2. *The Palacio de Bellas Artes* (Palace of Fine Arts) Contains the famous murals of Rivera, Siqueiros, and Orozco.
3. *La Ciudad Universitaria* (University City) An architectural and artistic wonder, the site of the past Olympic Games. The library building is completely covered with brilliantly covered mosaic tiles depicting the history of Mexico.
4. *La Torre Latinoamericana* The tallest building in Mexico. The magnificent view from the top gives you a bird's-eye view of the entire city.
5. *El Zócalo* The main square of the city. Here one finds the National Palace with its magnificent Diego Rivera murals.
6. *The Plaza de Garibaldi* The center for the Mariachis, strolling musicians who rent themselves out for tips.
7. *Floating Gardens of Xochimilco* The Venice of the Americas. Boats can be rented to travel through the miles of flower-lined canals.
8. *Teotihuacán* Famous Toltec ruins, which include the Pyramids of the Sun and of the Moon and the Temple of Quetzalcoatl.

ACAPULCO

Known as the "pearl of the Pacific," this famous beach resort is on the Pacific Ocean. The daring cliff divers at La Quebrada are an unforgettable experience.

CANCÚN AND THE ISLAND OF COZUMEL

Mexico's paradise on the Caribbean, noted for its swimming, scuba diving, snorkeling, and fishing.

ELSEWHERE IN MEXICO

1. *Chichén-Itzá* Famous Mayan ruins, located on the Yucatán Peninsula.
2. *Taxco* Famous for its silver shops and silver factories which line the streets.

PUERTO RICO

A tourist's delight, just 3½ hours from New York. When there, visit: San Juan's University at Rio Piedras, a large modern university with over 50,000 students. Also see Old San Juan, the original city built by the Spaniards in the 16th century. One main attraction is El Morro, a fortress constructed to ward off attacks by English pirates. Also in Puerto Rico, visit El Yunque, a luxurious rain forest with exotic vegetation, waterfalls, and tropical birds.

DOMINICAN REPUBLIC

Santo Domingo is the capital and largest city (half a million inhabitants) of this pleasant and friendly Caribbean island. The old cathedral is visited by tourists who come to see the tomb of Christopher Columbus. When here, also see:

1. *The Alcázar* The restored palace of Diego Columbus. It is richly furnished with paintings, furniture, and tapestries of the 16th century.
2. *Los Tres Ojos* (the three eyes) Located on the outskirts of the capital, this is a marvelous natural phenomenon of three underground springs.
3. *Puerto Plata* Noted for its white, sandy beaches on the northern coast of the island.

VENEZUELA

Caracas is the vibrant, modern capital of this oil-rich country, a sprawling metropolis of over three million people. In Venezuela, see also:

1. *Macuto Beach* Easily accessible, and very popular.
2. *Colonia Tovar* An authentic German village located in the mountains near Caracas.
3. *Margarita Island* An unspoiled and beautiful island in the Caribbean. Travelers go there from Caracas by plane or hydrofoil.

PERU

Lima, the capital, is a cosmopolitan city of over six million people. Two important areas are the Plaza San Martín and the Plaza de Armas. They are connected by the Jirón Unión, a major shopping street. See also:

1. *Cuzco* The ancient capital of the Incas. It combines both the Indian and Spanish colonial cultures.

2. *Machu Picchu* One of the wonders of the world; high in the Andes, this is the Lost City of the Incas.

COLOMBIA

Bogotá is the beautiful capital and principal city, known as the "Athens of South America." See also Cartagena, a coastal city on the Caribbean. It is a popular resort area.

There are many more countries and many more exciting places to visit. These suggestions are just a starter. *¡Buen Viaje!*

RELIGIOUS SERVICES

In addition to viewing the churches and cathedrals, you may wish to attend services.

Is there a ___ near here?	**¿Hay una ___ cerca de aquí?** *AH-ee oo-nah ___ SEHR-kah day ah-KEE*
Catholic church	**iglesia católica** *ee-GLAY-see-ah kah-TOHL-ee-kah*
Protestant church	**iglesia protestante** *ee-GLAY-see-ah pro-test-AHN-tay*
Synagogue	**sinagoga** *see-nah-GOH-gah*
Mosque	**mezquita** *mehs-KEE-tah*
When is the service (mass)?	**¿A qué hora es la misa?** *ah kay OH-rah ehs lah MEE-sah*
I want to speak to a ___.	**Quiero hablar con ___.** *kee-EHR-oh ah-BLAHR kohn*
priest	**un cura** *oon KOO-rah*
minister	**un ministro** *oon mee-NEES-troh*
rabbi	**un rabino** *oon rah-BEEN-oh*

PLANNING A TRIP

During your stay you may want to plan some excursions into the country or to other cities. In most countries you can move about by airplane, train, bus, boat, and car (see Driving a Car). For air travel within a country, look for signs to the domestic terminal (sometimes separate from the international terminal).

AIR SERVICES

Within Spain, two domestic airlines—Iberia and Avianco—fly to more than 36 cities. Unfortunately, to reach city A from B, you often have to go via Madrid and transfer. Barajas is ten miles from Madrid, but most airports are located within a few miles of a given city. A special ticket called "Visit Spain" gives unlimited air travel within Spain on Iberia for $149 for 45 days.

Flights within Mexico are easily arranged, particularly to other major tourist cities, such as Acapulco or the Yucatán. For trips among other Central and South American cities, consult your travel agent.

When is there a flight to ____?	**¿Cuándo hay un vuelo a ____?**	*KWAHN-doh AH-ee oon BWEHL-oh ah*
I would like a ____ ticket.	**Quisiera un billete ____.**	*kee-see-YEHR-ah oon bee-YEH-tay*
▀ round trip	**de ida y vuelta** *day EE-dah ee BWEHL-tah*	
▀ one way	**de ida** *day EE-dah*	
▀ tourist class	**en clase turista** *ehn KLAH-say toor-EES-tah*	
▀ first class	**en primera clase** *ehn pree-MEHR-ah KLAH-say*	
I would like a seat ____.	**Quisiera un asiento ____.**	*kee-see-YEHR-ah oon ah-SYEHN-toh*

■ in the smoking section	**en la sección de fumadores** *ehn lah sehk-SYOHN day foo-mah-DOHR-ehs*
■ in the nonsmoking section	**en la sección de no fumadores** *ehn lah sehk-SYOHN day noh foo-mah-DOHR-ehs*
■ next to the window	**de ventanilla** *day behn-tah-NEE-yah*
■ on the aisle	**de pasillo** *day pah-SEE-yoh*
What is the fare?	**¿Cuál es la tarifa?** *kwahl ehs lah tah-REE-fah*
Are meals served?	**¿Se sirven comidas?** *say seer-behn koh-MEE-dahs*
When does the plane leave (arrive)?	**¿A qué hora sale (llega) el avión?** *ah kay oh-ra SAH-lay (YEH-gah) ehl ah-BYOHN*
When must I be at the airport?	**¿Cuándo debo estar en el aeropuerto?** *KWAHN-doh deh-boh ehs-TAHR en ehl ah-ehr-oh-PWEHR-toh*
What is my flight number?	**¿Cuál es el número del vuelo?** *kwahl ehs ehl NOO-mehr-oh dehl BWEH-loh*
What gate do we leave from?	**¿De qué puerta se sale?** *day kay PWEHR-tah say sah-lay*
I want to confirm (cancel) my reservation for flight ____.	**Quiero confirmar (cancelar) mi reservación para el vuelo ____.** *kee-YEHR-oh kohn-feer-MAHR (kahn-say-LAHR) mee reh-sehr-bah-SYOHN pah-rah ehl BWEH-loh*
I'd like to check my bags.	**Quisiera facturar mis maletas.** *kee-SYEHR-ah fahk-too-RAHR mees mah-LEH-tahs*
I have only carry-on baggage.	**Tengo solo equipaje de mano.** *TEN-goh so-loh ay-kee-PAH-hay day MAH-noh*

| Can you pass my film (camera) through by hand? | **¿Podría inspeccionar el film (la cámara) a mano?** *poh-DREE-ah een-spek-syohn-AHR ehl feelm (lah KAH-mahr-ah) ah MAHN-oh* |

NOTE: Some high-speed film can be damaged by airport security x-rays. It is best to pack film in your suitcase, protected in a lead insulated bag. If you have film in your camera or carry-on baggage, avoid problems and ask the guard to pass it through by hand. If the guard refuses, bow to his wishes.

TRAIN SERVICE

RENFE offers a kilometric ticket that can save you up to 20% of your fare; round-trip fares on some routes save 25%. A *Tarjeta Dorado* (Gold Card) costs 25 pesetas and can save up to 50% on rail trips— available only to those 65 years or older.

The EURAILPASS is good in Spain, as well as 15 other countries. Tickets for unlimited train travel are available for 15 or 21 days or 1, 2 or 3 months.

The following is a brief description of the varieties of Spanish trains.

Talgo	A luxury diesel express with reclining seats and air conditioning. It operates between Madrid and major cities—Barcelona, Bilbao, Cadiz, Malaga, Sevilla, Valencia, Zaragoza.
Electrotren	A luxury train, but it is slower than Talgo, makes more stops, and covers more of the country. It is cheaper than Talgo.
TER	A luxury diesel express train, slower than Talgo and makes more stops.
TAF	A second-class diesel train.
Expreso	A long-distance night train, with only a few major stops.
Rápido	A fast train (slower than the Expreso).

Omnibuses or ferrobuses	Local trains.

A first (second) class ticket to _____ please.	**Un billete de primera (segunda) clase a _____ por favor.** *oon bee-YEH-teh day pree-MEHR-ah (say-GOON-dah) KLAH-say ah _____ pohr fah-BOHR*
▪ a half price ticket	**un medio billete** *oon MEH-dee-oh bee-YEH-teh*
▪ a round trip ticket	**un billete de ida y vuelta** *oon bee-YEH-teh day EE-dah ee BWEHL-tah*
▪ a one way ticket	**un billete de ida** *oon bee-YEH-teh day EE-dah*
I'd like a (no) smoking compartment.	**Quisiera un departamento para (no) fumadores.** *kee-SYEHR-ah oon day-pahr-tah-MEHN-toh pah-rah (noh) foo-mah-DOHR-ays*
When does the train arrive (leave)?	**¿Cuándo llega (sale) el tren?** *kwahn-doh YEH-gah (SAH-lay) ehl trehn*
From (at) what platform does it leave (arrive)?	**¿De (A) qué andén sale (llega)?** *day (ah) kay ahn-DEHN SAH-lay (YEH-gah)*
Does this train stop at _____?	**¿Para este tren en _____?** *PAH-rah ehs-tay trehn ehn*
Is the train late?	**¿Tiene retraso el tren?** *tee-YEH-nay ray-TRAH-soh ehl trehn*
How long does it stop?	**¿Cuánto tiempo para?** *kwahn-toh tee-EHM-poh PAH-rah*
Is there time to get a bite?	**¿Hay tiempo para tomar un bocado?** *ahy tee-EHM-poh PAH-rah toh-MAHR oon boh-KAH-doh*
Do we have to stand in line?	**¿Tenemos que hacer cola?** *tehn-EH-mohs kay ah-SEHR KOH-lah*

ON THE TRAIN

Passengers, all aboard!	**!Señores pasajeros, suban al tren!** *sehn-YOHR-ays pah-sah-HEHR-ohs soo-bahn ahl trehn*
Is there a dining car (sleeping car)?	**¿Hay coche-comedor (coche-cama)?** *ahy KOH-chay koh-may-DOHR (KOH-chay KAH-mah)*
Is it ____?	**¿Es ____?** *ehs*
■ a through train	**un tren directo** *oon trehn dee-REHK-toh*
■ a local	**un tren local (ómnibus, ordinario)** *oon trehn loh-KAHL (OHM-nee-boos, ohr-dee-NAH-ree-oh)*
■ an express	**un expreso (rápido)** *oon eks-PREHS-oh (RAH-pee-doh)*
Do I have to change trains?	**¿Tengo que trasbordar?** *TEHN-goh kay trahs-bohr-DAHR*
Is this seat taken?	**¿Está ocupado este asiento?** *ehs-TAH oh-koo-PAH-doh EHS-tay ah-SYEHN-toh*
Where are we now?	**¿Dónde estamos ahora?** *DOHN-day ehs-tah-mohs ah-OHR-ah*
Will we arrive on time (late)?	**¿Llegaremos a tiempo (tarde)?** *yeh-gahr-EH-mohs ah tee-EHM-poh (tahr-day)*
Can I check my bag through to ____?	**¿Puedo facturar mi maleta hasta ____?** *PWEH-doh fahk-toor-AHR mee mah-LEH-tah AHS-tah*
Excuse me, but you are in my seat.	**Perdón, creo que está ocupando mi asiento.** *pehr-DOHN, KRAY-oh key ehs-TAH oh-koo-PAHN-doh mee ah-SYEHN-toh*

SHIPBOARD TRAVEL

If you want to visit any surrounding islands, then you'll want to arrange to take the boat there.

Where is the dock?	**¿Dónde está el muelle?** *DOHN-day ehs-TAH ehl MWEH-yeh*
When does the next boat leave for ____?	**¿Cuándo sale el próximo barco para ____?** *KWAHN-doh SAH-lay ehl PROHKS-ee-moh BAHR-koh pah-rah*
How long does the crossing take?	**¿Cuánto dura la travesía?** *KWAHN-toh doo-rah lah trah-beh-SEE-ah*
Do we stop at any other ports?	**¿Hacemos escala en algunos puertos?** *ah-SAY-mohs ehs-KAH-lah ehn ahl-GOO-nohs PWEHR-tohs*
How long will we remain in the port?	**¿Cuánto tiempo permaneceremos en el puerto?** *KWAHN-toh tee-EHM-poh pehr-mah-neh-sehr-EH-mohs ehn ehl PWEHR-toh*

When do we land?	**¿Cuándo desembarcamos?** *KWAHN-doh dehs-ehm-bahr-KAH-mohs*
At what time do we have to be back on board?	**¿A qué hora debemos volver a bordo?** *ah kay OHR-ah deh-BAY-mohs bohl-BEHR ah BOHR-doh*
I'd like a _____ ticket.	**Quisiera un pasaje _____.** *kee-SYEHR-ah oon pah-SAH-hay*
▪ first class	**de primera clase** *day pree-MEHR-ah KLAH-say*
▪ tourist class	**de clase turista** *day KLAH-say toor-EES-tah*
▪ cabin	**para un camarote** *PAH-rah oon kah-mah-ROH-tay*
I don't feel well.	**No me siento bien.** *noh may SYEHN-toh byehn*
Can you give me something for sea sickness?	**¿Puede usted darme algo contra el mareo?** *PWEH-day oos-TEHD DAHR-may AHL-goh KOHN-trah ehl mah-RAY-oh*

TRAVEL TIP

Tired of waiting for your suitcase to come off the plane? You can avoid this delay by packing all your belongings into a small carry-on bag. Especially for those who travel light, the carry-on bag is sufficient to hold a week or two's clothing and personal goods. Avoid bags that are too large to fit under your seat on the plane, however, since not all airlines use planes with overhead bins capable of holding such bags. Some airlines have limits on the dimensions of carry-on bags, and if your bag exceeds those limits, you must check the item.

ENTERTAINMENTS AND DIVERSIONS

MOVIES, THEATER, CONCERTS, OPERA, BALLET

To find out what's doing in Madrid, consult the daily newspaper *ABC,* under the heading **"Espectáculos"**; *En Madrid,* a monthly English-Spanish leaflet available at the Madrid Tourist Office; or *Guía del Ocio* (Leisure Guide), a weekly listing of entertainment, hours, and admission fees.

The latest movies are at theaters along the Gran Vía in Madrid. The movies are dubbed into Spanish. Admission is usually 250 pesetas or less. Ushers should be tipped 5 pesetas.

There are 23 theaters in Madrid. **Teatro Zarzuela** is the most fun for tourists who are not well-versed in Spanish. Zarzuela consists of 19th-century light operas or operettas, with lots of music, dance, and pretty costumes. Classical Spanish theater can be seen at **Teatro Español** and **María Guerrero Theater.** Theater prices range from 200 to 1200 pesetas. Everything runs late in Spain. Matinees are at 7 or 7:30 p.m., evening performances are at 10:30 p.m.

Symphonic concerts can be heard at the beautiful 19th-century **Teatro Real,** the Madrid Cultural Center auditorium, **Fundación Juan March,** or Sundays in the Plaza del Maestro Villa in Retiro Park. Pop, rock, and jazz music can be heard in some discos, certain movie theaters, college auditoriums, and at various bars and pubs. Check the above-mentioned listings to determine where and when.

Theater and concert schedules and procedures vary throughout the rest of the Spanish-speaking world, so we advise you to check with your hotel concierge or the tourist office in the town in which you are staying in order to find out what is going on and where to get tickets.

Let's go to the ___.	**Vamos al ___.**	*BAH-mohs ahl*
movies (cinema)	**cine**	*SEE-nay*
theater	**teatro**	*tay-AH-troh*

What are they showing today?	**¿Qué ponen hoy?** *kay POH-nehn oy*
Is it a ___?	**¿Es ___?** *ehs*
mystery	**un misterio** *oon mee-STEHR-ee-oh*
comedy	**una comedia** *OO-nah koh-MEH-dee-ah*
drama	**un drama** *oon DRAH-mah*
musical	**una obra musical** *OO-nah OH-brah moo-see-KAHL*
romance	**una obra romántica** *OO-nah OH-brah roh-MAHN-tee-kah*
Western	**una película del Oeste** *OO-nah pehl-EE-koo-lah del OWEST-ay*
war film	**una película de guerra** *OO-nah pehl-EE-koo-lah day GHEHR-ah*
science fiction film	**una película de ciencia ficción** *oo-nah pehl-EE-koo-lah day see-EHN-see-ah feek-SYOHN*

cartoon	**una película de dibujos animados** *oo-nah pehl-EE-koo-lah day dee-BOO-hohs ah-nee-MAH-dohs*
Is it in English?	**¿Es hablada en inglés?** *ehs ah-BLAH-dah ehn een-GLAYSS*
Has it been dubbed?	**¿Ha sido doblada?** *ah SEE-doh doh-BLAH-dah*
Where is the box office?	**¿Dónde está la taquilla?** *DOHN-day ehs-TAH lah tah-KEE-yah*
What time does the (first) show begin?	**¿A qué hora empieza la (primera) función?** *ah kay OHR-ah ehm-PYEH-sah lah (pree-MEHR-ah) foon-SYOHN*
What time does the (last) show end?	**¿A qué hora termina la (última) función?** *ah kay OHR-ah tehr-MEEN-ah lah (OOL-tee-mah) foon-SYOHN*
I want a seat near the middle (front, rear).	**Quisiera un asiento en el centro (al frente, atrás).** *kee SYEHR-ah oon ah-SYEHN-toh ehn ehl SEHN-troh (ahl FREHN-tay, ah-TRAHS)*
Can I check my coat?	**¿Puedo dejar mi abrigo?** *PWEH-doh day-HAHR mee ah-BREE-goh*

BUYING TICKETS

I need two tickets for tonight.	**Necesito dos entradas para esta noche.** *neh-seh-SEE-toh dohs ehn-TRAH-dahs pah-rah ehs-tah NOH-chay*
orchestra	**de platea** *day plah-TAY-ah*
balcony	**de galería** *day gah-lehr-EE-ah*
mezzanine	**de anfiteatro** *day ahn-fee-tay-AH-troh*
We would like to attend ____.	**Quisiéramos asistir a ____.** *kee-SYEHR-ah-mohs ah-sees-TEER ah*
a ballet	**un ballet** *oon bah-LEH*
a concert	**un concierto** *oon kohn-SYEHR-toh*
an opera	**una ópera** *oo-nah OH-pehr-ah*

What are they playing (singing)?	**¿Qué están interpretando?** *kay ehs-TAHN een-tehr-pray-TAHN-doh*
Who is the conductor?	**¿Quién es el director?** *kee-YEHN ehs ehl dee-rehk-TOHR*
I prefer _____.	**Prefiero _____.** *preh-fee-YEHR-oh*
classical music	**la música clásica** *lah MOO-see-kah KLAH-see-kah*
popular music	**la música popular** *lah MOO-see-kah poh-poo-LAHR*
folk dance	**el ballet folklórico** *ehl bah-LEH foh-KLOHR-ee-koh*
ballet	**el ballet** *ehl bah-LEH*
Are there any seats for tonight's performance?	**¿Hay localidades para la representación de esta noche?** *AH-ee loh-kahl-ee-DAHD-ays pah-rah lah rep-reh-sen-tah-SYOHN day ehs-tah NOH-chay*
When does the season begin (end)?	**¿Cuándo empieza (termina) la temporada?** *KWAHN-doh ehm-PYEH-sah (tehr-MEEN-ah) lah tem-pohr-AH-dah*
Should I get the tickets in advance?	**¿Debo sacar las entradas de antemano?** *deh-boh sah-KAHR lahs ehn-TRAH-dahs day ahn-tay-MAH-noh*
Do I have to dress formally?	**¿Tengo que ir de etiqueta?** *TEN-goh kay eer day eh-tee-KEH-tah*
How much are the front row seats?	**¿Cuánto valen los asientos delanteros?** *KWAHN-toh bah-lehn lohs ahs-YEHN-tohs day-lahn-TEHR-ohs*
What are the least expensive seats?	**¿Cuáles son los asientos más baratos?** *KWAHL-ays sohn lohs ahs-YEHN-tohs mahs bah-RAH-tohs*

May I buy a program?	**¿Puedo comprar un programa?** *PWEH-doh kohm-PRAHR oon pro-GRAHM-ah*
What opera (ballet) are they performing?	**¿Qué ópera (ballet) ponen?** *kay OH-pehr-ah (bah-LEH) POH-nen*
Who's singing (tenor, soprano, baritone, contralto)?	**¿Quién canta (tenor, soprano, barítono, contralto)?** *kee-YEHN KAHN-tah (ten-OHR, soh-PRAH-noh, barítono, kohn-TRAHL-toh)*

NIGHTCLUBS, DANCING

There are **discotecas** and nightclubs and big Las Vegas-type shows at some of the larger, new hotels. There are even a few satirical reviews in cafe settings. Madrid is now as wide-open after dark as any European capital, more so than some. You will find **flamenco** performed in small clubs, such as Cafe de Chinitas, off the Gran Vía.

Hours at discos are approximately 7 p.m. to 3 a.m. Night club shows are at 11 p.m. or midnight or 1 a.m. **Tablao flamenco** places are open from 10 p.m. to 3 a.m., with shows at 12 and 1:30 or so. It is customary, but not required, to dine at the nightclub or flamenco place before the show, in which case you would arrive about 10 or 11 p.m., then stay for the midnight show.

Let's go to a nightclub.	**Vamos a un cabaret.** *BAH-mohs ah oon kah-bah-REH*
Is a reservation necessary?	**¿Hace falta una reserva?** *ah-say FAHL-tah oo-nah reh-SEHR-bah*
Is it customary to dine there as well?	**¿Se puede comer allá también?** *say PWEH-day koh-MEHR ah-YAH tahm-BYEHN*
Is there a good discotheque here?	**¿Hay aquí una buena discoteca?** *AH-ee ah-KEE oo-nah BWEH-nah dees-koh-TAY-kah*

Is there dancing at the hotel?	**¿Hay un baile en el hotel?** *AH-ee oon BAH-ee-lay ehn ehl oh-TEL*
We'd like a table near the dance floor.	**Quisiéramos una mesa cerca de la pista.** *kee-SYEHR-ah-mohs oo-nah MAY-sah sehr-kah day lah PEES-tah*
Is there a minimum (cover charge)?	**¿Hay un mínimo?** *AH-ee oon MEE-nee-moh*
Where is the checkroom?	**¿Dónde está el guardarropa?** *DOHN-day eh-STAH ehl gwahr-dah-ROH-pah*
At what time does the floor show go on?	**¿A qué hora empieza el espectáculo?** *ah kay OH-rah ehm-pee-EH-sah ehl ehs-peh-TAH-kool-oh*

QUIET RELAXATION

Tourists don't often take the time to relax, but you'll have a more enjoyable trip if you occasionally break from the sightseeing and have a quiet game of cards. You'll also find that games are an excellent way to meet Spanish people and begin to learn the language.

Where can I get a deck of cards?	**¿Dónde puedo conseguir una baraja?** *DOHN-day PWEH-doh kohn-seh-GHEER oo-nah bah-RAH-ha*
Do you want to play cards?	**¿Quiere usted jugar a las cartas?** *kee-YEHR-ay oos-TEHD hoo-GAHR ah lahs KAHR-tahs*
▪ bridge	**al bridge** *ahl breech*
▪ black jack	**al veintiuno** *ahl bayn-tee-OO-noh*
▪ poker	**al póker** *ahl POH-kehr*
I have the highest card.	**Tengo la carta más alta.** *TEN-goh lah KAHR-tah mahs AHL-tah*
▪ an ace	**un as** *oon ahs*

a king	**un rey** *oon ray*
a queen	**una reina** *OO-nah RAY-nah*
a jack	**una sota** *oo-nah SOH-tah*
Do you want to cut (shuffle)?	**¿Quiere usted cortar (barajar)?** *kee-YEHR-ay oos-TEHD kohr-TAHR (bahr-ah-HAHR)*
Do you have clubs (hearts, spades, diamonds)?	**¿Tiene usted bastos (copas, espadas, oros)?** *tee-YEH-nay oos-TEHD BAH-stohs (KOH-pahs, ehs-PAH-dahs, OHR-ohs)*
It's your turn (to deal).	**A usted le toca dar.** *ah oos-TEHD lay TOH-kah dahr*
Who opens?	**¿Quién abre?** *kee-EHN AH-bray*
What's your score?	**¿Cuántos tantos tiene usted?** *KWAHN-tohs TAHN-tohs tee-ehn-ay oos-TEHD*
I win (lose).	**Yo gano (pierdo).** *yoh GAH-noh (pee-YEHR-doh)*

BOARD GAMES

Do you want to play _____?	**¿Quiere jugar _____?** *kee-YEHR-ay hoo-GAHR*
checkers (draughts)	**a las damas** *ah lahs DAH-mahs*
chess	**al ajedrez** *ahl ah-hay-DREHS*
dominoes	**al dominó** *ahl dohm-ee-NOH*
We need a board.	**Necesitamos un tablero.** *neh-ses-ee-TAH-mohs oon tah-BLEHR-oh*
dice	**los dados** *lohs DAH-dohs*
the pieces	**las piezas** *lahs pee-AY-sahs*
the king	**el rey** *ehl ray*
the queen	**la reina** *lah RAY-nah*

the rook	**la torre**	*lah TOH-ray*
the bishop	**el alfil**	*ehl ahl-FEEL*
the knight	**el caballo**	*ehl kah-BAH-yoh*
the pawn	**el peón**	*ehl pay-OHN*
Check	**Jaque**	*HAH-kay*
Checkmate	**Jaque mate**	*HAH-kay MAH-tay*

SPECTATOR SPORTS

THE BULLFIGHT

The bullfight season in Spain runs from March to October. Sunday is the day, 5 or 7 p.m. the time. In Madrid there are two **plaza de toros**—the larger, most convenient is Plaza de Toros Monumental de las Ventas, the smaller is Plaza de Toros de Vista Alegre. Ticket prices range from 55 to 1,420 pesetas, depending on sun or shade locations. You can purchase tickets through your hotel concierge, at the **plaza de toros,** or at the official city box office at 3 Calle de la Victoria.

If you have not seen a bullfight before, it is wise to avoid a **Novillada,** a **corrida** with inexperienced matadors and under- or over-aged bulls.

el matador	kills the bull with his espada (sword).
el banderillero	thrusts three sets of long darts (banderillas) into the bull's neck to enfuriate him.
el picador	bullfighter mounted on a horse who weakens the bull with his lance (pica).
la cuadrilla	a team of helpers for the torero, who confuse and tire the bull with their capes (capas).
el monosabio	assistant who does various jobs in the redondel (bullring).

Is there a bullfight this afternoon? (every Sunday)?	**¿Hay una corrida de toros esta tarde (todos los domingos)?** *AH-ee oo-nah koh-REE-dah day TOH-rohs ehs-tah TAHR-day (toh-dohs lohs doh-MEEN-gohs)*
Take me to the bullring.	**Lléveme a la Plaza de Toros.** *YEH-bay-may ah lah PLAH-sah day TOHR-ohs*
I'd like a seat in the shade (in the sun).	**Quisiera un sitio a la sombra (al sol).** *kees-YEH-rah oon SEE-tee-oh ah lah SOHM-brah (ahl sohl)*
When does the parade of the bullfighters begin?	**¿Cuándo empieza el desfile de la cuadrilla?** *KWAHN-doh ehm-PYEH-sah ehl dehs-FEEL-ay day lah kwahd-REE-yah*
When does the first bull appear?	**¿Cuándo sale el primer toro?** *KWAHN-doh sah-lay ehl pree-MEHR TOH-roh*
How well that bullfighter works!	**¡Qué bien torea aquel matador!** *kay bee-EHN toh-RAY-ah ah-kehl mah-tah-DOHR*
Bravo!	**¡Olé!** *oh-LAY*

SOCCER

Soccer—called **fútbol**—is a popular sport in Spain and Latin America. In season, between September to June, you're sure to find a game somewhere any Sunday at 5 p.m. Madrid has two teams, *Atlético de Madrid* plays in the Vicente Calderón Stadium; *Real Madrid* team plays in Santiago Bernabeu stadium. Tickets are available through your hotel concierge or at the stadium. Cost is usually 500 to 2,500 pesetas, depending on location.

I'd like to watch a soccer match.	**Quisiera ver un partido de fútbol.** *kee-SYEHR-ah behr oon pahr-TEE-doh day FOOT-bohl*

Where's the stadium?	**¿Dónde está el estadio?** *DOHN-day ehs-TAH ehl ehs-TAH-dee-oh*
When does the first half begin?	**¿Cuándo empieza el primer tiempo?** *KWAHN-doh ehm-pee-EH-sah ehl pree-MEHR tee-EM-poh*
What teams are going to play?	**¿Qué equipos van a jugar?** *kay eh-kee-pohs bahn ah hoo-GAHR*
Who is playing _____?	**¿Quién es _____?** *kee-YEHN ehs*
▪ center	**el centro** *ehl SEN-troh*
▪ fullback	**el defensa** *ehl day-FEN-sah*
▪ halfback	**el medio** *ehl MED-ee-oh*
▪ wing	**el ala** *ehl AH-lah*
What was the score?	**¿Cuál fue la anotación?** *kwahl fway lah ah-noh-tah-SYOHN*

JAI ALAI

Pelota *(jai alai)* is a very fast Basque game played in a court called a **frontón.** There are two teams of two players each. The players each have a **cesta** (curved basket) to throw and catch the ball with. During the match, spectators may place bets on the teams. Hours are 5:30 p.m. daily, in Spain at Frontón de Madrid, 10 Calle Doctor Cortezo.

Are you a jai alai fan?	**¿Es usted aficionado a la pelota?** *ehs oos-TEHD ah-fee-syohn-AH-doh ah lah pel-OH-tah*
I'd like to see a jai alai match.	**Me gustaría ver un partido de pelota.** *may goos-tahr-EE-ah behr oon par-TEE-doh day pel-OH-tah*
Where can I get tickets?	**¿Dónde puedo conseguir billetes?** *DOHN-day pweh-doh kohn-seh-GEER bee-YEH-tays*
Where is the jai alai court?	**¿Dónde está el frontón?** *DOHN-day ehs-TAH ehl frohn-TOHN*

Who are the players?	**¿Quiénes son los jugadores?** *kee-YEHN-ehs sohn lohs hoo-gah-DOHR-ays*
Each team has a forward and a back.	**Cada equipo teine un delantero y un zaguero.** *kah-dah eh-kee-poh tee-EHN-ay oon day-lahn-TEHR-oh ee oon sah-GHER-oh*
Where do I place my bet?	**¿Dónde hago la apuesta?** *DOHN-day ah-goh lah ah-PWEH-stah*
▣ at that window	**en esa ventanilla** *ehn EH-sah ben-tah-NEE-yah*

HORSE RACING

There is no horse racing in Spain in the summer. In season, it is available at El Hippódromo de la Zarzuela on La Carretera de la Coruña.

Is there a race track here?	**¿Hay un hipódromo aquí?** *AH-ee oon ee-POH-droh-moh ah-KEE*
I want to see the races.	**Quiero ver las carreras de caballos.** *kee-EHR-oh behr lahs kahr-EHR-ahs day kah-BAH-yohs*

ACTIVE SPORTS

Do you play tennis?	**¿Sabe usted jugar al tenis?** *SAH-bay oos-TEHD hoo-GAHR ahl TEN-ees*
I (don't) play very well.	**(No) juego muy bien.** *(noh) hoo-AY-goh mwee bee-EHN*
Do you play singles (doubles)?	**¿Juega usted solo (en pareja)?** *HWAY-gah oos-TEHD SOH-loh (ehn pahr-AY-hah)*
Do you know where there is a court?	**¿Sabe usted dónde hay una cancha?** *SAH-bay oos-TEHD DOHN-day AH-ee oo-nah KAHN-chah*

Is it a private club? I'm not a member.	**¿Es un club privado? No soy socio.** *ehs oon kloob pree-BAH-do noh soy SOH-see-oh*
Can I rent a racquet?	**¿Se puede alquilar una raqueta?** *say PWEH-day ahl-kee-LAHR oo-nah rah-KAY-tah*
How much do they charge per hour (per day)?	**¿Cuánto cobran por hora (por día)?** *KWAHN-toh KOH-brahn pohr OH-rah (pohr DEE-ah)?*
Do you sell balls for a hard (soft) surface?	**¿Vende pelotas para una superficie dura (blanda)?** *BEN-day peh-LOH-tahs pah-rah oo-nah soo-pehr-FEE-syeh DOO-rah (BLAHN-dah)*
I serve (You serve) first.	**Yo saco (Usted saca) primero.** *yoh SAH-koh (oos-TEHD SAH-kah) pree-MEHR-oh*
You play very well.	**Usted juega muy bien.** *oos-TEHD hoo-EH-gah mwee bee-EHN*
You've won.	**Usted ha ganado.** *oos-TEHD ah gah-NAH-doh*
Where is a safe place to run (to jog)?	**¿Dónde hay un sitio seguro para correr?** *DOHN-day AH-ee oon SEE-tee-oh seh-GOOR-oh pah-rah kohr-EHR*
Where is there a health club (spa)?	**¿Dónde hay un gimnasio (balneario)?** *DOHN-day AH-ee oon heem-NAH-see-oh (bahl-nay-AHR-ee-oh)*

AT THE BEACH/POOL

Let's go to the beach (to the pool).	**Vamos a la playa (piscina).** *BAH-mohs ah lah PLAH-ee-ah (pee-SEEN-ah)*
Which bus will take us to the beach?	**¿Qué autobús nos lleva a la playa?** *kay AH-oo-toh-BOOS nohs yeh-bah ah lah PLAH-ee-ah*

Is there an indoor pool (outdoor) in the hotel?	**¿Hay una piscina cubierta (al aire libre) en el hotel?** *AH-ee oo-nah pee-SEE-nah (_____) ehn ehl oh-TEL*
I (don't) know how to swim well.	**(No) sé nadar bien.** *(noh) say nah-DAHR bee-EHN*
I just want to stretch out in the sand.	**Sólo quiero estirarme en la arena.** *SOH-loh kee-YEHR-oh ehs-tee-RAHR-may ehn lah ah-RAY-nah*
Is it safe to swim here?	**¿Se puede nadar aquí sin peligro?** *Say PWEH-day nah-DAHR ah-KEE seen peh-LEE-groh*
Is it dangerous for children?	**¿Hay peligro para los niños?** *AH-ee pel-EE-groh pah-rah lohs NEEN-yohs*
Is there a lifeguard?	**¿Hay salvavidas?** *AH-ee sahl-bah-BEE-dahs*
Where can I get _____?	**¿Dónde puedo conseguir _____?** *DOHN-day PWEH-doh kohn-seh-GHEER*
▪ an air mattress	**un colchón flotante** *oon kohl-CHOHN floh-tahn-tay*
▪ a bathing suit	**un traje de baño** *oon trah-hay day BAHN-yoh*
▪ a beach ball	**una pelota de playa** *oo-nah pel-OH-tah day PLAH-ee-ah*
▪ a beach chair	**un sillón de playa** *oon see-YOHN day PLAH-ee-ah*
▪ a beach towel	**una toalla de playa** *oo-nah toh-AH-yah day PLAH-ee-yah*
▪ a beach umbrella	**una sombrilla playera** *oo-nah sohm-BREE-yah plah-YEHR-ah*
▪ diving equipment	**equipo de buceo** *eh-KEE-poh day boo-SAY-oh*
▪ sunglasses	**gafas de sol** *GAH-fahs day sohl*

suntan lotion	**loción para broncear** *loh-SYOHN pah-rah brohn-SAY-ahr*
a surfboard	**una plancha de deslizamiento, un acuaplano** *OO-nah PLAHN-chah day dehs-lees-ah-mee-EHN-toh, oon ah-kwah-PLAH-noh*
water skis	**esquís acuáticos** *ehs-KEES ah-KWAHT-ee-kohs*

ON THE SLOPES

The main ski areas in Spain are the Pyrenees, the Guadarrama mountains, the Sierra Nevada, and the Cantabrian mountains. **Pistas** (ski runs) are marked with colored arrows according to their difficulty.

Green	very easy slopes
Blue	easy slopes
Red	difficult slopes for experienced skiers
Black	very difficult slopes for professionals

In South America, skiing choices are very limited. Most skiers head for the Andes, for resorts in Argentina and Chile.

Which ski area do you recommend?	**¿Qué sitio de esquiar recomienda usted?** *kay SEE-tee-oh day ehs-kee-AHR ray-koh-MYEHN-dah oos-TEHD*
I am a novice (intermediate, expert) skier.	**Soy principiante (intermedio, experto).** *soy preen-seep-YAHN-tay (een-tehr-MEHD-ee-oh, ehs-PEHR-toh)*
Is there enough snow at this time of year?	**¿Hay bastante nieve durante esta temporada?** *AH-ee bahs-TAHN-tay nee-EHB-ay door-ahn-tay ehs-tah temp-ohr-AH-dah*
How would I get to that place?	**¿Por dónde se va a ese sitio?** *pohr DOHN-day say bah ah eh-say SEE-tee-oh*

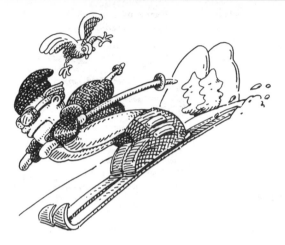

Can I rent _____ there?	**¿Puedo alquilar _____?** *PWEH-doh ahl-kee-lahr*
▪ equipment	**equipo** *eh-KEEP-oh*
▪ poles	**palos** *PAH-lohs*
▪ skis	**esquís** *ehs-KEES*
▪ ski boots	**botas de esquiar** *boh-tahs day ehs-kee-ahr*
Do they have ski lifts?	**¿Tienen funicular?** *TYEHN-eh foo-nee-koo-LAHR*
How much does the lift cost?	**¿Cuánto cobran?** *KWAHN-toh KOH-brahn*
Do they give lessons?	**¿Dan lecciones?** *dahn lek-SYOHN-ays*
Where can I stay at the summit?	**¿Dónde puedo alojarme en la cumbre?** *DOHN-day PWEH-doh ah-loh-HAHR-may ehn lah KOOM-bray*

ON THE LINKS

Is there a golf course?	**¿Hay un campo de golf?** *AH-ee oon KAHM-poh day gohlf*
Can one rent clubs?	**¿Se puede alquilar los palos?** *say PWEH-day ahl-kee-LAHR lohs PAH-lohs*

CAMPING

There are over 700 campgrounds in Spain. About 500 are located along the coast. Many of them have excellent facilities such as swimming pools, sport areas, restaurants, and supermarkets. The Spanish National Tourist Office furnishes a list of approved campsites.

Campsites (campings—**campamentos**) are classified as follows.

de lujo	luxury
primera clase	first class
segunda clase	second class
tercera clase	third class

In parts of Latin America, a tourist must have a permit to camp, and camping only in designated sights is recommended.

Is there a camping area near here?	**¿Hay un camping cerca de aquí?** *AH-ee oon KAHM-peeng sehr-kah day ah-KEE*
Do we pick our own site?	**¿Escogemos nuestro propio sitio?** *ehs-koh-HAY-mohs NWEHS-troh PROH-pee-oh SEE-tee-oh*
We only have a tent.	**Tenemos solo una tienda.** *ten-AY-mohs SOH-loh oo-nah TYEHN-dah*
Can we camp for one night only?	**¿Se puede acampar por una noche sola?** *say PWEH-day ah-kahm-pahr pohr oo-nah noh-chay SOH-lah*

Can we park our trailer (our caravan)?	**¿Podemos estacionar nuestro coche-vivienda (nuestra caravana)?** *poh-DAY-mos eh-stah-syohn-AHR-nwehs-troh KOH-chay bee-bee-EHN-dah (NWEHS-trah kahr-ah-BAHN-ah)*	

Is (are) there ____?   **¿Hay ____?** *AH-ee*

■ drinking water   **agua potable** *AH-gwah poh-TAH-blay*

■ showers   **duchas** *DOO-chahs*

■ fireplaces   **hogueras** *oh-GEHR-ahs*

■ picnic tables   **mesas de camping** *may-sahs day KAHM-peeng*

■ flush toilets   **servicios** *sehr-BEE-see-ohs*

■ electricity   **electricidad** *eh-lek-tree-see-DAHD*

■ a children's playground   **un parque infantil** *oon PAHR-kay een-fahn-TEEL*

■ a grocery store   **una tienda de comestibles** *oo-nah tee-EHN-dah day koh-mes-TEE-blays*

How much do they charge per person (per car)?   **¿Cuánto cobran por persona (por coche)?** *KWAHN-toh KOH-brahn pohr pehr-SOHN-ah (pohr koh-chay)*

We intend staying ____ days (weeks).   **Pensamos quedarnos ____ días (semanas).** *pen-SAH-mohs kay-DAHR-nohs ____ DEE-ahs (seh-MAHN-ahs)*

IN THE COUNTRYSIDE

Are there tours to the countryside?   **¿Hay excursiones al campo?** *AH-ee ehs-koor-SYOHN-ays ahl KAHM-poh*

What a beautiful landscape!   **¡Qué paisaje tan bonito!** *kay pah-ee-SAH-hay tahn boh-NEE-toh*

Look at _____.	Mire _____. *MEER-ay*
■ the barn	**el granero** *ehl grah-NEHR-oh*
■ the birds	**los pájaros** *lohs PAH-hahr-ohs*
■ the bridge	**el puente** *ehl PWEHN-tay*
■ the cottages	**las casitas** *lahs kah-SEE-tahs*
■ the farm	**la granja** *lah GRAHN-hah*
■ the fields	**los campos** *lohs KAHM-pohs*
■ the flowers	**las flores** *lahs FLOHR-ays*
■ the forest	**el bosque** *ehl BOHS-kay*
■ the hill	**la colina** *lah koh-LEE-nah*
■ the lake	**el lago** *ehl LAH-goh*
■ the mountains	**las montañas** *lahs mohn-TAHN-yahs*
■ the ocean	**el mar** *ehl mahr*
■ the plants	**las plantas** *lahs PLAHN-tahs*
■ the pond	**el estanque** *ehl ehs-TAHN-kay*
■ the river	**el río** *ehl REE-oh*
■ the stream	**el arroyo** *ehl ah-ROY-yoh*
■ the trees	**los árboles** *lohs AHR-boh-lays*
■ the valley	**el valle** *ehl BAH-yeh*
■ the village	**el pueblo** *ehl PWEHB-loh*
■ the waterfall	**la catarata** *lah kah-tahr-AH-tah*
Where does this path lead to?	**¿Adónde lleva el sendero?** *ah DOHN-day YEH-bah ehl sen-DEHR-oh*
These gardens are beautiful.	**Estos jardines son lindos.** *EHS-tohs hahr-DEEN-ays sohn LEEN-dohs*

FOOD AND DRINK

The Spanish-speaking world is a vast one, so any information on its food is, of necessity, very general. There are many similarities between the foods and eating habits of Spain and those of Latin America, since Latin American culture was largely shaped by Spanish invaders. Likewise, foods were brought back from the New World and rapidly incorporated into the cooking in Spain. But Latin American cooking is also greatly influenced by the preferences of its ancient peoples—the Incas, Aztecs, and Mayans. To sort all this out most clearly for you, we have divided the information in this chapter into two portions when appropriate: one for references to Spain, and the other for information on Latin America. Of the latter, most tips pertain to Mexico, with only minor variations for the remainder of Latin America.

IN SPAIN

Spanish restaurants are officially ranked from 5-fork (luxury) to 1-fork (4th class). The ratings—which you will see designated by forks on a sign outside each establishment—are based on the number of dishes served in specific categories, not on the quality of the establishment.

Dining hours in Spain, except for breakfast, are late: the mid-day meal, **comida,** is served from 1:30 to 4 p.m.; dinner, **cena,** from 8:30 p.m. to midnight. Outside Madrid, the hours are a little earlier. Restaurants post their menus outside their doors, so you may study the menu and make your decision before entering.

Madrid, as Spain's capital, has restaurants specializing in the cuisine of all its regions. You will find restaurants with Basque, Catalan, Galician, Asturian, Andalusian, and other specialties. Madrid, as the center of Castile, naturally has a wide number of Castilian restaurants, where roast pork and roast lamb are the premier specialties.

Some pointers about dining out in Spain: Spaniards customarily do their drinking and have their aperitifs in a bar or **tasca,** usually standing and socializing, before going into a restaurant to sit down and dine. Drinking at table usually consists of having wine with the meal. Many Spaniards have their large meal in mid-day, a light supper at night. At mid-day there are usually three courses consumed: appetizer or fish course, entree, and dessert. To call a waiter in Spain, it is customary to say **"Camarero"** (waiter), **"Oiga"** (listen), or **"Por favor"** (please). *Do not clap your hands or call "Chico" (boy).*

As in most countries, there is a variety of places in which you can obtain something to eat. Here we list a few of the common ones.

café	small place which serves alcoholic and nonalcoholic drinks, plus simple snacks; very casual
cafetería	not a self-service restaurant, as the name implies in English, but a cafe-type place specializing in informal food such as sandwiches, snacks, sweets, aperitifs, coffee, and tea
bar (tasca, taberna)	similar to a pub or bar in the U.S., in which drinks and small snacks (**tapas** or **pinchos**) are served
fonda (hostería, venta, posada)	small, informal inn which usually specializes in regional dishes
merendero (chirin-guito)	outdoor stall (usually at the beaches or piers) selling seafood, soft drinks, and ice cream
restaurante	traditional restaurant, varying in the extensiveness of their menu, usually offering a blending of regional specialties and more broad-based dishes; often also offers a tourist menu

IN LATIN AMERICA

In Mexico, people often eat several times a day. Breakfast (**desayuno**) is early, usually between 8 and 10 and often at a street vendor's stand or in the market. Lunch (**almuerzo**) is anywhere from 1 to 4 p.m. and can be a hearty meal. But sometime between breakfast and lunch, many people sneak in a snack (**antojo**), often a taco. Dinner (**cena**) is usually begun around 8 p.m., but can be served until midnight. Most other Latin American countries follow this basic timing as well.

In Mexico City, you'll find some restaurants that specialize in foods from other parts of Mexico as well. And in other regions of Mexico, you'll find a differing array of specialties from those areas. Mexican food is intriguing, with many fruits and vegetables that will be novel to British or American tourists. Much of the food is based on a variety of chilies, so the food often is firey hot especially if you are not accustomed to such spices. In other parts of Latin America, the food is not as richly developed but you'll find tasty variations of similar dishes as you move from country to country.

In general, the following categories of food establishments exist.

bar	serves drinks and **botanas** (snacks)
cantina	men's bar, usually also serving snacks; this is a place for the neighborhood men to gather
hacienda	a ranch-style restaurant, usually with a garden and dining out-of-doors; gracious, usually with regional specialties
hostería (fonda, posada)	a casual restaurant, usually with regional specialties
restaurante	varying from the most casual, neighborhood place to a fancy establishment catering to tourists

EATING OUT

Do you know a good restaurant?	**¿Conoce usted un buen restaurante?** *koh-NOH-say oos-TEHD oon bwehn rehs-tah-oo-RAHN-tay*
Is it very expensive?	**¿Es muy caro?** *ehs mwee KAH-roh*
Do you know a restaurant that serves native dishes?	**¿Conoce usted un restaurante típico?** *koh-NOH-say oos-TEHD oon rehs-tah-oo-RAHN-tay TEE-pee-koh*
Waiter!	**¡Camarero!** *kah-mah-REHR-oh*
Miss!	**¡Señorita!** *sen-yohr-EE-tah*

A table for two, please.	**Una mesa para dos, por favor.** *oo-nah MAY-sah pah-rah dohs pohr fa-BOHR*
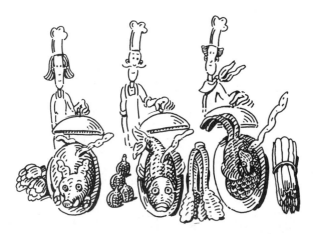in the corner	**en el rincón** *ehn ehl reen-KOHN*
near the window	**cerca de la ventana** *sehr-kah day lah ben-TAHN-ah*
on the terrace	**en la terraza** *ehn lah teh-RAH-sah*
I would like to make a reservation ____.	**Quisiera hacer una reserva ____.** *kee-see-EHR-ah ah-SEHR oo-nah ray-SEHR-bah*
for tonight	**para esta noche** *pah-rah ehs-tah NOH-chay*
for tomorrow evening	**para mañana por la noche** *pah-rah mahn-YAH-nah pohr lah NOH-chay*
for two (four) persons	**para dos (cuatro) personas** *pah-rah dohs (KWAH-troh) pehr-SOHN-ahs*

■ for 9 p.m.	**para las nueve** *pah-rah las NWEH-bay*
■ for 9:30	**para las nueve y media** *pah-rah lahs NWEH-bay ee MEHD-yah*
We'd like to have lunch now.	**Queremos almorzar ahora.** *kehr-AY-mohs ahl-mohr-SAHR ah-OHR-ah*
The menu, please.	**La carta, por favor.** *lah KAHR-tah pohr fa-BOHR*
I'd like the set menu.	**Quisiera el menú del día.** *kee-see-YEHR-ah ehl men-OO del DEE-ah*

Many restaurants have a special fixed-price meal called the **Plato Combinado, Menú Turístico,** or **Menú del Día.** There is a smaller selection to choose from, but the price is much less than choosing à la carte and the wine, tax, and tip are usually included. (The usual tip is 10 to 15 percent of bill. However if the service is included in the bill—**servicio incluído**—it is customary to leave a few pesetas as well.)

What's today's special?	**¿Cuál es el plato del día de hoy?** *KWAHL ehs ehl PLAH-toh del DEE-ah day oy*
What do you recommend?	**¿Qué recomienda usted?** *KAY reh-koh-mee-EHN-dah oos-TEHD*
What's the house specialty?	**¿Cuál es la especialidad de la casa?** *KWAHL ehs lah ehs-peh-see-ah-lee-DAHD day lah KAH-sah*
Do you serve children's portions?	**¿Hay platos especiales para niños?** *AH-ee PLAH-tohs ehs-peh-see-AHL-ays pah-rah NEEN-yohs*
I'm (not) very hungry.	**(No) tengo mucha hambre.** *(noh) TEN-goh moo-chah AHM-bray*
Are the portions small (large?)	**¿Son pequeños (grandes) las porciones?** *sohn peh-KAYN-yohs (GRAHN-days) lahs pohr-SYOHN-ays*

To begin with, please bring us _____.	**Para empezar, tráiganos _____ por favor.** *pahr-rah ehm-peh-SAHR, TRAH ee-gah-nohs _____ pohr fa-BOHR*
▪ an aperitif	**un aperitivo** *oon ah-pehr-ee-TEE-boh*
▪ a cocktail	**un coctel** *oon cohk-TEHL*
▪ some white (red) wine	**un vino blanco (tinto)** *oon BEE-noh BLAHN-koh (TEEN-toh)*
▪ some ice water	**agua helada** *AH-gwah eh-LAH-dah*
▪ a bottle of mineral water, with (without) gas	**una botella de agua mineral, con (sin) gas** *oo-nah boh-TEH-yah day AH-gwah mee-nehr-AHL, kohn (seen) gahs*
▪ a beer	**una cerveza** *oo-nah sehr-BEH-sah*
I'd like (to order now).	**Me gustaría (ordenar ahora).** *may goos-tahr-EE-ah (ohr-den-AHR-ah ah-OHR-ah)*

See the listings that follow for individual dishes, and also the regional specialties noted on pages 108–114.

Do you have a house wine?	**¿Tiene un vino de la casa?** *tee-YEHN-ay oon BEE-noh day lah KAH-SAH*
Is it dry (mellow, sweet)?	**¿Es seco (suave, dulce)?** *ehs SAY-koh (SWAH-bay, DOOL-say)*
Please also bring us _____.	**Tráiganos también _____.** *TRAH-ee-gah-nohs tahm-BYEHN*
▪ a roll	**un panecillo** *oon pah-neh-SEE-yoh*
▪ bread	**pan** *pahn*
▪ bread and butter	**pan y mantequilla** *pahn ee mahn-tay-KEE-yah*
▪ tortillas (Mexico)	**tortillas** *tohr-TEE-yahs*

Waiter, we need ——.	**Camerero, necesitamos ——.** *kah-mah-REH-roh, neh-seh-see-TAH-mohs*
▢ a knife	**un cuchillo** *oon koo-CHEE-yoh*
▢ a fork	**un tenedor** *oon ten-eh-DOHR*
▢ a spoon	**una cuchara** *oo-nah koo-CHAHR-ah*
▢ a teaspoon	**una cucharita** *oo-nah koo-chahr-EE-tah*
▢ a soup spoon	**una cuchara de sopa** *oo-nah koo-CHAH-rah day SOH-pah*
▢ a glass	**un vaso** *oon BAH-soh*
▢ a cup	**una taza** *oo-nah TAH-sah*
▢ a saucer	**un platillo** *oon plah-TEE-yoh*
▢ a plate	**un plato** *oon PLAH-toh*
▢ a napkin	**una servilleta** *oo-nah sehr-bee-YEH-tah*
▢ a toothpick	**un palillo** *oon pahl-EE-yoh*

APPETIZERS (STARTERS)

Tapas (bar snacks) are very popular in Spain. For a listing of typical tapas, see page 105, given with information on food specialties. The following are items you are likely to see on a restaurant menu.

alcachofas	artichokes
almejas	clams
anguilas ahumadas	smoked eels
calamares	squid
caracoles	snails
champiñones	mushrooms
chorizo	spicy sausage, usually pork
cigales	crayfish
gambas (Spain only)	shrimp
huevos	eggs

jamón serrano (Spain only)	cured ham
melón	melon
moluscos	mussels
ostras (ostiones)	oysters
quisquillas (Spain only)	small shrimp
sardinas	sardines

And in Latin America, there would be some of the following.

camarones	shrimp
guacamole	puréed avocado spread
tostadas	tortilla chips with various pepper and cheese toppings

SOUPS

Soups are wonderful, whether you are enjoying them in Spain or Latin America.

gazpacho	a highly variable purée of fresh, uncooked vegetables, including cucumbers, peppers, onions, and tomatoes; served cold
potaje madrileño	a thick soup of puréed chick peas, cod, and spinach
sopa de ajo	garlic soup
sopa de cebolla	onion soup
sopa de fideos	noodle soup
sopa de mariscos	seafood soup
sopa de gambas	shrimp soup
sopa de albóndigas	soup with meatballs
sopa de pescado	fish soup
sopa de verduras	soup made from puréed greens and vegetables

In Latin America, particularly Mexico, you are also likely to find:

| cazuela | a spicy soup-stew, simmered for a long time in an earthenware pot; can |

		be fish, vegetables, or meat
pozole		a hearty pork and hominy stew
sopa de aguacate		creamed avocado soup
sopa de huitlacoche		black corn soup made from the fungus that grows on corn cobs

ENTREES (MEAT AND FISH DISHES)

The "main course" of a meal in Spain is likely to be meat if you are inland and seafood if you are along the coast. First the meat.

carne de	*KAHR-nay day*	meat of
buey	*bway*	beef
cabrito	*kah-BREE-toh*	goat (kid)
carnero	*kahr-NEHR-oh*	mutton
cerdo	*SEHR-doh*	pork
cordero	*kohr-DEHR-oh*	lamb
ternera	*tehr-NEHR-ah*	veal
vaca, res	*BAH-kah, rehs*	beef

Some common cuts of meat, plus other terms you'll find on a menu.

albóndigas	*ahl-BOHN-dee-gahs*	meatballs
bistec	*bees-TEHK*	beef steak
carne picada	*kahr-nay pee-KAH-dah*	ground (minced) meat
chuletas	*choo-LEH-tahs*	chops
churrasco	*choo-RAHS-koh*	charcoal-grilled steak
cocido	*koh-SEE-doh*	stew
costilla	*kohs-TEE-yah*	cutlet

corazón	*koh-rah-SOHN*	heart
criadillas	*kree-ah-DEE-yahs*	sweetbreads
filete	*fee-LEH-tay*	filet
hígado	*EE-gah-doh*	liver
jamón	*ha-MOHN*	ham
lechón	*leh-CHOHN*	suckling pig
lengua	*LEN-gwah*	tongue
morcilla	*mohr-SEE-yah*	blood sausage
rabo de buey	*RAH-boh day BWAY*	oxtails
riñones	*reen-YOH-nays*	kidneys
salchichas	*sahl-CHEE-chahs*	sausages
sesos	*SAY-sohs*	brains
solomillo	*soh-loh-MEE-yoh*	pork tenderloin steak
tocino	*toh-SEE-noh*	bacon
tripas	*TREE-pahs*	tripe

You won't always recognize the types of fish available, since the waters around Spain or the Latin American countries are generally warmer, with more tropical varieties. Here is a general guide, with our advice that you sample what's offered and discover new types that you like.

almejas	*ahl-MAY-has*	clams
anchoas	*ahn-CHOH-ahs*	anchovies
anguilas	*ahn-GHEE-lahs*	eels
arenque, ahumado	*ah-REHN-kay, ah-oo-MAH-doh*	herring, smoked
atún	*ah-TOON*	tuna
bacalao	*bah-kah-LAH-oh*	codfish

besugo	*beh-SOO-goh*	sea bream
boquerones	*boh-keh-ROH-nehs*	whitebait
caballa	*kah-BAH-yah*	mackerel
calamares	*kahl-ah-MAHR-ayss*	squid
camarones	*kah-mah-ROH-nayss*	shrimp
cangrejos	*kahn-GRAY-hohs*	crabs
caracoles	*kahr-ah-KOH-layss*	snails
cigalas	*see-GAH-lahs*	large crayfish
congrio	*KOHN-gree-oh*	conger eel
gambas	*GAHM-bahs*	large shrimp
lampresas	*lahm-PRAY-sahs*	lamprey
langosta	*lahn-GOH-stah*	spiny lobster
langostino	*lahn-gohs-TEE-noh*	small crayfish
lenguado	*len-GWAH-doh*	flounder, sole
mejillones	*meh-hee-YOH-nayss*	mussels
mújol	*MOO-hohl*	mullet
merluza	*mehr-LOOS-ah*	bass, hake
pescadilla	*pehs-kah-DEE-yah*	whiting
pulpo	*POOL-poh*	octopus
quesquillas	*kehs-KEE-yahs*	shrimp
rape	*RAH-pay*	monkfish, angler-fish
salmón	*sahl-MOHN*	salmon
sardinas	*sahr-DEE-nahs*	sardines
trucha	*TROO-chah*	trout

And some terms for fowl and game:

capón	*kah-POHN*	capon
codorniz	*koh-dohr-NEES*	quail
conejo	*kohn-AY-hoh*	rabbit
faisán	*fah-ee-SAHN*	pheasant
ganso	*GAHN-soh*	goose
pato	*PAH-toh*	duck
pavo	*PAH-boh*	turkey
perdiz	*pehr-DEES*	partridge
pichón	*pee-CHOHN*	squab
pollo	*POH-yoh*	chicken
venado	*beh-NAH-doh*	venison
Is the meat _____?	**¿Es carne _____?**	*ehs KAHR-nay*
▪baked	**al horno**	*ahl-OHR-noh*
▪boiled	**guisada**	*ghee-SAH-dah*
▪braised (stewed)	**estofada**	*ehs-toh-FAH-dah*
▪broiled	**a la parrilla**	*ah lah pahr-EE-yah*
▪roasted	**asada**	*ah-SAH-dah*
▪poached	**escalfada**	*ehs-KAHL-fah-dah*
I like the meat _____.	**Me gustaría la carne _____.**	*may goos-tah-REE-ah lah KAHR-nay*
▪well done	**bien hecha**	*bee-EHN EH-chah*
▪medium	**término medio**	*TEHR-mee-noh MED-yoh*
▪rare	**poco hecha**	*POH-koh EH-chah*
▪tender	**tierna**	*tee-EHR-nah*

RICE DISHES

Rice forms the foundation of several dishes in Spain, especially **paella**. This specialty varies with the region, but always features saffron-flavored rice. You are likely to see it on a menu in any of these forms:

a la campesina	with ham, chicken, sausage, and small game birds
a la catalana	with sausages, pork, squid, chilies, and peas, or with chicken, snails, beans, and artichokes
alicantina	with rabbit, mussels, and shrimp
bruta	with pork, chicken, and whitefish
de mariscos	with crayfish, anglerfish, and other seafood
valenciana	with chicken, seafood, peas, and tomatoes—the most well-known version

TORTILLA-BASED DISHES

In Mexico particularly, the **tortilla** forms the basis for many dishes; this flat cornmeal cake is roughly the equivalent of bread there, and it is served along with some dishes as well as rolled and stuffed, layered with other ingredients and sauced, and fried until crisp. Here are some of the items you'll see on menus featuring tortilla dishes.

chalupas	tortillas that have been curled at the edges and filled with a ground pork filling, sauced with a green chili sauce
chilaquiles	layers of tortillas, alternated with beans, meat, chicken, and cheese, then baked
enchiladas	tortillas that have been fried, then rolled up and baked in a sauce
flautas	sort of a tortilla sandwich that is then rolled and deep-fried
quesadillas	tortillas that are stuffed with cheese and deep-fried

tacos		a tortilla with any of several fillings, usually eaten as a snack

SALADS

In Spain, salads are often part of the appetizer and consist of a zesty mixture of seafood or vegetables. In Latin America, the salad is frequently served along with the main course. (Tourists should be wary of ordering salads of raw vegetables or greens, since these items may have been washed in water that has not been treated for bacteria.) Here are some useful terms for ordering salads.

aceitunas	*ah-say-TOO-nahs*	olives
lechuga	*leh-CHOO-gah*	lettuce
pepino	*pep-EE-noh*	cucumber
tomate	*toh-MAH-tay*	tomato

EGG DISHES

In Spain, eggs are not usually eaten as a breakfast food, and when served usually are in an omelet **(tortilla)** with other ingredients such as ham, potatoes, peppers, shrimp, or mushrooms. Eggs are also served baked with a tomato sauce, or boiled with fish, or scrambled with vegetables.

eggs	**huevos**	*WEH-bohs*
omelet	**tortilla**	*tohr-TEE-yah*

In Latin America, if you want an omelet you can ask for a **tortilla** but in Mexico you are more likely to get a cornmeal cake. When in Mexico, ask for a **tortilla de huevo.** As for other egg preparations, you will find an English (American) breakfast is more common.

fried eggs	**huevos fritos**	*WEH-bohs FREE-tohs*
hard-boiled eggs	**huevos duros**	*WEH-bohs DOOR-ohs*
scrambled eggs	**huevos revueltos**	*WEH-bohs ray-BWEHL-tohs*

| soft-boiled eggs | **huevos pasados por agua** | *WEH-bohs pah-SAH-dohs pohr AH-gwah* |

On a menu, you are likely to see:

| **huevos con chorizo** | eggs with a spicy sausage |
| **huevos rancheros** | fried eggs with a spicy tomato sauce |

VEGETABLES

alcachofas	*ahl-kah-CHOH-fahs*	artichokes
apio	*AH-pee-oh*	celery
berenjena	*behr-ehn-HAY-nah*	eggplant (aubergine)
calabacín	*kah-lah-bah-SEEN*	zucchini
cebollas	*seh-BOH-yahs*	onions
col	*kohl*	cabbage
coliflor	*kohl-ee-FLOHR*	cauliflower
espinacas	*eh-spee-NAH-kahs*	spinach
espárragos	*ehs-PAHR-ah-gohs*	asparagus
champiñones	*chahm-peen-YOH-nays*	mushrooms
garbanzos	*gahr-BAHN-sohs*	chickpeas
guisantes	*ghee-SAHN-tays*	peas
judías	*hoo-DEE-ahs*	green beans
papas, patatas	*PAH-pahs, pah-TAH-tahs*	potatoes
papas fritas	*PAH-pahs FREE-tahs*	french fries
pimiento	*pee-MYEHN-toh*	pepper

puerros	*PWEHR-ohs*	leeks
maíz	*mah-EES*	corn
tomate	*toh-MAH-tay*	tomato
zanahorias	*sah-nah-OHR-ee-ahs*	carrots

In parts of Latin America you are likely also to see the following on a menu.

chile	*CHEE-lay*	chili peppers, of any variety (see pages 98–99)
frijoles	*free-HOH-lays*	beans, usually kidney or pinto
huitlacoche	*WEET-lah-koh-chay*	corn fungus
nopalito	*noh-pah-LEE-toh*	prickly pear cactus
yuca	*YOO-kah*	root vegetable, from yucca plant

SEASONINGS AND CONDIMENTS

Seasonings in Spain tend to be lively but not fiery hot. Personal preferences sometimes intercede, however, and you might want something additional for your meal. Here's how to ask for what you want.

butter	**la mantequilla**	*lah mahn-teh-KEE-yah*
horseradish	**el rábano picante**	*ehl RAH-bah-noh pee-KAHN-tay*
lemon	**limón**	*lee-MOHN*
margarine	**la margarina**	*lah mahr-gahr-EE-nah*
mayonnaise	**la mayonesa**	*lah mah-ee-oh-NAY-sah*

mustard	**la mostaza**	*lah mohs-TAH-sah*
oil	**el aceite**	*ehl ah-SAY-tay*
pepper (black)	**la pimienta**	*lah pee-mee-EHN-tah*
pepper (red) (Spain only)	**el pimiento**	*ehl pee-mee-EHN-toh*
pepper (red) (Latin America)	**ají**	*ah-HEE*
salt	**la sal**	*lah sahl*
sugar	**el azúcar**	*ehl ah-SOO-kahr*
saccharine	**la sacarina**	*lah sah-kah-REE-nah*
vinegar	**el vinagre**	*ehl bee-NAH-gray*
Worchestershire sauce	**la salsa inglesa**	*lah SAHL-sah een-GLAY-sah*

In Latin America, foods tend to be more heavily spiced, especially in Mexico. Here are some terms you might encounter on menus, describing the dish in terms of its major flavoring.

achiote	*ah-chee-OH-tay*	annatto
albahaca	*ahl-bah-AH-kay*	basil
azafrán	*ah-sah-FRAHN*	saffron
cilantro	*see-LAHN-troh*	coriander
orégano	*oh-REH-ga-noh*	oregano
romero	*roh-MEHR-oh*	rosemary

Descriptions of the different types of chilies could fill an entire book. Here we will mention a few of the major ones likely to be seen on menus.

ancho	mild to hot, with mild most common
chipotle	medium hot to hot, with a smokey flavor
jalapeño	hot, with a meaty flavor

pasilla	mild to medium hot, with a rich sweet flavor
pequín	hot
pimiento	sweet bell pepper
poblano	mild to hot, with a rich flavor
serrano	hot to very hot, with a bright flavor

And in sauces, you'll find:

salsa cruda	an uncooked tomato sauce, often served as a dip or table seasoning
salsa de tomatillo	delicate sauce made from Mexican green tomatoes (a husk tomato unlike the regular red tomato)
salsa de perejil	parsley sauce
ají de queso	cheese sauce
adobo	sauce made with ancho and pasilla chilies, sesame seeds, nuts, and spices
mole	a sauce of varying ingredients, made from chilies, sesame seeds, cocoa, and spices
pipián	sauce made from pumpkin seeds, chilies, coriander, and bread crumbs
verde	sauce of green chilies and green tomatoes

Oftentime, the Mexicans drink **atole,** a cornmeal drink that resembles a milkshake, with spicy foods. It is commonly served in a large pitcher for all at the table to drink.

DESSERTS—SWEETS
Desserts are not extensive in Spanish-speaking countries, but here are a few items that you may be offered.

arroz con leche	*ah-ROHS kohn LEH-chay*	rice pudding

crema catalana or flan	*krem-ah kah-tah-LAN-nah or flahn*	caramel custard
galletas	*gah-YEH-tahs*	cookies (biscuits)
helado	*ay-LAH-doh*	ice cream
▪ de chocolate	*day cho-koh-LAH-tay*	chocolate
▪ de pistacho	*day pees-TAH-choh*	pistachio
▪ de vainilla	*day bah-ee-NEE-yah*	vanilla
▪ de nueces	*day NWEH-says*	walnut
▪ de fresa	*day FRAY-sah*	strawberry
mazapán	*mah-sah-PAHN*	marzipan
merengue	*meh-REHN-gay*	meringue
natilla	*nah-TEE-yah*	cream pudding
pastel	*pahs-TEHL*	pastry
tarta	*TAHR-tah*	tart, usually fruit

FRUITS AND NUTS

In Spain, you'll find mostly fruits with which you are familiar. Here is a list of some frequent ones, with their translations.

What kind of fruit do you have?	**¿Qué frutas tiene?**	*kay FROO-tahs tee-YEHN-ay*
albaricoque	*ahl-bahr-ee-KOH-kay*	apricot
cereza	*sehr-AY-sah*	cherry
ciruela	*seer-WEH-lah*	plum
coco	*KOH-koh*	coconut
dátil	*DAH-teel*	date
frambuesa	*frahm-BWEH-sah*	raspberry

fresa	*FRAY-sah*	strawberry
higo	*EE-goh*	fig
lima	*LEE-mah*	lime
limón	*lee-MOHN*	lemon
mandarina	*mahn-dahr-EE-nah*	tangerine
manzana	*mahn-SAH-nah*	apple
melocotón	*mel-oh-koh-TOHN*	peach
melón	*meh-LOHN*	melon
naranja	*nah-RAHN-hah*	orange
pera	*PEH-rah*	pear
piña	*PEEN-yah*	pineapple
pomelo	*poh-MEH-loh*	grapefruit
sandía	*sahn-DEE-ah*	watermelon
uva	*OO-bah*	grape

In Latin American countries you'll find many more exotic fruits, including:

banana, plátano	*bah-NAH-nah, PLAH-ta-noh*	banana, plantain (green banana)
guayaba	*gwah-ee-AH-bah*	guava
mango	*MAHN-goh*	mango
jicama	*hee-KAH-mah*	jicama
tuna	*TOO-nah*	prickly pear

For some common varieties of nuts:

almendras	*ahl-MEN-drahs*	almonds
castañas	*kahs-TAHN-yahs*	chestnuts
avellanas	*ah-bay-YAHN-ahs*	hazelnuts (filberts)
nueces	*NWEH-sayss*	walnuts

SPECIAL CIRCUMSTANCES

Many travelers have special dietary requirements, so here are a few phrases that might help you get what you need or avoid what does you wrong.

I don't want anything fried (salted).	**No quiero nada frito (salado).**	*noh kee-YEHR-oh nah-dah FREE-toh (sah-LAH-doh)*
Do you have any-thing that is not spicy?	**¿Tiene algo que no sea picante?**	*tee-YEHN-ay AHL-goh kay noh SAY-ah pee-KAHN-tay*
I cannot eat anything made with ＿＿.	**No puedo comer nada hecho con ＿＿.**	*No PWEH-doh koh-MEHR NAH-dah AY-choh kohn*
Do you have any dishes without meat?	**¿Tiene platos sin carne?**	*tee-YEHN-ay PLAH-tohs seen KAHR-nay*

BEVERAGES

See pages 105–107 for information on Spanish wines and li-quors. As for other beverages, we give you the following phrases to help you ask for exactly what you wish.

Waiter, please bring me ＿＿.	**Camarero, tráiganos por favor ＿＿.**	*kah-mah-REHR-oh, TRAH-ee-gah-nohs pohr fah-BOHR*
coffee	**café**	*kah-FAY*
▪ black coffee	**café solo**	*kah-FAY SOH-loh*
▪ with cream	**café con crema**	*kah-FAY kohn KRAY-mah*
▪ with milk (regu-lar or American)	**un cortado**	*oon kohr-TAH-doh*
▪ espresso	**un exprés (un expreso)**	*oon ehs-PRESS (oon ehs-PRESS-oh)*

▨ half coffee/half milk (drunk in morning)	**café con leche**	*kah-FAY kohn LEH-chay*
▨ iced coffee	**café helado**	*kah-FAY eh-LAH-doh*
tea	**té**	*tay*
▨ with milk	**con leche**	*kohn LEH-chay*
▨ with lemon	**con limón**	*kohn lee-MOHN*
▨ with sugar	**con azúcar**	*kohn ah-SOO-kahr*
▨ iced tea	**té helado**	*tay eh-LAH-doh*
chocolate (hot)	**chocolate**	*choh-koh-LAH-tay*
water	**agua**	*AH-gwah*
▨ cold	**agua fría**	*AH-gwah FREE-ah*
▨ ice	**agua helada**	*AH-gwah ay-LAH-dah*
▨ mineral, with gas (without gas)	**agua mineral, con gas (sin gas)**	*AH-gwah mee-nehr-AHL, kohn gahs (seen gahs)*
cider	**una sidra**	*oo-nah SEE-drah*
juice	**un jugo**	*oon HOO-goh*
lemonade	**una limonada**	*oo-nah lee-moh-NAH-dah*
milk	**la leche**	*lah LEH-chay*
▨ malted milk	**una leche malteada**	*oo-nah LEH-chay mahl-tay-AH-dah*
▨ milk shake	**un batido de leche**	*oon bah-TEE-doh day LEH-chay*
orangeade	**una naranjada**	*oo-nah nahr-ahn-HAH-dah*

punch	**un ponche**	*oon POHN-chay*
soda	**una gaseosa**	*oo-nah gah-say-OH-sah*
tonic water	**un tónico**	*oon TOH-nee-koh*

You might also wish to try an old Spanish favorite, **horchata de chufas,** an ice-cold drink made from ground earth almonds. It is a thin, milk-like substance that is mildly sweet and very refreshing on a hot day. Usually it is scooped up from large vats that are kept chilled, and served in a tall glass.

The check, please.	**La cuenta, por favor.** *lah KWEHN-tah pohr fah-BOHR*
Separate checks.	**Cuentas separadas.** *KWEHN-tahs sep-ahr-AH-dahs*
Is the service (tip) included?	**¿Está incluída la propina?** *ehs-TAH een-kloo-EE-dah lah proh-PEE-nah*
I haven't ordered this.	**No he pedido ésto.** *noh ay ped-EE-doh EHS-toh*
I don't think the bill is right.	**Me parece que hay un error en la cuenta.** *may pah-RAY-say kay AH-ee oon ehr-OHR ehn lah KWEHN-tah*
This is for you.	**Esto es para usted.** *EHS-toh ehs pah-rah oos-TEHD*
We're in a hurry.	**Tenemos prisa.** *ten-EH-mohs PREE-sah*

DRINKS AND SNACKS

In Spain, bars and cocktail lounges sometimes also call themselves pubs. **Cervecerías** are tascas or pubs that specialize in German beer in the barrel, as well as wine. Some pubs are more like piano bars, others are like classical music coffee houses.

Spanish beer, a German-style brew, is both national (San Miguel and Aguila brands) and local (such as Alhambra in Granada, Vitoria in Malaga, Cruz Campo in Sevilla) in nature. Regular, light, and dark (**negra**) are the types, usually served ice cold.

Sidra, or cider, is available still or sparkling. Most famous sparkling sidra is produced in the north in Asturias and is called **sidra champagna.** Look for El Gaitero brand.

TAPAS (BAR SNACKS)

One of the delights of Spain is its **tapas,** light snacks that are varied samplings of Spanish cuisine. These hors d'oeuvre might include some of the following items.

aceitunas	olives
alcachofas a la vinagreta	artichokes with vinaigrette dressing
almejas en salsa de ajo	clams in a garlic sauce
angulas	fried baby eels
calamares a la romana	batter-fried squid strips
caracoles en salsa	snails in a tomato sauce
chorizo al diablo	sausage, especially spicy
entremesas variados	platter of assorted snacks
gambas a la plancha	grilled shrimp
huevos rellenos	stuffed hard-cooked eggs
palitos de queso	cheese straws
pan con jamón	toast slices with ham
pinchitos	kebabs
salchichón	salami

SPANISH WINES

Wine is as much the "drink of the country" in Spain as in France and Italy. Premier table wines are the Bordeaux and Burgundy types produced in the Rioja area along the Ebro River in the north. Sherry, Spain's most famous white wine, is produced in the south. There are five sherry types: fino, man-

WINE	REGION	DESCRIPTION	ORDER WITH
Chacoli	Basque	A light, re-freshing petil-lant white	Seafood, poultry
Espumoso	Catalonia	Superb, cham-pagne-like white	Celebrations, desserts
Málaga	Malaga	Heavy, sweet muscatel	Desserts, after-dinner
Panades	Catalonia	Fine, robust reds, some with great character	Meats, game
		—also some pleasant whites	Seafood, poultry
Priorato	Tarragona	Astringent whites,	Seafood
		—table reds	Meats
Ribeiro	Galicia	Light, refresh-ing, crackling whites	Seafood, cheese
Rioja	Old Castile, Navarra	Long-lived, deep rich reds of great charac-ter	Meats, game, spicy foods
		—also riesling-type whites	Seafood, Cheese
Sherry	Andalucia	*fino* (very dry)	aperitif
		manzanilla (dry)	aperitif
		amontillado (slightly sweet)	Dessert, cheese
		oloroso (sweet and nutty)	Dessert or af-ter-dinner
		Cream (sweet, syrupy nectar)	After-dinner

zanilla, amontillado, oloroso, and cream. Fino and manzanilla are the driest and are favorite aperitifs. The others are served with dessert or as after-dinner drinks.

Spanish brandy and numerous liqueurs are produced in Spain and are inexpensive.

I would like ____.	**Quisiera ____.** *kee-SYEHR-ah*
▨ a glass of wine	**una vaso de vino** *oon BAH-soh day BEE-noh*
▨ a bottle of wine	**una botella de vino** *oo-nah boh-TEH-yah day BEE-noh*
Is it ____?	**¿Es ____?** *ehs*
▨ red	**tinto** *TEEN-toh*
▨ white	**blanco** *BLAHN-koh*
▨ rosé	**rosado** *roh-SAH-doh*
light	**ligero** *lee-GEH-roh*
sparkling	**espumoso** *ehs-poo-MOH-soh*
dry	**seco** *SAY-koh*
sweet	**dulce** *DOOL-say*

Sangría is a refreshing fruit punch made from red wine, brandy, fruit, sugar, and soda water. It is usually enjoyed on picnics and in the afternoon, but not at dinner.

LATIN AMERICAN DRINKS

From the Caribbean come a variety of colorful drinks, most of which use rum combined with tropical fruits such as the pineapple, coconut, passion fruit, and papaya. Many of these drinks are also available in other Latin American countries, including Mexico. First we list a few of these, then give you descriptions of some of the less familiar Mexican drinks that are particular to that country.

In Mexico **tequila** is a very popular drink, drunk neat (straight) with salt and lime and often also jalapeño peppers. It is distilled from the juice of the agave (maguey) plant (a cactus-like succulent) and comes in both clear and amber; the amber has been aged and has a more mellow flavor.

cuba libre	rum, lime juice, and Coca Cola
margarita	tequila, lime juice, and salt
piña colada	coconut cream, pineapple juice, and rum
ponche	fruit juice and rum or tequila
pulque	the fermented juice of the agave (maguey) plant, often with flavorings added such as herbs, pineapple, celery; available in special pulque bars
tequila sunrise	orange juice, grenadine, tequila

SOUTH AMERICAN WINES

Wine grapes only grow well in moderate climates, so the countries with any wines at all are Argentina, Chile, Uruguay, and parts of Brazil. Argentina produces the most wine (quite a bit, as compared with North America), and most of it is consumed there. The wines from Chile are better, however, so if you are in that country or a neighboring one, ask for those. Elsewhere, you will be able to enjoy European wines and California wines in the larger hotels and restaurants that cater to tourists.

FOOD SPECIALTIES OF SPAIN

There are no hard-and-fast rules for Spanish cooking. Seasonings and ingredients will vary from region to region, depending on what's available and what the background is of the people. In Basque country, the helpings are large and the food is heavy with seafood: fried cod, fried eels, squid, and sea bream. Along the Cantabrian coast are excellent cheeses and exquisite sardines. **Sopa montañesa** (a regional soup) is famous, as are **caracoles a la santona** (snails) and **tortilla a la montañesa,** the regional omelet. In Asturias, have a good plate of **fabada,** the beans and blood sausage stew. Tripe is also good. In Galicia, the **pote gallego** (hot pot) is tasty, as is **merluza a la gallega** (hake). Santiago clams, spider crabs, and rock barnacle (**centollos** and **percebes**), are succulent.

Along the eastern coast, in Catalonia, you'll sample **escudella i carn d'olla,** a vegetable and meat stew, or **butifarra con judías,** pork sausage with beans. **Habas estofadas** is stewed broad beans. Toward Valencia is the land of **paella,** the famous saffron-tinted rice which is mixed with a variety of seafood and meats. If you travel to the Balearic Islands, sample **sopas mallorqinas** (soups), sausages, sardine omelet, or Ibiza-style lobster.

Castilian cuisine is famous for a chickpea and blood sausage stew (**cocido a la madrileña**). In Segovia and Sepúlveda you should eat the lamb and suckling pig. **Chorizo** and smoked ham (**jamón serrano**) are world famous. In Toledo, enjoy the **huevos a caballo,** stewed partridge, and marzipan.

Andalusian food is famous for **gazpacho,** a cold spicy soup of raw tomatoes, peppers, cucumber, and other ingredients depending on the cook. Also here try the mixed fried fishes.

Some other specialties include the following:

bacalao a la vizcaína	salt cod stewed with olive oil, peppers, tomatoes and onions
calamares en su tinta	baby squid cooked in its own ink
callos a la andaluza	tripe stew, with sausages, vegetables and seasonings
camarones en salsa verde	shrimps in a green sauce
capón relleno a la catalana	roasted capon stuffed with meat and nuts
carnero verde	stewed lamb with herbs and pignolis
cocido madrileño	mixed meat stew with chickpeas and vegetables
criadillas fritas	fried testicles
empanadas	deep-fried pies filled with meat and vegetables
fabada asturiana	spicy mixture of white beans, pork, and sausages
gallina en pepitoria	chicken dish with nuts, rice, garlic, and herbs
langosta a la barcelonesa	spiny lobster sauteed with chicken and tomatoes, garnished with almonds

lenguado a la andaluza	stuffed flounder or sole with a vegetable sauce
liebre estofada	hare and green beans, cooked in a tart liquid
marmitako	Basque tuna stew
pescado a la sal	a white fish, packed in salt and roasted
pisto manchego	vegetable stew of tomatoes, peppers, onions, eggplant, and zucchini
sesos en caldereta	calves brains, simmered in wine
zarzuela	fish stew; varies greatly depending on region but usually similar to a bouillabaisse

SOME MEXICAN SPECIALTIES

The Mexican restaurants that proliferate throughout the U.S. are not truly representative of Mexican cooking. What is most familiar to non-Mexicans are the tortilla-based dishes described on page 94 and other dishes such as tamales but Mexicans view these as snacks. True Mexican cooking is as varied as the country itself, with much seafood along the coasts and other unusual dishes inland. Almost all Mexican cooking, however, is united in its use of chilies—those marvelously varied flavoring agents that range from very sweet to fiery hot. Also serving to unify Mexican cuisine are corn, beans, and rice, plus the herbs coriander and cumin and the spices cinnamon and cloves. As mentioned earlier, tortillas are the bread of this culture. Most often they are made from cornmeal, but in some parts of the country they are made from wheat flour instead.

In the vicinity of Mexico City, the food is fairly sophisticated, with a variety of ingredients appearing in dishes made with chicken, seafood, and various types of meat. Perhaps most famous is the **mole poblano,** in which turkey is served with a dark brown sauce that contains a variety of spices, ground poblano chilies, and a hint of chocolate.

Along the Mexican coast around Acapulco, as well as along the Gulf Coast, the dishes are mostly made with fresh ingredients, including seafood and fruit. In the Yucatán, the dishes reflect very strongly the ancient Mayan culture, with **pollo pibil,** a chicken dish that is colored with annato, rolled in banana leaves, and steamed in a pit.

Wherever you are, ask for the local specialties. You are apt to sample one of the following.

amarillito	chicken or pork stew with green tomatoes, pumpkin, and chilies
carne asada	marinated pieces of beef that have been grilled
ceviche acapulqueño	raw fish or shellfish marinated in lime juice
chile relleno	stuffed chile (usually with cheese), that is coated with a light batter and fried
cochinita pibil	a suckling pig stuffed with fruits, chilies, and spices, then wrapped and baked in a pit
coloradito	chicken stew made with ancho chilies, tomatoes, and red peppers
frijoles refritos	kidney or pinto beans that have been cooked then mashed and re-heated, often with chilies
guajolote relleno	turkey stuffed with fruit, nuts, and chilies and braised in wine
gorditas	bits of meat and cheese, fried and served with guacamole
guacamole	a purée of avocado, onion, garlic, and chilies, used as a condiment and a sauce for a variety of dishes
huachinango a la veracruzana	red snapper marinated in lime juice and baked with tomatoes, olives, capers, and chilies
jaibas en chilpachole	crabs cooked in a tomato sauce, flavored with the Mexican spice epazote
mancha manteles	a stew of chicken or pork, with a mixture of vegetables and in a sauce of nuts, green tomatoes, and chilies

muk-bil pollo	chicken pie with a cornmeal topping
papazul	rolled tortillas in a pumpkin sauce
panuchos	chicken dish baked with black beans and eggs
puchero	a stew made from a variety of meats, vegetables, fruits; served as a soup, then a main course
sopa de lima	a chicken soup laced with lime

SOUTH AND CENTRAL AMERICAN FOODS

This is a large area to cover, and any attempt to describe all the dishes is likely to be a bit foolish. Nevertheless, whereas Spain and Mexico have established readily identifiable cuisines, most countries in South and Central America have some special dishes. Many of the dishes are variations on what you will also find in Mexico or Spain.

Peru and Ecuador, and parts of Bolivia and Chile, have a heritage of Incan culture and so the food is a combination of Indian and Spanish. Here are some specialties of this region.

anticuchos	skewered chunks of marinated beef heart, served with a hot sauce
caldillo de congrio	conger eel in a stew
humitas	cornmeal bits flavored with onion, peppers, and spices
llapingachos	potato-cheese croquettes
papas a la huancaína	potatoes in a spicy cheese sauce

Argentina, Uruguay, and Paraguay are countries that favor beef, so some of their notable dishes include **carbonada,** a stew of meat with vegetables served in a pumpkin shell. **Carne con cuero** is roasted beef (done in the skin), and **matambre** is a large steak stuffed with spinach, eggs, and carrots, then braised. The **parillada** is a type of English mixed grill, but just about every part of the animal is served. **Yerbe mate** is a tea drunk in this region made by steeping leaves from a holly bush.

Colombia and Venezuela are noted for their **arepas,** which are cornmeal buns filled with meat, chicken or cheese. **Buñuelos** are balls of fried cornmeal, dusted with powdered sugar. **Empanadas** are also popular here, and these pies are usually stuffed with meat, onions, and dried fruits. **Hallacas** is a seasoned mixture of meat stuffed into cornmeal dough and wrapped in banana leaves—sort of a tamale. For fish, the Colombians have **vindo de pescado,** a fish stew that is cooked on an outdoor grill.

Bolivia is well known for its roast suckling pig, as well as **picante de pollo,** a fried chicken that is rather spicy. **Lomo montado** is a steak topped with a fried egg.

The Central American countries reflect the tastes and dishes of the Spanish, but incorporate many tropical fruits in their food. Look for **gallo en sidra** (chicken in cider), tripe and vegetable stews, and a whole range of meat stews-soups.

FOODS OF THE CARIBBEAN

There are some Spanish influences in Caribbean cooking, but you'll also find that West Africans have contributed to this food as have the French. If we concentrate on those islands where Spanish is spoken, the following items are likely to be found on menus.

asopao	a chicken and rice soup-stew with ham, peas, and peppers
chicharrones	deep-fried pork cracklings
frituras de bacalao (bacalaítos)	fish cakes that are fried in hot oil
mondongo	thick stew of beef tripe, potatoes, tomatoes, pumpkin, chickpeas and other tropical vegetables
moros y cristianos	black beans and rice
pasteles	a mixture of plaintain and seasonings, steamed in a banana leaf
picadillo	mixture of chopped meat with peppers, olives, raisins, and tomatoes

plátanos fritos	sliced, fried green bananas (plantains)
relleno de papa	potato dough stuffed with a mixture of meat, olives, and tomatoes
ropa vieja	literally "old clothes," this is shredded beef cooked with tomatoes and peppers
sancocho	a vegetable stew with potatoes, tomatoes, and tropical vegetables
yuca con mojo	stewed yucca root (cassava), in a garlic sauce

TRAVEL TIP

When you purchase goods in a foreign country, save the receipts in case you have to prove the value of those purchases to customs agents upon returning home. Before you leave home, find out which goods you are likely to purchase that are not subject to duty and which are items you cannot bring back into the country. Consider also, especially if you plan to purchase a large number of heavy items, whether it is more advantageous to ship your purchases home or to pay airline charges for overweight.

MEETING PEOPLE

Here are some greetings, introductions, and invitations, plus some phrases you might need if dating.

SMALL TALK

My name is _____.	**Me llamo _____.**	*may YAH-mo*
Do you live here?	**¿Vive usted aquí?**	*BEE-bay oos-TEHD ah-KEE*
Where are you from?	**¿De dónde es usted?**	*day DOHN-day ehs oos-TEHD*
I am _____.	**Soy _____.**	*soy*

- from the United States
  de Estados Unidos *day ehs-TAH-dohs oo-NEE-dohs*

- from Canada
  del Canadá *del cah-nah-DAH*

- from England
  de Inglaterra *day een-glah-TEHR-ah*

- from Australia
  de Australia *day ow-STRAHL-yah*

I like Spain (South America) very much.	**Me gusta mucho España (Sud América).**	*may GOOS-tah MOO-choh ehs-PAHN-yah (sood ah-MEHR-ee-kah)*
I would like to go there.	**Me gustaría ir allá.**	*may goos-tahr-EE-ah eer ah-YAH*
How long will you be staying?	**¿Cuánto tiempo va a quedarse?**	*KWAHN-toh tee-EHM-poh bah ah kay-DAHR-say*
I'll stay for a few days (a week).	**Me quedaré unos días (una semana).**	*may kay-dahr-AY oo-nohs DEE-ahs (oo-nah sehm-AHN-ah)*
What hotel are you at?	**¿En qué hotel está?**	*ehn kay oh-TEL ehs-TAH*

What do you think of ____?	**¿Qué le parece ____?** *kay lay pah-REH-say*
I (don't) like it very much.	**(No) me gusta mucho.** *(noh) may GOOS-tah MOO-choh*
I think it's ____.	**Creo que es ____.** *KREH-oh kay ehs*
■ (very) beautiful	**(muy) bonito(a)** *(mwee) bohn-EE-toh(ah)*
■ interesting	**interesante** *een-tehr-ehs-AHN-tay*
■ magnificent	**magnífico(a)** *mahg-NEEF-ee-koh(kah)*
■ wonderful	**maravilloso(a)** *mahr-ah-bee-YOH-soh(sah)*

INTRODUCTIONS

May I introduce my ____?	**Le presento a mi ____?** *lay pray-SENT-oh ah mee*
■ brother (sister)	**hermano(a)** *ehr-MAH-noh(nah)*
■ father (mother)	**padre (papá) [madre (mamá)]** *PAH-dray (pah-PAH) MAH-dray (mah-MAH)*
■ friend	**amigo(a)** *ah-MEE-goh(gah)*
■ husband (wife)	**marido (esposa)** *mahr-EE-doh (ehs-POH-sah)*
■ sweetheart	**novio(a)** *NOH-bee-oh(ah)*
■ son (daughter)	**hijo(a)** *EE-hoh(hah)*
How do you do (Glad to meet you).	**Mucho gusto (en conocerle).** *MOO-choh GOOS-toh (ehn koh-noh-SEHR-lay)*
How do you do (The pleasure is mine).	**El gusto es mío.** *ehl GOOS-toh ehs MEE-oh*
I am a ____.	**Soy ____.** *soy*
■ teacher	**maestro(a)** *mah-EHS-troh(trah)*

◾doctor	**médico** *MED-ee-koh*
◾lawyer	**abogado** *ah-boh-GAH-doh*
◾businessperson	**persona de negocios** *pehr-SOHN-ah day neh-GOH-see-ohs*
◾student	**estudiante** *ehs-too-DYAHN-tay*
Would you like a picture (snapshot)?	**¿Quiere una foto?** *kee-YEHR-ay oo-nah FOH-toh*
Stand here (there).	**Párese aquí (_____).** *PAH-ray-say ah-KEE*
Don't move.	**No se mueva.** *noh say MWEH-bah*
Smile. That's it.	**Sonría. ¡Así es!** *sohn-REE-ah ah-SEE-ehs*
Will you take a picture of me (us)?	**¿(Nos)Me quiere sacar una foto?** *(nos)may kee-YEHR-ay sah-KAHR oo-nah FOH-toh*

DATING AND SOCIALIZING

May I have this dance?	**¿Quiere usted bailar?** *kee-YEHR-ay oos-TEHD bah-ee-LAHR*
Yes, of course.	**Sí, con mucho gusto.** *see kohn MOO-choh GOOS-toh*
Would you like a cigarette (drink)?	**¿Quiere fumar (tomar algo)?** *kee-YEHR-ay foo-MAHR (toh-MAHR AHL-goh)*
Do you have a light (a match)?	**¿Tiene fuego (un fósforo)?** *tee-YEH-nay FWAY-goh (oon FOHS-fohr-oh)*
Do you mind if I smoke?	**¿Le molesta que fume?** *lay moh-LEHS-tah kay FOO-may*
May I take you home?	**¿Me permite llevarle a casa?** *may pehr-MEE-tay yeh-BAHR-lay ah KAH-sah*

| May I call you? | **¿Puedo llamarle?** *PWEH-doh yah-MAHR-lay* |

| Are you doing anything tomorrow? | **¿Está libre mañana?** *eh-STAH LEE-bray mahn-YAH-nah* |

| Are you free this evening? | **¿Está usted libre esta tarde?** *eh-STAH oos-TEHD LEE-bray ehs-tah TAHR-day* |

| Would you like to go _____ together? | **¿Quiere acompañarme a _____?** *kee-YEHR-ay ah-kohm-pahn-YAHR-may ah* |

| I'll wait for you in front of the hotel. | **Le espero delante del hotel.** *lay ehs-PEHR-oh del-AHN-tay del oh-TEL* |

| I'll pick you up at your house (hotel). | **Le recogeré en su casa (hotel).** *lay ray-koh-hehr-AY ehn soo KAH-sah (oh-TEL)* |

| What is your telephone number? | **¿Cuál es su número de teléfono?** *kwahl ehs soo NOO-mehr-oh day tel-EH-foh-noh* |

| Here's my telephone number (address). | **Aquí tiene mi número de teléfono (mi dirección).** *ah-KEE tee-EH-nay mee NOO-mehr-oh day tel-EH-foh-noh (mee dee-rehk-SYOHN)* |

| Will you write to me? | **¿Me escribirá?** *may ehs-kree-beer-AH* |

| I'm single (married). | **Soy soltero, a (casado, a).** *soy sohl-TEHR-oh, ah (koh-SAH-doh, ah)* |

| Is your husband (wife) here? | **¿Está aquí su esposo (esposa)?** *eh-STAH ah-KEE soo ehs-POH-soh (sah)* |

| I'm here with my family. | **Estoy aquí con mi familia.** *ehs-TOY ah-KEE kohn mee fah-MEEL-yah* |

| Do you have any children? | **¿Tiene usted hijos?** *tee-EH-nay oos-TEHD EE-hohs* |

| How many? | **¿Cuántos?** *KWAHN-tohs* |

SAYING GOOD-BYE

Nice to have met you.
Ha sido un verdadero gusto. *ah SEED-oh oon behr-dah-DEHR-oh GOOS-toh*

The pleasure was mine.
El gusto ha sido mío. *ehl GOOS-toh ah SEE-doh MEE-oh*

Regards to ___.
Saludos a ___ de mi parte. *sah-LOO-dohs ah ___ day mee PAHR-tay*

Thanks for a wonderful evening.
Gracias por su invitación. Ha sido una noche extraordinaria. *GRAH-see-ahs pohr soo een-bee-tah-SYOHN. Ah see-doh oo-nah NOH-chay ehs-trah-ohr-dee-NAHR-ee-ah*

I must go home now.
Tengo que marcharme ahora. *TEN-goh kay mahr-CHAR-may ah-OH-rah*

You must come to visit us.
Debe venir a visitarnos. *DEH-bay ben-EER ah bee-see-TAHR-nohs*

SHOPPING

Spain is a country and Madrid a city where you can still have clothes, suits, shoes, boots, and other things custom-made. Prices are not cheap, but for fine workmanship, the price is still considerably lower than in many other countries. Ready-to-wear shoes are also good value—in style, workmanship and price.

Handcrafts, such as pottery, leather work, weaving, and embroideries, are traditional and still found in many regions of Spain. Official government handcraft stores, called **Artespaña,** are located in cities throughout Spain. There are three in Madrid alone. There are regional specialties, such as pottery, in Talavera (near Toledo) and Manises (near Valencia); damascene ware and steel knives and swords in Toledo; weaving and rug-making in Granada; fans, dolls, combs, and mantillas in Sevilla; leatherwork in Cordoba and Mallorca and Menorca; olive wood products, pottery, embroideries, glassware, and artificial pearls in Mallorca; and trendy, boutique sports clothes and jewelry in Ibiza.

Antiques are also widely available in Spain, ranging from **santos** (small wooden sculptures of saints) and rare books to painted cabinets, portable desks, and glass paintings. Many fine antiques shops in Madrid are located along Calle de Prado, Carrera de San Jerónimo, and in El Rastro. There is a stamp-and-coin market held every Sunday morning from 10 a.m. to 2 p.m. on the Plaza Mayor in Madrid.

Modern art is also a good buy, especially in Madrid and Barcelona, especially works by internationally known Spanish artists such as Miró, Tapies, Sempere, and others. Kreisler II, Galería Vijande, and Galería Egam are among many reputable galleries in Madrid. In Barcelona there are many galleries along Rambla de Cataluña.

Madrid has three major department stores with branches in many other cities. They are: Galerías Preciados, with three Madrid locations; El Corte Inglés, with four Madrid locations; and Celso García, with two Madrid stores. You will also find Woolworth and Sears in Madrid.

Prices are fixed in department stores and most shops. In flea markets, antique shops, and some art galleries and custom workshops, you can attempt to "negotiate" prices if you wish.

In Mexico, because of recent devaluations, your money will bring you great values for crafts and hand-made goods. In particular, Mexico has to offer some fine embroidery, silver items, and paper goods. You'll also find small, detailed figurines made from straw, wood carvings, pottery, and leather goods. Since it is such a large country, with so many different specialties, we can only suggest that you look about where you are, go to local markets, and see what you like. In the markets you will have to bargain for what you want; in shops, the prices are often fixed or there is only a small margin for bargaining.

The remainder of Latin America is too vast an area to be able to offer tips on specialty items. We suggest you read some tourist guides before leaving on your trip. In Latin American countries, shops are generally open from about 9 a.m. to 1 p.m., then open again about 3 p.m. and remain open until early evening, about 7. On Sunday, most shops are closed, but some markets are open and bustling.

GOING SHOPPING

Where can I find ____?	**¿Dónde se puede encontrar ____?** *DOHN-day say pweh-day ehn-kohn-TRAHR*
a bakery	**una panadería** *OO-nah pah-nah-dehr-EE-ah*
a book store	**una librería** *OO-nah leeb-rehr-EE-ah*
a butcher shop	**una carnicería** *OO-nah kahr-nee-sehr-EE-ah*
a camera shop	**una tienda de fotografía** *OO-nah tee-EHN-dah day foh-toh-grah-FEE-ah*
a candy store	**una confitería** *OO-nah kohn-fee-tehr-EE-ah*

▪ a clothing store	**una tienda de ropa** *OO-nah tee-YEHN-dah day ROH-pah*
▪ a delicatessen	**una tienda de ultramarinos** *OO-nah tee-YEHN-dah day ool-trah-mah-REE-nohs*
▪ a department store	**un almacén** *oon ahl-mah-SEHN*
▪ a pharmacy (chemist)	**una farmacia** *OO-nah fahr-MAH-see-ah*
▪ a florist	**una florería** *OO-nah flohr-ehr-EE-ah*
▪ a gift (souvenir) shop	**una tienda de regalos (recuerdos)** *OO-nah tee-YEHN-dah day ray-GAHL-ohs (ray-kwehr-dohs)*
▪ a grocery store	**una tienda de comestibles** *OO-nah tee-YEHN-dah day koh-mehs-TEE-blays*
▪ a hardware store (ironmonger)	**una ferretería** *OO-nah feh-reh-teh-REE-ah*
▪ a jewelry store	**una joyería** *OO-nah hoy-ehr-EE-ah*
▪ a liquor store	**una licorería** *OO-nah lee-kohr-ehr-EE-ah*
▪ a newsstand	**un puesto de periódicos** *oon PWEHS-toh day peh-ree-OH-dee-kohs*
▪ a record store	**una tienda de discos** *OO-nah tee-yehn-dah day DEES-kohs*
▪ a shoe store	**una zapatería** *OO-nah sah-pah-tehr-EE-ah*
▪ a supermarket	**un supermercado** *oon SOO-pehr-mehr-KAH-doh*
▪ a tobacco shop	**un estanco** *oon ehs-TAHN-koh*
▪ a toy store	**una juguetería** *OO-nah hoo-get-ehr-EE-ah*

BEING HELPED

Young man. Can you wait on me?	**Joven. ¿Puede usted atenderme?** *HOH-ben PWEH-day oos-TEHD ah-ten-DEHR-may?*
Miss. Can you help me?	**Señorita. ¿Me podría ayudar?** *sehr-yohr-EE-tah may poh-DREE-ah ah-yoo-DAHR*
Do you take credit cards?	**¿Acepta tarjetas de crédito?** *ah-SEP-tah tahr-HAY-tahs day KRED-ee-toh*
Can I pay with a traveler's check?	**¿Puedo pagar con un cheque de viajero?** *PWEH-doh pah-GAHR kohn oon CHEH-kay day bee-ah-HEHR-oh*

BOOKS

Is there a store that carries English-language books?	**¿Hay una tienda que lleve libros en inglés?** *AH-ee oo-nah TYEHN-dah kay YEH-bay LEE-brohs ehn een-GLAYS*
What is the best (biggest) bookstore here?	**¿Cuál es la mejor librería (la librería más grande) de aquí?** *kwahl ehs lah may-HOHR lee-brehr-EE-ah (lah lee-brehr-EE-ah mahs grahn-day) day ah-KEE*
I'm looking for a copy of ____.	**Busco un ejemplar de ____.** *boos-koh oon eh-hem-PLAHR day*
I don't know the title (author).	**No sé el título (autor).** *noh say ehl TEE-too-loh (AH-oo-TOHR)*
I'm just looking.	**Estoy solo mirando.** *ehs-TOY SOH-loh meer-AHN-doh*
Do you have books (novels) in English?	**¿Tiene usted libros (novelas) en inglés?** *tee-EHN-eh oos-TEHD LEE-brohs (noh-BEL-ahs) ehn een-GLAYSS*

Do you have paper-back copies?	**¿Tiene usted ejemplares en rústi-ca?** *tee-EHN-ay oos-TEHD eh-hem-PLAHR-ays ehn ROOS-tee-kah*
I want a ____.	**Quiero ____.** *kee-EHR-oh*
▪ guide book	**una guía** *oon-ah GHEE-ah*
▪ map of this city	**un plano de esta ciudad** *oon PLAH-noh day ehs-tah see-oo-DAHD*
▪ pocket dictionary	**un diccionario de bolsillo** *oon deek-syohn-AHR-ee-oh day bohl-SEE-yoh*
▪ Spanish-English dictionary	**un diccionario español-inglés** *oon deek-syohn-AHR-ee-oh ehs-pahn-YOHL-een-GLAYSS*
Where can I find ____?	**¿Dónde están ____?** *DOHN-day ehs-TAHN*
▪ detective stories	**las novelas policíacas** *lahs noh-BEH-lahs poh-lee-SEE-ah-kahs*
▪ history books	**los libros de historia** *lohs lee-brohs day ee-STOHR-ee-ah*
▪ short story books	**los libros de cuentos** *lohs lee-brohs day KWEHN-tohs*
▪ cookbooks	**los libros de cocina** *lohs LEE-brohs day koh-SEE-nah*
I'll take these books.	**Me quedo con estos libros.** *may kay-doh kohn EHS-tohs LEE-brohs*
Will you wrap them, please?	**¿Quiere envolverlos, por favor?** *kee-YEHR-ay ehn-bohl-BEHR-lohs pohr fah-BOHR*

CLOTHING

| Would you please show me ____? | **¿Quiere enseñarme ____, por fa-vor?** *kee-YEHR-ay ehn-sehn-YAHR-may pohr fah-BOHR* |

a belt	**un cinturón** *oon seen-toor-OHN*
a blouse	**una blusa** *oo-nah BLOO-sah*
a bra	**un sostén** *oon soh-STEHN*
a dress	**un vestido** *oon bes-tee-doh*
an evening gown	**un traje de noche** *oon TRAH-hay day NOH-chay*
leather (suede) gloves	**guantes de cuero (de gamuza)** *GWAHN-tays day KWEHR-oh (day gah-MOOS-ah)*
handkerchiefs	**pañuelos** *pahn-yoo-EH-lohs*
a hat	**un sombrero** *oon sohm-BREHR-oh*
a jacket	**una chaqueta** *oo-nah chah-KAY-tah*
an overcoat	**un abrigo** *oon ah-BREE-goh*
pants	**pantalones** *pahn-tah-LOHN-ays*
pantyhose	**pantimedias** *pahn-tee-MEHD-ee-ahs*
a raincoat	**un impermeable** *oon eem-pehr-may-AH-blay*
a robe	**una bata** *oo-nah BAH-tah*
a shirt	**una camisa** *oo-nah kah-MEES-ah*
(a pair of) shoes	**(un par de) zapatos** *(oon pahr day) sah-PAH-tohs*
shorts (briefs)	**calzoncillos** *kahl-sohn-SEE-yohs*
Do you have something ____?	**¿Tiene algo ____?** *tee-EH-nay AHL-goh*
else	**más** *mahs*
larger	**más grande** *mahs grahn-day*
less expensive	**menos caro** *may-nohs KAHR-oh*
longer	**más largo** *mahs LAHR-goh*

■ of better quality	**de más alta calidad** *day mahs AHL-tah kahl-ee-DAHD*
■ shorter	**más corto** *mahs KOHR-toh*
■ smaller	**más pequeño** *mahs peh-KAYN-yoh*

COLORS AND FABRICS

I (don't) like the color.	**(No) me gusta este color.** *(noh) may GOOS-tah ehs-tay koh-LOHR*
Do you have it in ____?	**¿Tiene algo en ____?** *tee-EHN-ay ahl-goh ehn*
■ black	**negro** *NEH-groh*
■ blue	**azul** *ah-SOOL*
■ brown	**marrón, pardo** *mah-ROHN, PAHR-doh*
■ gray	**gris** *grees*
■ green	**verde** *BEHR-day*
■ orange	**anaranjado** *a-nah-rahn-HAH-do*
■ pink	**rosado** *roh-SAH-doh*

red	**rojo** *ROH-hoh*
white	**blanco** *BLAHN-koh*
yellow	**amarillo** *ah-mah-REE-yoh*
I want something in _____.	**Quiero algo en _____.** *kee-YEHR-oh AHL-goh ehn*
chiffon	**gasa** *GAH-sah*
corduroy	**pana** *PAH-nah*
cotton	**algodón** *ahl-goh-DOHN*
denim	**dril de algodón, tela tejana** *dreel day ahl-goh-DOHN, TEH-la tay-HAH-nah*
felt	**fieltro** *fee-EHL-troh*
flannel	**franela** *frah-NEHL-ah*
gabardine	**gabardina** *gah-bahr-DEEN-ah*
lace	**encaje** *ehn-KAH-hay*
leather	**cuero** *KWEHR-oh*
linen	**hilo** *EE-loh*
nylon	**nilón** *nee-LOHN*
satin	**raso** *RAH-soh*
silk	**seda** *SAY-dah*
suede	**gamuza** *gah-MOO-sah*
taffeta	**tafetán** *tah-fay-TAHN*
terrycloth	**tela de toalla** *TEHL-ah-day toh-AH-yah*
velvet	**terciopelo** *tehr-see-oh-PEHL-oh*
wool	**lana** *LAH-nah*
worsted	**estambre** *ehs-TAHM-bray*
synthetic (polyester)	**sintético** *seen-TET-ee-koh*

I prefer ____.	**Prefiero** ____. *preh-FYEHR-oh*
permanent press	**algo inarrugable** *AHL-goh een-ah-roo-GAH-blay*
wash and wear	**algo que no necesita planchar** *AHL-goh kay noh neh-seh-SEE-tah plahn-CHAHR*
Show me something ____.	**Muéstreme algo** ____. *MWEHS-tray-may AHL-goh*
in a solid color	**de color liso** *day koh-LOHR LEE-soh*
with stripes	**de rayas** *day RAH-ee-ahs*
with polka dots	**de lunares** *day loo-NAHR-ays*
in plaid	**de cuadros** *day KWAH-drohs*
Please take my measurements.	**¿Quiere tomarme la medida?** *kee-YEHR-ay toh-MAHR-may lah meh-DEE-dah*
I take size (My size is) ____.	**Llevo el tamaño (Mi talla es)** ____. *YEH-boh ehl tah-MAHN-yoh (mee TAH-yah ehs)*
small	**pequeño(a)** *peh-KAYN-yoh(yah)*
medium	**mediano(a)** *meh-dee-AH-noh(yah)*
large	**grande** *GRAHN-day*
Can I try it on?	**¿Puedo probármelo?** *PWEHD-oh proh-BAHR-may-loh*
Can you alter it?	**¿Puede arreglarlo?** *PWEH-day ah-ray-GLAHR-loh*
Can I return the article?	**¿Puedo devolver el artículo?** *PWEH-doh day-bohl-BEHR ehl ahr-TEE-koo-loh*
Do you have something hand made?	**¿Tiene algo hecho a mano?** *tee-YEH-nay ahl-goh ay-choh ah mah-noh*

CLOTHING MEASUREMENTS

MEN

SHOES

American	7	8	9	10	11	12
British	6	7	8	9	10	11
Continental	39	41	43	44	45	46

SUITS, COATS

American	34	36	38	40	42	44	46	48
British	44	46	48	50	54	56	58	60
Continental	44	46	48	50	52	56	58	60

SHIRTS

American	14	$14\frac{1}{2}$	15	$15\frac{1}{2}$	16	$16\frac{1}{2}$	17	$17\frac{1}{2}$
British	14	$14\frac{1}{2}$	15	$15\frac{1}{2}$	16	$16\frac{1}{2}$	17	$17\frac{1}{2}$
Continental	36	37	38	39	40	41	42	43

WOMEN

SHOES

American	4	5	6	7	8	9
British	3	4	5	6	7	8
Continental	35	36	37	38	39	40

DRESSES, SUITS

American	8	10	12	14	16	18
British	10	12	14	16	18	20
Continental	36	38	40	42	44	46

BLOUSES, SWEATERS						
American	32	34	36	38	40	42
British	34	36	38	40	42	44
Continental	40	42	44	46	48	50

The zipper doesn't work.	**No funciona la cremallera.** *noh foon-SYOHN-ah lah kray-mah-YEH-rah*
It doesn't fit me.	**No me queda bien.** *noh may KAY-dah BYEHN*
It fits very well.	**Me queda muy bien.** *may KAY-dah mwee BYEHN*
I'll take it.	**Me lo llevo.** *may loh YEH-boh*
Will you wrap it?	**¿Quiere envolverlo?** *kee-YEHR-ay ehn-bohl-BEHR-loh*
I'd like to see the pair of shoes (boots) in the window.	**Quisiera ver el par de zapatos (botas) de la vitrina.** *kee-see-YEH-rah behr ehl pahr day sah-PAH-tohs (BOH-tahs) day lah bee-TREE-nah*
They're too narrow (wide).	**Son demasiado estrechos (anchos).** *sohn day-mahs-ee-AH-doh ehs-TRAY-chohs (AHN-chohs)*
I'll take them.	**Me los llevo.** *may lohs YEH-boh*
I also need shoe-laces.	**También necesito cordones de zapato.** *tahm-BYEHN neh-say-SEE-toh kohr-DOHN-ays day sah-PAH-toh*
That's all I want for now.	**Eso es todo por ahora.** *eh-soh ehs TOH-doh pohr ah-OHR-ah*

ELECTRICAL APPLIANCES

When buying any electrical items, check the voltage because it may not correspond with that you have at home.

I want to buy _____.	**Quiero comprar** _____.	*kee-YEHR-oh kohm-PRAHR*
a battery	**una pila**	*OO-nah PEE-lah*
an electric shaver	**una máquina de afeitar eléctrica**	*oo-nah MAH-kee-nah day ah-fay-TAHR eh-LEK-tree-kah*
a hair dryer	**un secador de pelo**	*oon say-kah-DOHR day PEH-loh*
a (portable) radio	**una radio (portátil)**	*oo-nah RAH-dee-oh (pohr-TAH-teel)*
a tape recorder	**una grabadora de cinta**	*oo-nah grah-bah-DOHR-ah day SEEN-tah*

FOODS AND HOUSEHOLD ITEMS

Always keep in mind the restrictions you will face at customs when you return to your own country. Fresh foods often are not permitted. When you go to a food market or shop, bring your own bag along with you to tote home your groceries. A collapsible net bag is very useful.

I'd like _____.	**Quisiera** _____.	*kee-SYEHR-ah*
a bar of soap	**una pastilla de jabón**	*OO-nah pahs-TEE-yah day hah-BOHN*
a bottle of juice	**una botella de jugo**	*OO-nah boh-TEH-yah day HOO-goh*
a box of cereal	**una caja de cereal**	*OO-nah KAH-hah day sehr-ay-AHL*
a can (tin) of tomato sauce	**una lata de salsa de tomate**	*OO-nah LAH-tah day SAHL-sah day toh-MAH-tay*
a dozen eggs	**una docena de huevos**	*OO-nah doh-SAY-nah day WAY-bohs*

■ a jar of coffee | **un pomo de café** *oon POH-moh day kah-FAY*

■ a kilo of potatoes (2.2 lbs) | **un kilo de papas (patatas)** *oon KEE-loh day PAH-pahs (pah-TAH-tahs)*

■ a half-kilo of cherries | **medio kilo de cerezas** *MED-ee-oh KEE-loh day sehr-AY-sahs*

■ a liter of milk | **un litro de leche** *oon LEE-troh day LEH-chay*

■ a package of candies | **un paquete de dulces** *oon pah-KEH-tay day dool-sayss*

■ 100 grams of cheese | **cien gramos de queso** *see-EHN GRAH-mohs day KAY-soh*

■ a roll of toilet paper | **un rollo de papel higiénico** *oon ROH-yoh day pah-pel ee-hee-EHN-ee-koh*

What is this (that)? | **¿Qué es esto (eso)?** *kay ehs EHS-toh (EHS-oh)*

Is it fresh? | **¿Está fresco?** *ehs-TAH FRES-koh*

I'd like a kilo (about 2 pounds) of oranges.* | **Quisiera un kilo de naranjas.** *kee-SYEHR-ah oon KEE-loh day nah-RAHN-hahs*

■ a half-kilo of butter | **medio kilo de mantequilla** *MED-ee-oh kee-loh day mahn-tay-KEE-yah*

■ 200 grams (about $\frac{1}{2}$ pound) of cookies (cakes) | **doscientos gramos de galletas (pasteles)** *dohs-SYEHN-tohs GRAH-mohs day gah-YEH-tahs*

■ 100 grams (about $\frac{1}{4}$ pound) of ham | **cien gramos de jamón** *SYEHN GRAH-mohs day hah-MOHN*

---

*NOTE: Common measurements for purchasing foods are a kilo, or fractions thereof, and 100, 200, and 500 grams. See also the pages on numbers, 13–16.

METRIC WEIGHTS AND MEASURES

SOLID MEASURES
(APPROXIMATE MEASUREMENTS ONLY)

OUNCES	GRAMS (GRAMOS)	GRAMS	OUNCES
$\frac{1}{4}$	7	10	$\frac{1}{3}$
$\frac{1}{2}$	14	100	$3\frac{1}{2}$
$\frac{3}{4}$	21	300	$10\frac{1}{2}$
1	28	500	18

POUNDS	KILOGRAMS (KILOS)	KILOGRAMS	POUNDS
1	$\frac{1}{2}$	1	$2\frac{1}{4}$
5	$2\frac{1}{4}$	3	$6\frac{1}{2}$
10	$4\frac{1}{2}$	5	11
20	9	10	22
50	23	50	110
100	45	100	220

LIQUID MEASURES
(APPROXIMATE MEASUREMENTS ONLY)

OUNCES	MILLILITERS (MILILITROS)	MILLILITERS	OUNCES
1	30	10	$\frac{1}{3}$
6	175	50	$1\frac{1}{2}$
12	350	100	$3\frac{1}{2}$
16	475	150	5

GALLONS	LITERS (LITROS)	LITERS	GALLONS
1	$3\frac{3}{4}$	1	$\frac{1}{4}$ (1 quart)
5	19	5	$1\frac{1}{3}$
10	38	10	$2\frac{1}{2}$

JEWELRY

I'd like to see _____.   **Quisiera ver _____.** *kee-SYEHR-ah-behr*

◼ a bracelet **un brazalete** *oon brah-sah-LAY-tay*

◼ a brooch **un broche** *oon BROH-chay*

◼ a chain **una cadena** *oo-nah kah-DAY-nah*

◼ a charm **un dije** *oon DEE-hay*

◼ some earrings **unos aretes (in Spain, pendientes)** *OO-nohs ah-REH-tays (pen-DYEHN-tays)*

◼ a necklace **un collar** *oon koh-YAHR*

◼ a pin **un alfiler** *oon ahl-fee-LEHR*

◼ a ring **un anillo (una sortija)** *oon ahn-EE-yoh (OO-nah sohr-TEE-hah)*

◼ a rosary **un rosario** *oon roh-SAHR-ee-oh*

◼ a (wrist) watch **un reloj (de pulsera)** *oon ray-LOH (day pool-SEHR-ah)*

Is this _____?   **¿Es esto _____?** *ehs EHS-toh*

◼ gold **oro** *OH-roh*

◼ platinum **platino** *plah-TEE-noh*

◼ silver **plata** *PLAH-tah*

◼ stainless steel **acero inoxidable** *ah-SEHR-oh een-ohks-ee-DAH-blay*

Is it solid or gold plated?   **¿Es macizo o dorado?** *ehs mah-SEE-soh oh dohr-AH-doh*

How many carats is it?   **¿De cuántos quilates es?** *day KWAHN-tohs kee-LAH-tays ehs*

What is that stone?   **¿Qué es esa piedra?** *kay ehs EHS-ah pee-YEHD-drah*

I want ____.	**Quiero ____.** *kee-YEHR-oh*
an amethyst	**una amatista** *oo-nah ah-mah-TEES-tah*
an aquamarine	**una aguamarina** *oo-nah ah-gwah-mah-REE-nah*
a diamond	**un diamante** *oon dee-ah-MAHN-tay*
an emerald	**una esmeralda** *oo-nah ehs-mehr-AHL-dah*
ivory	**marfil** *mahr-FEEL*
jade	**jade** *HAH-day*
onyx	**ónix** *OH-neeks*
pearls	**perlas** *PEHR-lahs*
a ruby	**un rubí** *oon roo-BEE*
a sapphire	**un zafiro** *oon sah-FEER-oh*
a topaz	**un topacio** *oon toh-PAH-see-oh*
turquoise	**turquesa** *toor-KAY-sah*
How much is it?	**¿Cuánto vale?** *KWAHN-toh BAH-lay*

NEWSPAPERS AND MAGAZINES

Do you carry English newspapers (magazines)?	**¿Tiene usted periódicos (revistas) en inglés?** *tee-YEHN-ay oos-TEHD peh-ree-OH-dee-kohs (ray-BEES-tahs) en een-GLAYSS*
I'd like to buy some (picture) post cards.	**Quisiera comprar postales (ilustradas).** *kee-SYEHR-ah kohm-PRAHR pohs-TAHL-ays (ee-loos-TRAH-dahs)*
Do you have stamps?	**¿Tiene sellos?** *tee-YEHN-ay SEH-yohs*
How much is that?	**¿Cuánto es?** *KWAHN-toh ehs*

PHOTOGRAPHIC SUPPLIES

For phrases dealing with camera repairs, see page 153.

Where is there a camera shop?	**¿Dónde hay una tienda de artículos fotográficos?** *DOHN-day AH-ee oo-nah tee-YEHN-dah day ahr-TEEK-oo-lohs foh-toh-GRAHF-ee-kohs*
Do you develop film here?	**¿Aquí revelan películas?** *ah-KEE ray-BEHL-ahn pel-EE-koo-lahs*
How much does it cost to develop a roll?	**¿Cuánto cuesta revelar un carrete?** *KWAHN-toh KWEHS-tah ray-behl-AHR oon kahr-reh-tay*
I want _____.	**Quiero _____.** *kee-YEHR-oh*
one print of each	**una copia de cada uno** *oo-nah KOH-pee-ah day kah-dah OO-noh*
an enlargement	**una ampliación** *oo-nah ahm-plee-ah-SYOHN*
with a glossy (matte) finish	**con acabado brillante (mate)** *kohn ah-kah-bah-doh bree-YAHN-tay (MAH-tay)*
I want a roll of color (black and white) film.	**Quiero un rollo de películas en colores (en blanco y negro).** *kee-YEHR-oh oon roh-yoh day pehl-EE-koo-lahs ehn koh-lohr-ays (ehn BLAHN-koh ee NEH-groh)*
When can I pick up the pictures?	**¿Cuándo puedo recoger las fotos?** *KWAHN-doh PWEH-doh ray-koh-HEHR lahs FOH-tohs*
Do you sell cameras?	**¿Vende usted cámaras?** *ben-day oos-TEHD KAH-mah-rahs*
I want an inexpensive camera.	**Quiero una cámara barata.** *kee-YEHR-oh oo-nah KAH-mah-rah bah-RAH-tah*

RECORDS AND TAPES

Is there a record shop around here?	**¿Hay una tienda de discos por aquí?** *AH-ee oo-nah tee-yehn-dah day DEES-kohs pohr ah-kee*
Do you sell ____?	**¿Vende usted ____?** *BEN-day oos-TEHD*
cassettes	**casetas** *kah-SAY-tahs*
records	**discos** *DEES-kohs*
tapes	**cintas** *SEEN-tahs*
Do you have an album of ____?	**¿Tiene un álbum de ____?** *tee-EHN-ay oon AHL-boon day*
L.P. (33 r.p.m.)	**un elepé** *oon ehl-ay-PAY*
45 r.p.m.	**un cuarenta y cinco** *oon kwahr-EHN-tah ee SEEN-koh*
Where is the ____ section?	**¿Dónde está la sección de ____?** *DOHN-day ehs-TAH lah sek-SYOHN day*
classical music	**la música clásica** *lah MOO-see-kah KLAHS-ee-kuh*
folk music	**la musica folklórica** *lah MOO-see-kah fohl-KLOHR-ee-kah*
latest hits	**los últimos éxitos** *lohs OOL-tee-mohs EHK-see-tohs*
rock 'n roll	**el rocanrol** *ehl rohk-ahn-ROHL*
opera	**la ópera** *lah OH-pehr-ah*
popular music	**la música popular** *lah MOO-see-kah poh-poo-LAHR*
Spanish music	**la música española** *lah MOO-see-kah ehs-pahn-YOH-lah*
Latin music	**la música latina** *lah MOO-see-kah lah-TEEN-ah*

SOUVENIRS, HANDICRAFTS

I'd like ____.	**Quisiera ____.** *kee-SYEHR-ah*
a pretty gift	**un regalo bonito** *oon ray-GAH-loh boh-NEE-toh*
a small gift	**un regalito** *oon ray-gah-LEE-toh*
a souvenir	**un recuerdo** *oon ray-KWEHR-doh*
It's for ____.	**Es para ____.** *ehs pah-rah*
I don't want to spend more than ____ dollars.	**No quiero gastar más de ____ dólares.** *noh kee-YEHR-oh gahs-TAHR mahs day ____ DOH-lahr-ays*
Could you suggest something?	**¿Podría usted sugerir algo?** *poh-DREE-ah oos-TEHD soo-hehr-EER AHL-goh*
Would you show me your selection of ____?	**¿Quiere enseñarme su surtido de ____?** *kee-YEHR-ay ehn-sen-YAHR-may soo soor-TEE-doh day*
blown glass	**vidrio soplado** *BEE-dree-oh soh-PLAH-doh*
carved objects	**objetos de madera tallada** *ohb-HET-ohs day mah-DEHR-ah tah-YAH-dah*
cut crystal	**vidrio tallado** *BEE-dree-oh tah-YAH-doh*
dolls	**muñecas** *moon-YEH-kahs*
earthenware (pottery)	**loza** *LOH-sah*
fans	**abanicos** *ah-bah-NEE-kohs*
jewelry	**joyas** *HOY-ahs*
lace	**encaje** *ehn-KAH-hay*

■ leathergoods **objetos de cuero** *ohb-HET-ohs day KWEHR-oh*

■ liqueurs **licores** *lee-KOHR-ays*

■ musical instruments **instrumentos musicales** *een-stroo-MEN-tohs moo-see-KAHL-ays*

■ perfumes **perfumes** *pehr-FOO-mays*

■ pictures **dibujos** *dee-BOO-hohs*

■ posters **carteles** *kahr-TEHL-ays*

■ religious articles **artículos religiosos** *ahr-TEE-koo-lohs ray-lee-hee-OH-sohs*

LITTLE TREASURES

Is this an antique? **¿Es una antigüedad?** *ehs oo-nah ahn-tee-gway-DAHD*

How old is it? **¿Cuántos años tiene?** *KWAHN-tohs anh-yohs tee-YEHN-ay*

Is it a reproduction? **¿Es una reproducción?** *ehs oo-nah ray-proh-dook-SYOHN*

Tell me its history. **¿Puede decirme algo de su historia?** *PWEH-day day-SEER-may AHL-go day soo ee-STOHR-ee-ah*

Is the artist well known? **¿Es conocido el artista?** *ehs kohn-oh-SEE-doh ehl ahr-TEES-tah*

Where has he (she) exhibited? **¿Dónde está exhibiendo?** *DOHN-day ehs-TAH eks-ee-BYEHN-doh*

What materials are used? **¿De qué está hecho?** *day KAY ehs-TAH AY-choh*

What does this signify? **¿Qué quiere decir esto?** *Kay KYEHR-ay day-SEER EHS-toh*

Is this hand-made? **¿Está hecho a mano?** *eh-STAH AY-choh ah MAH-noh*

What is the name of the type of work?	**¿Cómo se llama este tipo de traba-jo?** *KOH-moh say YAH-mah EHS-tay TEE-poh day trah-BAH-ho*
Is this a specialty of this region? this town?	**¿Es una especialidad de esta re-gión? de este pueblo?** *ehs oo-nah ehs-pehs-yah-lee-DAHD day ehs-tah ray-HYOHN day ehs-tay PWEHB-loh*
What are the local specialties of _____?	**¿Cuáles son las especialidades lo-cales de _____?** *KWAHL-ays sohn lahs ehs-pehs-yah-lee-DAHD-ays loh-KAHL-ays day*
Is this washable?	**¿Es lavable?** *ehs lah-bah-blay*
Will it shrink?	**¿Se encoge?** *say ehn-KOH-hay*
Should it be washed by hand?	**¿Debe lavarse a mano?** *DEH-bay lah-BAHR-say ah MAH-noh*
in cold water	**¿en agua fría?** *ehn AH-gwah FREE-ah*
Can it go in the dry-er?	**¿Se puede meter en la secadora?** *say PWEHD-ay meh-TEHR ehn lah seh-kah-DOHR-ah*
Can this go in the dishwasher?	**¿Se puede meter esto en el lava-platos?** *say PWEH-day meh-TEHR ehs-toh ehn ehl lah-bah-PLAH-tohs*
Is it ovenproof?	**¿Está a prueba de horno?** *ehs-TAH ah PRWEH-bah day OR-hohs*
Is this safe to use for cooking?	**¿Se puede usar sin peligro para cocinar?** *say PWEH-day oo-SAHR SEEN pe-LEE-groh pah-rah koh-see-NAHR*
What is the lead con-tent?	**¿Qué contenido de plomo tiene?** *kay kohn-ten-EE-doh day PLOH-moh tee-YEHN-ay*
Did you make this yourself?	**¿Lo ha hecho usted?** *loh ah AY-choh oos-TEHD*

BARGAINING

In Latin America, especially in the markets, you will be expected to bargain for everything you want to purchase. The key to successful bargaining is to end up with a price that is fair for both you and the merchant. Begin by asking the price, then make your own offer about half to two-thirds of the asking price. Usually the merchant will make another offer and you can listen and consider the object, perhaps finding a little problem with it—a tear, a scrape, some unevenness. A little discussion back and forth, and you'll soon have it at a fair price. If you do not understand numbers, then the seller will write the number down for you. At the conclusion, smile and thank the merchant, expressing your happiness with the result.

Please, madam, how much is this?	**Por favor, señora, ¿Cuánto vale esto?** *pohr fah-BOHR sehn-YOHR-ah KWAHN-toh BAH-lay EHS-toh*
Oh, no, that is more than I can spend.	**Ay, no, eso es más de lo que puedo gastar.** *AH-ee noh EHS-oh ehs MAHS day loh kay PWEH-doh gahs-TAHR*
How about _____?	**¿Y si le doy _____?** *EE see lay doy*
No, that is too high. Would you take _____?	**No, eso es demasiado. ¿Aceptaría _____?** *noh EHS-oh ehs day-mahs-ee-AH-doh ah-sep-tahr-EE-ah*
But there seems to be a scratch (tear) here.	**Me parace que hay un arañazo (un roto) aquí.** *may pahr-ay-say kay AH-ee oon ah-rahn-YAH-soh ah-KEE*
Yes, that's fine. I'll take it.	**Así esta bien. Me lo llevo.** *ah-SEE ehs-TAH byehn may loh YEH-boh*
Thank you. Have a nice day.	**Gracias. Qué lo pase bien.** *GRAH-see-ahs kay loh PAH-say byehn*

STATIONERY ITEMS

I want to buy ____.	**Quiero comprar** ____. *kee-YEHR-oh kohm-PRAHR*
a ball-point pen	**un bolígrafo** *oon boh-lee-grah-foh*
a deck of cards	**una baraja** *oo-nah bahr-AH-hah*
envelopes	**sobres** *SOH-brays*
an eraser	**una goma de borrar** *oo-nah GOH-mah day bohr-AHR*
glue	**cola de pegar** *koh-lah day peh-GAHR*
a notebook	**un cuaderno** *oon kwah-DEHR-noh*
pencils	**lápices** *LAH-pee-sayss*
a pencil sharpener	**un sacapuntas** *oon sah-kah-POON-tahs*
a ruler	**una regla** *oo-nah REHG-lah*
Scotch Tape	**cinta adhesiva** *SEEN-tah ahd-ehs-EE-bah*
some string	**cuerda** *KWEHR-dah*
typing paper	**papel de máquina** *pah-PEL day MAH-kee-nah*
wrapping paper	**papel de envolver** *pah-PEL day ehn-bohl-BEHR*
a writing pad	**un bloc de papel** *oon blohk day pah-PEL*

TOBACCO

In Latin America you can buy cigarettes and other related items at a **tabaquería** *(tah-bah-kehr-EE-ah)*.

In Spain, you would go to an **estanco** *(ehs-TAHN-koh)*.

A pack (carton) of cigarettes, please.	**Un paquete (cartón) de cigarrillos, por favor.** *oon pah-KAY-tay (kahr-TOHN) day see-gahr-EE-yohs pohr fah-BOHR*
filtered	**con filtro** *kohn FEEL-troh*
unfiltered	**sin filtro** *seen FEEL-troh*
menthol	**de mentol** *day mehn-TOHL*
king-size	**extra largos** *EHS-trah LAHR-gohs*
Are these cigarettes (very) strong (mild)?	**¿Son (muy) fuertes (suaves) estos cigarrillos?** *sohn (mwee) FWEHR-tays (SWAH-bays) ehs-tohs see-gahr-EE-yohs*
Do you have American cigarettes?	**¿Tiene usted cigarrillos norteamericanos?** *tee-YEHN-ay oos-TEHD see-gahr-EE-yohs nohr-tay-ah-mehr-ee-KAH-nohs*
What brands?	**¿De qué marcas?** *day kay MAHR-kahs*
Please give me a pack of matches also.*	**Déme una caja de fósforos también.** *DAY-may oo-nah kah-hah day FOHS-for-ohs tahm-bee-EHN*
Do you sell ____?	**¿Vende usted ____?** *BEHN-day oo-STEHD*
a cigarette holder	**una boquilla** *oo-nah boh-KEE-yah*
cigars	**cigarros** *see-GAHR-rohs*
flints	**piedras de encendedor** *pee-EH-drahs day ehn-sen-day-DOHR*
lighter fluid	**líquido de encendedor** *LEE-kee-doh day ehn-sen-day-DOHR*
lighters	**encendedores** *ehn-sen-day-DOHR-ays*

*Matches are often not free; you must pay for them.

▣ pipes	**pipas**	*PEE-pahs*
▣ pipe tobacco	**tobaco de pipa**	*tah-BAH-koh day PEE-pah*

TOILETRIES

In Spain, a drugstore (chemist) doesn't carry toiletries. There you will have to go to a **perfumería**. In Latin America, however, you'll find cosmetics and other toiletries at a drugstore as well.

Do you have ____?	**¿Tiene usted ____?** *tee-YEHN-ay oo-STEHD*
▣ bobby pins	**horquillas** *ohr-KEE-yahs*
▣ a brush	**un cepillo** *oon sep-EE-yoh*
▣ cleansing cream	**crema limpiadora** *KRAY-mah leem-pee-ah-DOHR-ah*
▣ a comb	**un peine** *oon PAY-nay*
▣ a deodorant	**un desodorante** *oon dehs-oh-dohr-AHN-tay*
▣ (disposable) diapers	**pañales (desechables)** *pahn-YAH-lays (dehs-ay-CHAH-blays)*
▣ emery boards	**limas de cartón** *LEE-mahs day kahr-TOHN*
▣ eye liner	**un lápiz de ojos** *oon LAH-pees day OH-hohs*
▣ hair spray	**laca** *LAH-kah*
▣ lipstick	**lápiz de labios** *LAH-pees day LAH-bee-ohs*
▣ make-up	**maquillaje** *mah-kee-YAH-hay*
▣ mascara	**rimel** *ree-MEHL*
▣ a mirror	**un espejo** *oon ehs-PAY-ho*

■ mouthwash	**un lavado bucal** *oon lah-bah-doh boo-kahl*
■ nail clippers	**un cortauñas** *oon kohr-tah-oon-yahs*
■ a nail file	**una lima de uñas** *oo-nah lee-mah day OON-yahs*
■ nail polish	**esmalte de uñas** *ehs-MAHL-tay day OON-yahs*
■ nail polish remover	**un quita-esmalte** *oon kee-tah ehs-MAHL-tay*
■ a razor	**una navaja** *oo-nah nah-BAH-hah*
■ razor blades	**hojas de afeitar** *OH-hahs day ah-fay-TAHR*
■ sanitary napkins	**servilletas higiénicas** *sehr-bee-YEH-tahs ee-HYEHN-ee-kahs*
■ (cuticle) scissors	**tijeras (de cutículas)** *tee-HAIR-ahs (day koo-TEE-kool-ahs)*
■ shampoo	**champú** *chahm-POO*
■ shaving lotion	**loción de afeitar** *loh-SYOHN day ah-fay-TAHR*
■ soap	**jabón** *hah-BOHN*
■ a sponge	**una esponja** *oo-nah ehs-POHN-hah*
■ tampons	**tapones** *tah-POHN-ays*
■ tissues	**pañuelos de papel** *pahn-yoo-EH-lohs day pah-PEL*
■ toilet paper	**papel higiénico** *pah-PEL ee-hy-EHN-ee-koh*
■ a tooth brush	**un cepillo de dientes** *oon sep-EE-yoh day dee-YEHN-tays*
■ toothpaste	**pasta de dientes** *pah-stah day dee-YEHN-tays*
■ tweezers	**pinzas** *PEEN-sahs*

PERSONAL CARE AND SERVICES

If your hotel doesn't offer these services, ask the attendant at the desk to recommend someone nearby.

AT THE BARBER

Where is there a good barber shop?	**¿Dónde hay una buena barbería?** *DOHN-day AH-ee oo-nah BWEH-nah bahr-behr-EE-ah*
Do I have to wait long?	**¿Tengo que esperar mucho?** *ten-goh kay ehs-pehr-AHR MOO-choh*
Am I next?	**¿Me toca a mí?** *may TOH-kay ah mee*
I want a shave.	**Quiero que me afeiten.** *kee-YEHR-oh kay may ah-FAY-tehn*
I want a haircut (razorcut).	**Quiero un corte de pelo (a navaja).** *kee-YEHR-oh oon KOHR-tay day PEH-loh (ah nah-BAH-hah)*
Short in back, long in front.	**Corto por detrás, largo por delante.** *KOHR-toh pohr day-TRAHS, lahr-goh pohr day-LAHN-tay*
Leave it long.	**Déjelo largo.** *DAY-hay-loh LAHR-goh*
I want it (very) short.	**Lo quiero (muy) corto.** *loh kee-YEHR-oh (mwee) KOHR-toh*
You can cut a little ____.	**Puede cortar un poquito ____.** *PWEH-day kohr-TAHR oon poh-KEE-toh*
▪ in back	**por detrás** *pohr day-TRAHS*
▪ in front	**por delante** *pohr day-LAHN-tay*
▪ off the top	**de arriba** *day ah-REE-bah*

◼ on the sides	**a los lados** *ah lohs LAH-dohs*
Cut a little bit more here.	**Córteme un poco más aquí.** *KOHR-tay-may oon POH-koh mahs ah-KEE*
That's enough.	**Eso es bastante.** *EH-soh ehs bah-STAHN-tay*
I (don't) want ____.	**(No) quiero ____.** *(noh) kee-YEHR-oh*
◼ shampoo	**champú** *chahm-POO*
◼ tonic	**tónico** *TOHN-ee-koh*
Use the scissors only.	**Use sólo las tijeras.** *oo-say soh-loh lahs tee-HAIR-ahs*
Please trim my ____.	**Recórteme ____ por favor.** *ray-KOHR-tay-may ____ pohr fah-BOHR*
◼ beard	**la barba** *lah bahr-bah*
◼ moustache	**el bigote** *ehl bee-GOH-tay*
◼ sideburns	**las patillas** *lahs pah-TEE-yahs*
I'd like to look at myself in the mirror.	**Quisiera mirarme al espejo.** *kee-SYEHR-ah meer-AHR-may ahl ehs-PAY-hoh*
How much do I owe you?	**¿Cuánto le debo?** *KWAHN-toh lay DEH-boh*
Is service included?	**¿Está incluída la propina?** *eh-STAH een-kloo-EE-dah lah proh-PEE-nah*

AT THE BEAUTY PARLOR

Is there a beauty parlor (hairdresser) near the hotel?	**¿Hay un salón de belleza (una peluquería) cerca del hotel?** *AH-ee oon sah-LOHN day beh-YEH-sah (OO-nah pel-oo-kehr-EE-ah) SEHR-kah del oh-TEL*

| I'd like an appointment for this afternoon (tomorrow). | **Quisiera hacer una cita para esta tarde (mañana).** *kee-SYEHR-ah ah-SEHR oo-nah SEE-tah pah-rah EHS-tah TAHR-day (mahn-YA-nah)* |
| Can you give me ____? | **¿Puede darme ____?** *PWEH-day DAHR-may* |

■ a color rinse — **un enjuague de color** *oon ehn-hoo-AH-gay day koh-LOHR*

■ a facial massage — **un masaje facial** *oon mah-SAH-hay fah-see-AHL*

■ a haircut — **un corte de pelo** *oon KOHR-tay day PEH-loh*

■ a manicure — **una manicura** *oo-nah mah-nee-KOOR-ah*

■ a permanent — **una permanente** *oon-nah pehr-mah-NEN-tay*

■ a shampoo — **un champú** *oon chahm-POO*

■ a tint — **un tinte** *oon TEEN-tay*

■ a touch up	**un retoque** *oon ray-TOH-kay*
■ a wash and set	**un lavado y peinado** *oon lah-bah-doh ee pay-NAH-doh*
I'd like to see a color chart.	**Quisiera ver un muestrario.** *kee-SYEHR-ah behr oon mwehs-TRAHR-ee-oh*
I want _____.	**Quiero _____.** *kee-YEHR-oh*
■ auburn	**rojizo** *roh-HEE-soh*
■ (light) blond	**un rubio (claro)** *oon ROO-bee-oh (KLAHR-oh)*
■ brunette	**castaño** *kahs-TAHN-yo*
■ a darker color	**un color más oscuro** *oon koh-LOHR mahs oh-SKOOR-oh*
■ a lighter color	**un color más claro** *oon koh-LOHR mahs KLAH-roh*
■ the same color	**el mismo color** *ehl MEES-moh koh-LOHR*
Don't apply any hair-spray.	**No me ponga laca.** *noh may POHN-gah lah-kah*
Not too much hair-spray.	**Sólo un poco de laca.** *SOH-loh oon POH-koh day LAH-kah*
I want my hair _____.	**Quiero el pelo _____.** *kee-YEHR-oh ehl peh-loh*
■ with bangs	**con flequillo** *kohn fleh-KEE-yoh*
■ in a bun	**con un moño** *kohn oon MOHN-yoh*
■ in curls	**con bucles** *kohn boo-KLAYS*
■ with waves	**con ondas** *kohn OHN-dahs*
I'd like to look at myself in the mirror.	**Quiero mirarme al espejo.** *kee-YEHR-oh meer-AHR-may ahl ehs-PAY-hoh*

How much do I owe you?	**¿Cuánto le debo?** *KWAHN-toh lay DEH-boh*
Is service included?	**¿Está incluída la propina?** *es-TAH een-kloo-EE-dah lah proh-PEE-nah*

LAUNDRY AND DRY CLEANING

Where is the nearest laundry (dry cleaners)?	**¿Dónde está la lavandería (la tintorería) más cercana?** *DOHN-day ehs-TAH lah lah-bahn-deh-REE-ah (lah teen-TOHR-ehr-EE-ah) mahs sehr-KAH-nah*
I have a lot of (dirty) clothes to be _____.	**Tengo mucha ropa (sucia) que _____.** *ten-goh moo-chah ROH-pah (SOO-see-ah) kay*
■ (dry) cleaned	**limpiar (en seco)** *leem-pee-AHR (ehn SEH-koh)*
■ washed	**lavar** *lah-BAHR*
■ mended	**arreglar** *ah-ray-GLAHR*
■ ironed	**planchar** *plahn-CHAHR*
Here's the list.	**Aquí tiene la lista.** *ah-KEE tee-EH-neh lah LEES-tah*
■ 3 shirts (men's)	**tres camisas (de hombre)** *trays kah-mee-sahs (day OHM-bray)*
■ 12 handkerchiefs	**doce pañuelos** *doh-say pahn-yoo-AY-lohs*
■ 6 pairs of socks	**seis pares de calcetines** *sayss pah-rays day kahl-say-TEEN-ays*
■ 1 blouse (nylon)	**una blusa (de nilón)** *oo-nah BLOO-sah (day nee-LOHN)*
■ 4 shorts (underwear)	**cuatro calzoncillos** *KWAH-troh kahl-sohn-SEEL-yohs*
■ 2 pyjamas	**dos pijamas** *dohs pee-HAHM-ahs*

☐ 2 suits	**dos trajes** *dohs TRAH-hays*
☐ 3 ties	**tres corbatas** *trays kohr-BAH-tahs*
☐ 2 dresses (cotton)	**dos vestidos (de algodón)** *dohs behs-tee-dohs (day ahl-go-DOHN)*
☐ 2 skirts	**dos faldas** *dohs FAHL-dahs*
☐ 1 sweater (wool)	**un suéter (de lana)** *oon soo-EH-tehr (day LAH-nah)*
☐ 1 pair of gloves	**un par de guantes** *oon pahr day GWAHN-tays*
I need them for _____.	**Las necesito para _____.** *lahs neh-seh-SEE-toh PAH-rah*
☐ tonight	**esta noche** *EHS-tah NOH-chay*
☐ tomorrow	**mañana** *mahn-YAH-nah*
☐ next week	**la semana próxima** *lah seh-MAH-nah PROHK-see-mah*
☐ the day after tomorrow	**pasado mañana** *pah-SAH-doh mahn-YAH-nah*
When will you bring it back?	**¿Cuándo la traerá?** *kwahn-doh lah trah-ehr-AH*
When will it be ready?	**¿Cuándo estará lista?** *kwahn-doh ehs-tah-RAH lees-tah*
There's a button missing.	**Falta un botón.** *fahl-tah oon boh-TOHN*
Can you sew it on?	**¿Puede usted coserlo?** *pweh-deh oos-TEHD koh-SEHR-loh*
This isn't my laundry.	**Esta no es mi ropa.** *EHS-tah noh ehs mee ROH-pah*

SHOE REPAIRS

A shoemaker, **el zapatero** *(ehl sah-pah-TEHR-oh)* will repair shoes.

Can you fix these shoes (boots)?	**¿Puede arreglar estos zapatos (estas botas)?** *PWEH-day ah-ray-GLAHR ehs-tohs sah-PAH-tohs (ehs-tahs BOH-tahs)*
Put on (half) soles and rubber heels.	**Póngales (medias) suelas y tacones de goma.** *POHN-gah-lays (MED-ee-ahs) SWAY-lahs ee tah-KOHN-ays day GOH-mah*
I'd like to have my shoes shined too.	**Quiero que me limpien los zapatos también.** *kee-YEHR-oh kay may LEEM-pee-ehn lohs sah-PAH-tohs tahm-BYEHN*
When will they be ready?	**¿Para cuándo los tendrá?** *pah-rah KWAHN-doh lohs ten-DRAH*
I need them by Saturday (without fail).	**Los necesito para el sábado (sin falta).** *lohs nes-ehs-see-toh pah-rah ehl SAH-bah-doh (seen FAHL-tah)*

WATCH REPAIRS

A watchmaker, in his shop, **la relojería** *(ray-loh-hehr-EE-ah)* will repair watches and clocks.

Can you fix this watch (alarm clock) (for me)?	**¿(Me) puede arreglar este reloj (despertador)?** *(may) PWEH-day ah-ray-GLAHR EHS-tay ray-LOH (dehs-pehr-tah-dohr)*
Can you clean it?	**¿Puede usted limpiarlo?** *PWEH-day oos-TEHD leem-pee-AHR-loh*
I dropped it.	**Se me cayó.** *say may kah-YOH*
It's running slow (fast).	**Se atrasa (se adelanta).** *say ah-TRAH-sah (Say ah-deh-LAHN-tah)*
It's stopped.	**Está parado.** *ehs-TAH pah-RAH-doh*
I wind it everyday.	**Le doy cuerda todos los días.** *lay doy KWEHR-dah toh-dohs lohs DEE-ahs*

I need ____.	**Necesito ____.** *neh-say-SEE-toh*
a crystal, glass	**un cristal** *oon kree-STAHL*
an hour hand	**un horario** *oon ohr-AH-ee-oh*
a minute hand	**un minutero** *oon mee-noo-TEHR-oh*
a stem	**un tornillo** *oon tohr-NEE-yoh*
a second hand	**un segundario** *oon say-goon-DAH-ree-oh*
a battery	**una pila** *oo-nah PEE-lah*
When will it be ready?	**¿Cuándo estará listo?** *KWAHN-doh ehs-tah-RAH LEES-toh*
May I have a receipt?	**¿Me puede dar un recibo?** *may PWEH-day dahr oon ray-SEE-boh*

CAMERA REPAIRS

Can you fix this camera?	**¿Puede usted arreglar esta cámara?** *PWEHD-eh oos-TEHD ah-ray-GLAHR ehs-tah KAH-mah-rah*
The film doesn't advance.	**El carrete no se mueve.** *ehl kah-REH-tay noh say MWEH-bay*
I think I need new batteries.	**Creo que necesito una nueva pila.** *KRAY-oh kay reh-seh-SEE-toh oo-nah NWEH-bah PEE-lah*
How much will the repair cost?	**¿Cuánto costará el arreglo?** *KWAHN-toh kohs-tah-RAH ehl ah-REG-loh*
When can I come and get it?	**¿Cuándo puedo venir a buscarla?** *KWAHN-doh PWEHD-oh ben-EER ah boos-KAHR-lah*
I need it as soon as possible.	**La necesito lo más pronto posible.** *lah neh-say-SEE-toh loh mahs PROHN-toh poh-SEE-blay*

MEDICAL CARE

THE PHARMACY (CHEMIST)

La farmacia *(fahr-MAH-see-ah)* in Spain can be recognized by its sign with a green cross. If it is closed, look for a list on the door which has the nearest stores which are open. Note that a pharmacy mainly sells drugs; for toiletries, you must go to a **perfumería.**

Where is the nearest (all-night) pharmacy (chemist)?	**¿Dónde está la farmacia (de guardia) más cercana?** *DOHN-day ehs-TAH lah fahr-MAH-see-ah (day GWAHR-dee-ah) mahs sehr-KAH-nah*
At what time does the pharmacy open (close)?	**¿A qué hora se abre (se cierra) la farmacia?** *ah kay OH-rah say AH-bray (say SYEHR-ah) lah fahr-MAH-see-ah*
I need something for ____.	**Necesito algo para ____.** *neh-seh-SEE-toh AHL-goh pah-rah*
a cold	**un catarro** *oon kah-TAH-roh*
constipation	**el estreñimiento (constipación estomacal)** *ehl ehs-trayn-yee-MYEHN-toh*
a cough	**la tos** *lah-tohs*
diarrhea	**la diarrea** *lah dee-ahr-RAY-ah*
a fever	**la fiebre** *lah fee-YEHB-ray*
hay fever	**la fiebre del heno** *lah fee-YEHB-ray del AY-noh*
a headache	**un dolor de cabeza** *oon doh-LOHR day kah-BAY-sah*
insomnia	**el insomnio** *ehl een-SOHM-nee-oh*
nausea	**náuseas** *NAH-oo-say-ahs*
sunburn	**la quemadura del sol** *lah kay-mah-DOOR-ah del SOHL*

a toothache	**un dolor de muelas** *oon doh-LOHR day MWEH-lahs*
an upset stomach	**la indigestión** *lah een-dee-hes-TYOHN*
I do not have a prescription.	**No tengo la receta.** *noh TEN-goh lah reh-SAY-tah*
May I have it right away?	**¿Me la puede dar en seguida?** *May lah PWEH-day DAHR ehn seh-GHEE-dah*
It's an emergency!	**¡Es urgente!** *ehs oor-HEN-tay*
How long will it take?	**¿Cuánto tiempo tardará?** *KWAHN-toh tee-YEHM-poh tahr-dahr-AH*
When can I come for it?	**¿Cuándo puedo venir a recogerla?** *KWAHN-doh PWEH-doh ben-EER ah ray-koh-HAIR-lah*
I would like ____.	**Quisiera ____.** *kee-see-YEHR-ah*
adhesive tape	**esparadrapo** *ehs-pah-rah-DRAH-poh*
alcohol	**alcohol** *ahl-koh-OHL*
an antacid	**un antiácido** *oon ahn-tee-AH-see-doh*
an antiseptic	**un antiséptico** *oon ahn-tee-SEP-tee-koh*
aspirins	**aspirinas** *ahs-peer-EE-nahs*
Band-Aids	**curitas** *koor-EE-tahs*
contraceptives	**contraceptivos** *kohn-trah-sep-TEE-bohs*
corn plasters	**callicidas** *kah-yee-SEE-dahs*
cotton	**algodón** *ahl-goh-DOHN*
cough drops	**pastillas para la tos** *PAHS-TEE-yahs pah-rah lah TOHS*

cough syrup	**jarabe para la tos** *hah-RAH-bay pah-rah lah TOHS*
ear drops	**gotas para los oídos** *goh-tahs pah-rah lohs oh-EE-dohs*
eye drops	**gotas para los ojos** *goh-tahs pah-rah lohs OH-hohs*
iodine	**yodo** *YOH-doh*
a (mild) laxative	**un laxante (ligero)** *oon lahk-SAHN-tay (lee-HEHR-oh)*
milk of magnesia	**la leche de magnesia** *lah leh-chay day mahg-NAY-see-ah*
prophylactics	**profilácticos** *pro-fee-LAHK-tee-kohs*
sanitary napkins	**servilletas higiénicas** *sehr-bee-YEH-tahs ee-HYEHN-ee-kahs*
suppositories	**supositorios** *soo-pohs-ee-TOHR-ee-ohs*
talcum powder	**polvos de talco** *POHL-bohs day TAHL-koh*
tampons	**tapones** *tah-POHN-ays*
a thermometer	**un termómetro** *oon tehr-MOH-met-roh*
tranquilizers	**un tranquilizante** *oon trahn-kee-lee-SAHN-tay*
vitamins	**vitaminas** *bee-tah-MEE-nahs*

WITH THE DOCTOR

I don't feel well.	**No me siento bien.** *noh may SYEHN-toh BYEHN*
I need a doctor.	**Necesito un médico.** *neh-seh-SEE-toh oon MEH-dee-koh*

Do you know a doctor who speaks English?	**¿Conoce un médico que hable inglés?** *koh-NOH-say oon MEH-dee-koh kay ah-blay een-GLAYSS*
Where is his office (surgery)?	**¿Dónde está su consultorio?** *DOHN-day ehs-TAH soo kohn-sool-TOHR-ee-oh*
Will the doctor come to the hotel?	**¿Vendrá el medico al hotel?** *ben-DRAH ehl MED-ee-koh ahl oh-TEL*
I feel dizzy.	**Estoy mareado.** *ehs-TOY mahr-ay-AH-doh*
I feel weak.	**Me siento débil.** *may SYEHN-toh DAY-beel*
My temperature is normal (37°C).	**Tengo la temperatura normal (treinta y siete grados).** *TEN-goh lah tem-pehr-ah-TOOR-ah nohr-MAHL (trayn-tah ee see-EH-tay GRAH-dohs)*
I (think I) have _____.	**(Creo que) tengo _____.** *KRAY-oh kay TEN-goh*
an abscess	**un absceso** *oon ahb-SEHS-oh*
a broken bone	**un hueso roto** *oon WAY-soh ROH-toh*
a bruise	**una contusión** *oo-nah kohn-too-SYOHN*
a burn	**una quemadura** *oo-nah kay-mah-DOOR-ah*
something in my eye	**algo en el ojo** *AHL-goh ehn ehl OH-hoh*
the chills	**escalofríos** *ehs-kah-loh-FREE-ohs*
a chest (head) cold	**un catarro (resfriado)** *oon kah-TAHR-oh (res-free-AH-doh)*
constipation	**el estreñimiento** *ehl ehs-trayn-yee-mee-YENT-oh*
stomach cramps	**calambres** *kahl-AHM-brays*

a cut **una cortadura** *oo-nah kohr-tah-DOOR-ah*

diarrhea **la diarrea** *lah dee-ah-RAY-ah*

a fever **fiebre** *fee-YEHB-bray*

a fracture **una fractura** *oo-nah frahk-TOOR-ah*

a headache **un dolor de cabeza** *oon doh-lohr day kah-BAY-sah*

an infection **una infección** *oo-nah een-fek-SYOHN*

a lump **un bulto** *oon BOOL-toh*

a sore throat **un dolor de garganta** *oon doh-lohr day gahr-GAHN-tah*

a stomach ache **un dolor de estómago** *oon doh-lohr day ehs-TOH-mah-goh*

It hurts me here. **Me duele aquí.** *may DWEH-lay ah-KEE*

My whole body hurts. **Me duele todo el cuerpo.** *may DWEH-lay toh-doh ehl KWEHR-poh*

PARTS OF THE BODY

ankle	**el tobillo** *ehl toh-BEE-yoh*
appendix	**el apéndice** *ehl ah-PEN-dee-say*
arm	**el brazo** *ehl BRAH-soh*
back	**la espalda** *lah ehs-PAHL-dah*
breast	**el pecho** *ehl PAY-choh*
cheek	**la mejilla** *lah meh-HEE-yah*
ear	**el oído** *ehl oh-EE-doh*
elbow	**el codo** *ehl KOH-doh*
eye	**el ojo** *ehl OH-hoh*
face	**la cara** *lah KAH-rah*
finger	**el dedo** *ehl DAY-doh*
foot	**el pie** *ehl pee-AY*
glands	**las glándulas** *lahs GLAHN-doo-lahs*
hand	**la mano** *lah MAHN-oh*
head	**la cabeza** *lah kah-BAY-sah*
heart	**el corazón** *ehl kohr-ah-SOHN*
hip	**la cadera** *lah kah-DEHR-ah*
knee	**la rodilla** *lah roh-DEE-yah*
leg	**la pierna** *lah pee-YEHR-nah*
lip	**el labio** *ehl LAH-bee-oh*
liver	**el hígado** *ehl EE-gah-doh*
mouth	**la boca** *lah BOH-kah*
neck	**el cuello** *ehl KWEH-yoh*
nose	**la nariz** *lah nah-REES*
shoulder	**el hombro** *ehl OHM-broh*
skin	**la piel** *lah pee-YEHL*

thumb	**el pulgar** *ehl pool-GAHR*
throat	**la garganta** *lah gahr-GAHN-tah*
toe	**el dedo del pie** *ehl DAY-doh del pee-YEH*
tooth	**el diente** *ehl dee-YEHN-tay*
wrist	**la muñeca** *lah moon-YEH-kah*

TELLING THE DOCTOR

I've had this pain since yesterday.	**Tengo este dolor desde ayer.** *ten-goh ehs-tay doh-LOHR des-day ah-YEHR*
There's a (no) history of asthma (diabetes) in my family.	**(No) hay incidencia de asma (diabetes) en mi familia.** *(noh) AH-ee een-see-DEN-see-ah day AHS-mah (dee-ah-BEH-tays) ehn mee fah-MEEL-yah.*
I'm (not) allergic to antibiotics (penicillin).	**(No) soy alérgico(a) a los antibióticos (penicilina).** *(noh) soy ah-LEHR-hee-koh (kah) ah lohs ahn-tee-bee-OH-tee-kohs (pen-ee-see-LEE-nah).*
I have a pain in my chest.	**Tengo dolor en el pecho.** *TEN-goh doh-LOHR ehn ehl PAY-choh*
I had a heart attack _____ year(s) ago.	**Tuve un ataque al corazón hace _____ año(s).** *TOO-bay oon ah-TAH-kay ahl kohr-ah-SOHN ah-say _____ ahn-yoh(s)*
I'm taking this medicine (insulin).	**Tomo esta medicina (insulina).** *toh-moh ehs-tah med-ee-SEE-nah (een-soo-LEE-nah)*
I'm pregnant.	**Estoy embarazada.** *ehs-toy ehm-bahr-ah-SAH-dah*
I feel better (worse).	**Me siento mejor (peor).** *may see-YEN-toh may-HOHR (pay-OHR)*
Is it serious (contagious)?	**¿Es grave (contagioso)?** *ehs GRAH-bay (kohn-tah-hee-OH-soh)*

Do I have to go to the hospital?	**¿Tengo que ir al hospital?** *ten-goh kay eer ahl ohs-pee-TAHL*
When can I continue my trip?	**¿Cuándo puedo continuar mi viaje?** *KWAHN-doh PWEH-doh kon-teen-oo-AHR mee bee-AH-hay*

DOCTOR'S INSTRUCTIONS

Abra la boca.	Open your mouth.
Saque la lengua.	Stick out your tongue.
Tosa.	Cough.
Respire fuerte.	Breathe deeply.
Quítese la ropa	Take off your clothing .
Acuéstese.	Lie down.
Levántese.	Stand up.
Vístase.	Get dressed.

FOLLOWING UP

Are you giving me a prescription?	**¿Va a darme una receta?** *bah ah DAHR-may oo-nah ray-SAY-tah?*
How often must I take this medicine (these pills)?	**¿Cuántas veces al día tengo que tomar esta medicina (estas píldoras)?** *KWAHN-tahs BEH-says ahl DEE-ah ten-goh kay toh-MAHR ehs-tah med-ee-SEE-nah (EHS-tahs PEEL-dohr-ahs)*
(How long) do I have to stay in bed?	**¿(Cuánto tiempo) tengo que quedarme en cama?** *(KWAHN-toh tee-YEHM-poh) ten-goh kay kay-DAHR-may ehn KAH-mah*
Thank you (for everything), doctor.	**Muchas gracias (por todo), doctor.** *MOO-chahs GRAH-see-ahs (pohr TOH-doh) dohk-TOHR*
How much do I owe you for your services?	**¿Cuánto le debo?** *KWAHN-toh lay DEHB-oh*

IN THE HOSPITAL (ACCIDENTS)

Help!	**¡Socorro!** *soh-KOH-roh*
Get a doctor, quick!	**¡Busque un médico, rápido!** *BOO-skay oon MED-ee-koh, RAH-pee-doh*
Call an ambulance!	**¡Llame una ambulancia!** *YAH-may oo-nah ahm-boo-LAHN-see-ah*
Take him to the hospital!	**¡al hospital!** *ahl ohs-pee-TAHL*
I've fallen.	**Me he caído.** *may ay kah-EE-doh*
I was knocked down (run over).	**Fui atropellado(a).** *fwee ah-troh-peh-YAH-doh*
I think I've had a heart attack.	**Creo que he tenido un ataque al corazón.** *KRAY-oh kay ay ten-EE-doh oon ah-TAH-kay ahl kohr-ah-SOHN*
I burned myself.	**Me quemé.** *may kay-MAY*
I cut myself.	**Me corté.** *may kohr-TAY*
I'm bleeding.	**Estoy sangrando.** *ehs-toy sahn-GRAHN-doh*
I think the bone is broken (dislocated).	**Creo que el hueso está roto (dislocado)** *KRAY-oh kay ehl WAY-soh ehs-TAH ROH-toh (dees-loh-kah-doh)*
The leg is swollen.	**La pierna está hinchada.** *lah pee-EHR-nah ehs-TAH een-CHAH-dah*
I have sprained (twisted) my wrist (ankle).	**Me he torcido la muñeca (el tobillo).** *may ay tohr-SEE-doh lah moon-YEH-kah (ehl toh-BEE-yoh)*
I can't move my elbow (knee).	**No puedo mover el codo (la rodilla).** *noh pweh-doh moh-BEHR ehl koh-doh (lah roh-DEE-yah)*
I have medical insurance.	**Tengo seguro médico.** *ten-goh seh-GOO-roh MED-ee-koh*

AT THE DENTIST

Can you recommend a dentist?	**¿Puede recomendar un dentista?** *PWEH-day reh-koh-men-DAHR oon den-TEES-tah*
I have a toothache that's driving me crazy.	**Tengo un dolor de muela que me vuelve loco.** *ten-goh oon doh-LOHR day MWEH-lah kay may BWEHL-bay loh-koh*
I've lost a filling.	**Se me ha caído un empaste.** *say may ah kah-EE-doh oon ehm-PAHS-tay*
I've broken a tooth.	**Me rompí un diente.** *may rohm-PEE oon dee-EHN-tay*
My gums hurt me.	**Me duelen las encías.** *may DWEH-len lahs ehn-SEE-ahs*
Is there an infection?	**¿Hay una infección?** *AH-ee oo-nah een-fehk-SYOHN*
Will you have to extract the tooth?	**¿Tendrá que sacar la muela (el diente)?** *ten-DRAH kay sah-kahr lah MWEH-lah (ehl dee-EHN-tay)*
Can you fill it _____?	**¿Podría empastarlo _____?** *poh-DREE-ah ehm-pahs-TAHR-loh*
with amalgam	**con platino** *kohn plah-TEE-noh*
with gold	**con oro** *kohn OHR-oh*
with silver	**con plata** *kohn PLAH-tah*
for now	**por ahora** *pohr ah-OHR-ah*
temporarily	**temporalmente** *tem-pohr-ahl-MEN-tay*
Can you fix _____?	**¿Puede usted reparar _____?** *PWEH-day oo-STEHD ray-pah-RAHR*
this bridge	**este puente** *EHS-tay PWEHN-tay*
this crown	**esta corona** *ehs-tah kohr-OH-nah*

■ these dentures	**estos dientes postizos** *ehs-tohs dee-EHN-tays pohs-TEE-sohs*
When should I come back?	**¿Cuándo debo volver?** *KWAHN-doh DEH-boh bohl-BEHR*
How much do I owe you for your services?	**¿Cuánto le debo?** *KWAHN-toh lay DEH-boh*

WITH THE OPTICIAN

Can you repair these glasses (for me)?	**¿Puede usted arreglar(me) estas gafas?** *PWEH-day oos-TEHD ah-ray-GLAHR (may) ehs-tahs GAH-fahs*
I've broken a lens (the frame).	**Se me ha roto un cristal (la armadura).** *say may ah ROH-toh oon krees-TAHL (lah ahr-mah-DOOR-ah)*
Can you put in a new lens?	**¿Puede usted ponerme un cristal nuevo?** *PWEH-day oos-TEHD poh-NEHR-may oon krees-TAHL NWEH-boh*
I do not have a prescription.	**No tengo receta.** *noh TEN-goh ray-SAY-tah*
Can you tighten the screws?	**¿Puede usted apretar los tornillitos?** *PWEH-day oos-TEHD ah-pray-tahr lohs tohr-NEE-yee-tohs*
I need the glasses as soon as possible.	**Necesito las gafas urgentemente.** *neh-seh-SEE-toh lahs GAH-fahs oor-hen-tay-MEN-tay*
I don't have any others.	**No tengo otras.** *noh TEN-goh OH-trahs*
I've lost a contact lens.	**Se me ha perdido una lente de contacto.** *say may ah pehr-DEE-doh oo-nah LEN-tay day kohn-TAHK-toh*
Can you replace it quickly?	**¿Puede reemplazarla rápidamente?** *PWEH-day ray-ehm-plah-SAHR-lah rah-pee-dah-MEN-tay*

COMMUNICATIONS

POST OFFICE

Post cards and stamps can be purchased at **estancos** (tobacconists) and kiosks (these can be distinguished by their red and yellow signs) in addition to the official post office (**Correos y Telégrafos**).

The post office is open from 9:00 to 1:30 and from 4:00 to 7:00 Monday to Saturday.

I want to mail a letter.	**Quiero echar una carta al correo.** *kee-YEHR-oh ay-CHAHR OO-nah KAHR-tah ahl kohr-AY-oh*
Where's the post office?	**¿Dónde está correos?** *DOHN-day ehs-TAH kohr-AY-ohs*
Where's a letterbox?	**¿Dónde hay un buzón?** *DOHN-day AH-ee oon boo-SOHN*
What is the postage on _____ to the United States (Canada, England, Australia)?	**¿Cuánto es el franqueo de _____ a los Estados Unidos (al Canadá, a Inglaterra, a Australia)?** *KWAHN-toh ehs ehl frahn-KAY-oh day _____ ah lohs ehs-TAH-dohs oo-NEE-dohs (ahl kahn-ah-DAH, ah eeng-lah-TEHR-ah, ah ow-STRAHL-yah)*
▪ a letter	**una carta** *oo-nah KAHR-tah*
▪ an insured letter	**una carta asegurada** *oo-nah KAHR-tah ah-say-goor-AH-dah*
▪ a registered mail	**una carta certificada** *oo-nah KAHR-tah sehr-teef-ee-KAH-dah*
▪ a special delivery letter	**una carta urgente** *oo-nah KAHR-tah oor-HEN-tay*
▪ a package	**un paquete postal** *oon pah-kay-tay pohs-TAHL*
▪ a post card	**una postal** *oo-nah pohs-TAHL*

When will it arrive?	**¿Cuándo llegará?** *KWAHN-doh yeh-gahr-AH*
Which is the _____ window?	**¿Cuál es la ventanilla de _____?** *kwahl ehs lah ben-tah-NEE-yah day*
◼ general delivery	**la lista de correos** *lah LEES-tah day kohr-AY-ohs*
◼ money order	**los giros postales** *lohs HEER-ohs pohs-TAHL-ays*
◼ stamp	**los sellos** *lohs SEH-yohs*
Are there any letters for me? My name is _____.	**¿Hay cartas para mí? Me llamo _____.** *AH-ee KAHR-tahs pah-rah mee may YAH-moh*
I'd like _____.	**Quisiera _____.** *kee-see-YEHR-ah*
◼ 10 envelopes	**diez sobres** *dee-EHS SOH-brays*
◼ 6 postcards	**seis postales** *sayss pohs-TAHL-ays*
◼ 5 (air mail) stamps	**cinco sellos (aéreos)** *SEEN-koh SEH-yohs (ah-EHR-ay-ohs)*
◼ Do I fill out a customs receipt?	**¿Hay un recibo de advana?** *AH-ee oon ray-SEE-boh day ah-DWAHN-ah*

TELEGRAMS

Where's the telegraph office?	**¿Dónde está el Correos y Telégrafos?** *DOHN-day ehs-TAH ehl kohr-AY-ohs ee tel-AY-grah-fohs*
How late is it open?	**¿Hasta cuándo está abierto?** *AH-stah KWAHN-doh ehs-TAH ah-bee-YEHR-toh*
I'd like to send a telegram (night letter) to _____.	**Quisiera mandar un telegrama (un cable nocturno) a _____.** *kee-see-YEHR-ah mahn-DAHR oon teh-lay-GRAH-mah (oon KAH-blay nohk-TOOR-noh) ah*

How much it is per word?	**¿Cuánto cuesta por palabra?** *KWAHN-toh KWEHS-tah pohr pah-LAH-brah*
I need to send a telex.	**Tengo que enviar un "telex."** *TEN-goh kay ehm-bee-AHR oon TEL-eks*
I want to send it collect.	**Quiero mandarlo con cobro revertido.** *kee-YEHR-oh mahn-DAHR-loh kohn KOH-broh reh-behr-TEE-doh*
When will it arrive?	**¿Cuándo llegará?** *KWAHN-doh yeh-gahr-AH*

TELEPHONES

In Spain telephones use coins of 5, 25, and 50 pesetas.

To call another country, dial 07, wait for a dial tone and then dial the country code followed by the area code and the number.

Public telephones can be found in many stores and cafes; there are also many telephone booths (**cabinas telefónicas**)

or you can call at the telephone exchange (**la central telefónica**).

Many telephone booths are for local calls only. To call another city or country, you must find a booth with a green stripe across the top marked "**interurbano**."

If you have difficulty operating the telephone or feel you will not be able to understand the person who answers the call, ask the clerk at your hotel to place the call for you.

Where is ____?	**Donde hay ____?** *DOHN-day AH-ee*
▪ a public telephone	**un teléfono público** *oon tel-EHF-oh-noh POO-blee-koh*
▪ a telephone booth	**una cabina telefónica** *oo-nah kah-BEE-nah tel-eh-FOHN-ee-kah*
▪ a telephone directory	**una guía telefónica** *oo-nah GHEE-ah tel-eh-FOHN-ee-kah*
May I use your phone?	**¿Me permite usar su teléfono?** *may pehr-MEE-tay oo-sahr soo tel-EHF-oh-noh*
I want to make a ____.	**Quiero hacer una llamada ____.** *kee-YEHR-oh ah-sehr oo-nah yah-MAH-dah*
▪ local	**local** *loh-kahl*
▪ long distance	**a larga distancia** *ah LAHR-gah dees-TAHN-see-ah*
▪ person to person	**personal** *pehr-SOHN-ahl*
▪ collect	**a cobro revertido** *ah KOH-broh ray-behr-TEE-doh*
Can I call direct?	**¿Puedo marcar directamente?** *PWEH-doh mahr-KAHR dee-rehk-tah-MEN-tay*
Do I need tokens for the phone?	**¿Necesito fichas para el teléfono?** *neh-seh-SEE-toh fee-chahs pah-rah ehl tel-EHF-oh-no*

How do I get the operator?	**¿Cómo puedo conseguir la central?** *KOH-moh PWEH-doh kon-seh-GHEER lah sehn-TRAHL*
Operator, can you get me number ____?	**Señorita, quiere comunicarme con ____?** *sehn-yohr-EE-tah, kee-YEHR-ay koh-moo-nee-KAHR-may kohn*
My number is ____.	**Mi número es ____.** *mee NOO-mehr-oh ehs*
May I speak to ____?	**¿Puedo hablar con ____?** *PWEH-doh ah-BLAHR kohn*
Speaking.	**Con él habla.** *kon ehl AH-blah*
Hello.	**Diga.** *DEE-gah*
Who is this?	**¿Con quién hablo?** *kohn kee-YEHN AH-bloh*
I can't hear.	**No oigo.** *noh OY-goh*
Speak louder, please.	**Hable más alto, por favor.** *AH-blay mahs AHL-toh pohr fah-BOHR*
Don't hang up. Hold the wire.	**No cuelgue.** *noh KWEHL-gay*
This is ____.	**Habla ____.** *AH-blah*
Operator, there's no answer (they don't answer).	**Señorita, no contestan.** *sen-yohr-EE-tah, noh kohn-TEST-ahn*
The line is busy.	**La línea está ocupada.** *lah LEE-nay-ah ehs-TAH oh-koo-PAH-dah*
You gave me (that was) a wrong number.	**Me ha dado (fue) un número equivocado.** *may ah DAH-doh (fway) oon NOO-mehr-oh ay-kee-boh-KAH-doh*
I was cut off.	**Me han cortado.** *may ahn kohr-TAH-doh*
Please dial it again.	**Llame otra vez, por favor.** *YAH-may OH-trah bes, pohr fah-BOHR*

I want to leave a message.	**Quiero dejar un recado.** *kee-YEHR-oh day-HAHR oon ray-KAH-doh*
How much do I have to pay?	**¿Cuanto tengo que pagar?** *KWAHN-toh TEN-goh kay pah-GAHR?*
Will you help me place a long-distance call?	**¿Podría ayudarme a hacer una llamada a larga distancia?** *poh-DREE-ah ah-yoDAHR-may ah-SEHR oo-nah yah-MAH-dah ah LAHR-gah dees-TAHN-see-ah*

BUSINESS SERVICES

Deluxe hotels in Madrid and certain other major cities usually can arrange secretarial services in English, French, and German for business guests. Some hotels have telexes available.

I need to send a telex.	**Tengo que enviar un telex.** *TEN-goh kay ehm-bee-AHR oon TEL-ehks*
Do you take shorthand?	**¿Sabe taquigrafía?** *SAH-bay tah-kee-grah-FEE-ah*
Do you know how to type a business letter?	**¿Sabe escribir una carta de negocio?** *SAH-bay ehs-kree-BEER oo-nah KAHR-tah day neh-GOH-see-oh*

TRAVEL TIP

Even if you are fluent in the language of your host country, you may crave news of home in the form of an English-language newspaper. In over 150 countries, the *International Herald Tribune* brings the events of the world to its English-speaking readers. This is a top-quality newspaper assembled jointly by the New York *Times* and the Washington *Post*. It is available at most foreign newsstands.

DRIVING A CAR

Car is an easy way to travel in Spain. Roads are generally good, though there are just a few super highways (**autopistas**). More common are national and country roads, which are usually two- or three-lane asphalt roads. Roads are well marked with international highway symbols. Mileage is designated in kilometers. A mile is ⅝'s of a kilometer; see chart on page 176). Gas prices are the same at stations all over the country. In smaller towns, gas stations are few and far between, so it is wise to "gas up" when you can. Note that seat belts are mandatory. If stopped by the police, you will be fined for not wearing a belt.

CAR RENTALS

Rentals can be arranged before departure through a travel agent or upon arrival at a rental office in the major airports or in or near the railroad station in a larger city or town. You'll find Hertz, Avis, Atesa (Budget-Rent-A-Car), Europcar, and Godfrey Davis, among other car rental agencies. The usual rate is by the day or week, with a charge per kilometer. Requirements: you must be 18 years old or older and hold a valid U.S. or international driver's license. A credit card is the preferred method of payment.

Where can I rent _____?	**¿Dónde puedo alquilar _____?** *dohn-day PWEH-doh ahl-kee-LAHR*
a car	**un coche** *oon KOH-chay*
a motorcycle	**una motocicleta** *oo-nah moh-toh-see-KLAY-tah*
a bicycle	**una bicicleta** *oo-nah bee-see-KLAY-tah*
I want a _____.	**Quiero _____.** *kee-EH-roh*
small car	**un coche pequeño** *oon KOH-chay peh-KAYN-yoh*

large car **un coche grande** *oon KOH-chay GRAHN-day*

sports car **un coche deportivo** *oon KOH-chay day-pohr-TEE-boh*

I prefer automatic transmission. **Prefiero el cambio automático.** *preh-fee-EHR-oh ehl KAHM-bee-oh AH-oo-toh-MAH-tee-koh*

How much does it cost ____? **¿Cuánto cuesta ____?** *KWAHN-toh KWEHS-tah*

per day **por día** *pohr DEE-ah*

per week **por semana** *pohr seh-MAHN-ah*

per kilometer **por kilómetro** *pohr kee-LOH-meht-roh*

for unlimited mileage **con kilometraje ilimitado** *kohn kee-loh-may-TRAH-hay ee-lee-mee-TAH-doh*

How much is the insurance? **¿Cuánto es el seguro?** *KWAHN-toh ehs ehl seh-GOOR-oh*

Is the gas included? **¿Está incluída la gasolina?** *ehs-TAH een-kloo-EE-dah lah gahs-oh-LEEN-ah*

Do you accept credit cards? **¿Acepta usted tarjetas de crédito?** *ah-sehp-tah oos-TEHD tahr-HAY-tahs day KREH-dee-toh*

Here's my driver's license. **Aquí tiene mi licencia de conducir.** *ah-KEE tee-EH-nay mee lee-SEN-see-ah day kohn-doo-SEER*

Do I have to leave a deposit? **¿Tengo que dejar un depósito?** *ten-goh kay day-hahr oon day-POHS-ee-toh*

I want to rent the car here and leave it in ____. **Quiero alquilar el coche aquí y dejarlo en ____.** *kee-YEHR-oh ahl-kee-LAHR ehl koh-chay ah-KEE ee day-HAHR-loh ehn*

What kind of gasoline does it take?	**Que tipo de gasolina necesita?** *kay TEE-poh day gah-so-LEE-nah neh-seh-SEE-tah*

PARKING

In a town or city, park only in designated places, usually marked by a sign with a big "E" or "P" (for parking). If you park in a no-parking zone, you run the very real risk of having your car towed.

Is this a legal parking place?	**¿Es esto un lugar para estacionar?** *ehs EHS-toh oon loo-GAHR pah-rah ehs-tah-syohn-AHR*
What is the parking fee?	**¿Cuánto cuesta estacionar aquí?** *KWAHN-toh KWEHS-tah ehs-tah-syohn-AHR ah-KEE*
Where can I find a place to park?	**¿Dónde puedo encontrar un sitio de estacionamiento?** *DOHN-day PWEHD-oh ehn-kohn-TRAHR oo SEE-tee-oh day ehs-tah-syohn-ah-mee-YEHN-toh*

ON THE ROAD

In Spain turnpikes are called **autopistas** and are marked as "A" roads on the map. **Autopistas de peaje** are toll roads.

National highways are called **carreteras nacionales** and are marked with a red "N" on the map. Regional highways are reasonably good and are numbered with the prefix "C." Speed limits are:

autopistas	120 km/h (74½ m.p.h.)
double-lane highways	100 km/h (62 m.p.h.)
other roads	90 km/h (56 m.p.h.)
populated areas	60 km/h (37 m.p.h.)

And pay attention to speed limits. They are enforced. Radar control is commonplace, and if you exceed the limit, you may receive a ticket by mail after you have returned home. Driving in a city can be confusing. Many streets are one-way and are very narrow, twisting, and crowded.

Excuse me, can you tell me ____?	**Por favor, ¿puede usted decirme ____?** *pohr fah-BOHR, pweh-day oos-TEHD day-SEER-may*
Which way is it to ____?	**¿Por dónde se va a ____?** *pohr DOHN-day say bah ah*
How do I get to ____?	**¿Cómo se va a ____?** *KOH-moh say bah ah*
I think we're lost.	**Creo que estamos perdidos.** *KRAY-oh kay ehs-TAH-mohs pehr-DEE-dohs*
Is this the way to ____?	**¿Es éste el camino a ____?** *ehs EHS-tay ehl kah-MEE-noh ah*
Is it a good road?	**¿Es buena la carretera?** *ehs BWAY-nah la kahr-ray-TEHR-ah*

Where does this highway go to?	**¿Adónde va esta carretera?** *ah DOHN-day bah ehs-tah kah-ray-TEHR-ah*
Is this the shortest way?	**¿Es éste el camino más corto?** *ehs EHS-tay ehl kah-MEE-noh mahs KOHR-toh*
Are there any detours?	**¿Hay desviaciones?** *AH-ee des-bee-ah-SYOHN-ays*
Do I go straight?	**¿Sigo derecho?** *see-goh deh-RAY-choh*
Do I turn to the right (to the left)?	**¿Doblo a la derecha (a la izquierda)?** *DOH-bloh ah lah deh-RAY-chah (ah lah ees-kee-YEHR-dah)*
How far is it from here to the next town?	**¿Cuánta distancia hay de aquí al primer pueblo?** *KWAHN-tah dees-TAHN-see-ah ah-ee day ah-KEE-ahl pree-MEHR PWEH-bloh*
How far away is ____?	**¿A qué distancia está ____?** *ah kay dees-TAHN-see-ah ehs-tah*
Do you have a road map?	**¿Tiene usted un mapa de carreteras?** *tee-yehn-ay-oos-TEHD oon MAH-pah day kahr-ray-TEHR-ahs*
Can you show it to me on the map?	**¿Puede indicármelo en el mapa?** *PWEH-day een-dee-KAHR-may-loh ehn ehl MAH-pah*

AT THE SERVICE STATION

Gasoline (petrol) is sold by the liter in Europe, and for the traveler accustomed to gallons, it may seem confusing, especially if you want to calculate your mileage per gallon (kilometer per liter). Here are some tips on making those conversions.

LIQUID MEASURES (APPROXIMATE)		
LITERS	U.S. GALLONS	IMPERIAL GALLONS
30	8	$6\frac{1}{2}$
40	$10\frac{1}{2}$	$8\frac{3}{4}$
50	$13\frac{1}{4}$	11
60	$15\frac{3}{5}$	13
70	$18\frac{1}{2}$	$15\frac{1}{2}$
80	21	$17\frac{1}{2}$

DISTANCE MEASURES (APPROXIMATE)	
KILOMETERS	MILES
1	.62
5	3
10	6
20	12
50	31
100	62

Where is there a gas (petrol) station?	**¿Dónde hay una estación de gasolina?** *DOHN-day AH-ee oo-nah ehs-tah-SYOHN day gahs-oh-LEE-nah*
Fill it up with ____.	**Llénelo con ____.** *YAY-nay-loh kohn*
diesel	**diesel** *dee-EH-sel*
regular (90 octane)	**normal** *nohr-MAHL*
super (96 octane)	**super** *SOO-pehr*
extra (98 octane)	**extra** *EHS-trah*
Give me ____ liters.	**Déme ____ litros.** *day-may ____ LEE-trohs*
Please check ____.	**¿Quiere inspeccionar ____.** *kee-YEHR-ay eens-pehk-syohn-ahr*
the battery	**la batería** *lah bah-tehr-EE-ah*

TIRE PRESSURE	
POUNDS/SQUARE INCH	KILOGRAMS/CM²
17	1.2
18	1.3
20	1.4
21	1.5
23	1.6
24	1.7
26	1.8
27	1.9
28	2.0
30	2.1
31	2.2
33	2.3
34	2.4
36	2.5
37	2.6
38	2.7
40	2.8

■ the carburetor	**el carburador** *ehl kahr-boor-ah-DOHR*	
■ the oil	**el aceite** *ehl ah-SAY-tay*	
■ the spark plugs	**las bujías** *lahs boo-HEE-ahs*	
■ the tires	**las llantas, las ruedas** *lahs YAHN-tahs, RWAY-dahs*	
■ the tire pressure	**la presión de las llantas** *lah preh-SYOHN day lahs YAHN-tahs*	
■ the antifreeze	**el agua del radiador** *ehl ah-GWAH del rah-dee-ah-DOHR*	
Change the oil.	**Cambie el aceite.** *KAHM-bee-ay ehl ah-SAY-tay*	
Lubricate the car.	**Engrase el coche.** *ehn-GRAH-say ehl KOH-chay*	

Charge the battery.	**Cargue la batería.** *KAHR-gay lah bah-tehr-EE-ah*
Change the tire.	**Cambie esta llanta.** *KAHM-bee-ay ehs-tah YAHN-tah*
Wash the car.	**Lave el coche.** *LAH-bay ehl KOH-chay*

ACCIDENTS AND REPAIRS

My car has broken down.	**Mi coche se ha averiado.** *mee KOH-chay say AH ah-behr-ee-AH-doh*
It overheats.	**Se calienta demasiado.** *say kahl-YEN-tah day-mahs-ee-AH-doh*
It doesn't start.	**No arranca.** *noh ah-RAHN-kah*
I have a flat tire.	**Se me ha pinchado una rueda.** *say may ah peen-CHAH-doh oon-ah RWEH-dah*
The radiator is leaking.	**El radiador tiene un agujero.** *ehl rah-dee-ah-dohr tee-YEHN-ay oon ah-goo-HEHR-oh*
The battery is dead.	**Tengo la batería descargada.** *ten-goh lah bah-tehr-EE-ah des-kahr-GAH-dah*
The keys are locked inside the car.	**Las puertas están cerradas con las llaves adentro.** *lahs PWEHR-tahs ehs-TAHN sehr-AH-dahs kohn lahs YAH-bays ah-DEN-troh*
Is there a garage (repair shop) near here?	**¿Hay un garage (taller) por aquí?** *AH-ee oon gah-RAH-hay (tah-YEHR) pohr ah-KEE*
I need a mechanic (tow truck).	**Necesito un mecánico (remolcador).** *neh-seh-SEE-toh oon meh-KAHN-ee-koh (ray-mohl-kah-DOHR)*

Can you _____? **¿Puede usted _____?** *PWEH-day oos-TEHD*

■ give me a push **empujarme** *ehm-poo-HAHR-may*

■ help me **ayudarme** *ah yoo DAHR may*

I don't have any tools. **No tengo herramientas.** *noh ten-goh ehr-ah-MYEHN-tahs*

Can you lend me _____? **¿Puede usted prestarme _____?** *PWEH-day oos-TEHD prehs-TAHR-may*

■ a flashlight **una linterna** *oo-nah leen-TEHR-nah*

■ a hammer **un martillo** *oon mahr-TEE-yoh*

■ a jack **un gato** *oon GAH-toh*

■ a monkey wrench **una llave inglesa** *oo-nah YAH-beh een-GLAY-sah*

■ pliers **alicates** *ah-lee-KAH-tays*

■ a screwdriver **un destornillador** *oon des-tohrn-EE-yah-DOHR*

I need _____. **Necesito _____.** *neh-seh-see-toh*

■ a bolt **un perno** *oon PEHR-noh*

■ a bulb **una bombilla** *oo-nah bohm-BEE-yah*

■ a filter **un filtro** *oon FEEL-troh*

■ a nut **una tuerca** *oo-nah TWEHR-kah*

Can you fix the car? **¿Puede usted arreglar el coche?** *PWEH-day oos-TEHD ah-ray-GLAHR ehl KOH-chay*

Can you repair it temporarily? **¿Puede repararlo temporalmente?** *PWEH-day ray-pahr-AHR-loh tem-pohr-AHL-men-tay*

Do you have the part? **¿Tiene la pieza?** *tee-EHN-ay lah pee-ay-sah*

I think there's something wrong with ____.	**Creo que pasa algo con ____.** *KRAY-oh kay PAH-sah AHL-goh kohn*
the directional signal	**el indicador de dirección** *ehl een-dee-kah-DOHR day dee-rek-SYOHN*
the door handle	**el tirador de puerta** *ehl teer-ah-DOHR day PWEHR-tah*
the electrical system	**el sistema eléctrico** *ehl sees-tay-mah eh-LEK-tree-koh*
the fan	**el ventilador** *ehl ben-tee-lah-DOHR*
the fan belt	**la correa de ventilador** *lah koh-ray-ah day ben-tee-lah-DOHR*
the fuel pump	**la bomba de gasolina** *lah bohm-bah day gahs-oh-LEE-nah*
the gear shift	**el cambio de velocidad** *ehl kahm-bee-oh day beh-lohs-ee-DAHD*
the headlight	**el faro delantero** *ehl fah-ROH deh-lahn-TEHR-oh*
the horn	**la bocina** *lah boh-SEEN-ah*
the ignition	**el encendido** *ehl ehn-sen-DEE-doh*
the radio	**la radio** *lah RAH-dee-oh*
the starter	**el arranque** *ehl ah-RAHN-kay*
the steering wheel	**el volante** *ehl boh-LAHN-tay*
the tail light	**el faro trasero** *ehl fah-ROH trah-SEHR-oh*
the transmission	**la transmisión** *lah trahns-mee-SYOHN*
the water pump	**la bomba de agua** *lah BOHM-bah day AH-gwah*
the windshield (windscreen) wiper	**el limpiaparabrisas** *ehl LEEM-pee-ah-pah-rah-BREE-sahs*

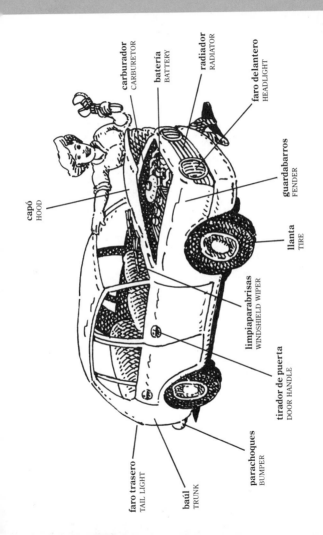

carburador
CARBURETOR

batería
BATTERY

radiador
RADIATOR

faro delantero
HEADLIGHT

guardabarros
FENDER

capó
HOOD

llanta
TIRE

limpiaparabrisas
WINDSHIELD WIPER

tirador de puerta
DOOR HANDLE

parachoques
BUMPER

faro trasero
TAIL LIGHT

baúl
TRUNK

Guarded railroad crossing   Yield   Stop

Right of way   Dangerous intersection ahead   Gasoline (petrol) ahead

Parking   No vehicles allowed   Dangerous curve

Pedestrian crossing   Oncoming traffic has right of way   No bicycles allowed

No parking allowed   No entry   No left turn

No U-turn

No passing

Border crossing

Traffic signal ahead

Speed limit

Traffic circle (roundabout) ahead

Minimum speed limit

All traffic turns left

End of no passing zone

One-way street

Detour

Danger ahead

Entrance to expressway

Expressway ends

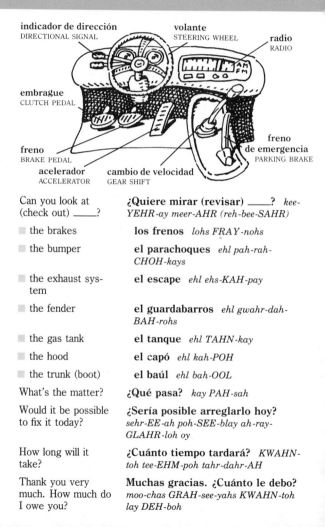

indicador de dirección
DIRECTIONAL SIGNAL

volante
STEERING WHEEL

radio
RADIO

embrague
CLUTCH PEDAL

freno
BRAKE PEDAL

freno
de emergencia
PARKING BRAKE

acelerador
ACCELERATOR

cambio de velocidad
GEAR SHIFT

Can you look at (check out) _____?	**¿Quiere mirar (revisar) _____?** *kee-YEHR-ay meer-AHR (reh-bee-SAHR)*
▪ the brakes	**los frenos** *lohs FRAY-nohs*
▪ the bumper	**el parachoques** *ehl pah-rah-CHOH-kays*
▪ the exhaust system	**el escape** *ehl ehs-KAH-pay*
▪ the fender	**el guardabarros** *ehl gwahr-dah-BAH-rohs*
▪ the gas tank	**el tanque** *ehl TAHN-kay*
▪ the hood	**el capó** *ehl kah-POH*
▪ the trunk (boot)	**el baúl** *ehl bah-OOL*
What's the matter?	**¿Qué pasa?** *kay PAH-sah*
Would it be possible to fix it today?	**¿Sería posible arreglarlo hoy?** *sehr-EE-ah poh-SEE-blay ah-ray-GLAHR-loh oy*
How long will it take?	**¿Cuánto tiempo tardará?** *KWAHN-toh tee-EHM-poh tahr-dahr-AH*
Thank you very much. How much do I owe you?	**Muchas gracias. ¿Cuánto le debo?** *moo-chas GRAH-see-yahs KWAHN-toh lay DEH-boh*

GENERAL INFORMATION

TELLING TIME

What time is it?	**¿Qué hora es?**	*kay OH-rah ehs*

When telling time in Spanish, *It is* is expressed by **Es la** for 1:00 and **Son las** for all other numbers.

It's 1:00.	**Es la una.**	*ehs lah OO-nah*
It's 2:00.	**Son las dos.**	*sohn lahs dohs*
It's 3:00, etc.	**Son las tres, etc.**	*sohn lahs trehs*

The number of minutes after the hour is expressed by adding **y** (and) followed by the number of minutes.

It's 4:10.	**Son las cuatro y diez.**	*sohn lahs KWAH-troh ee dyehs*
It's 5:20.	**Son las cinco y veinte.**	*sohn lahs SEEN-koh ee BAYN-tay.*

A quarter after and half past are expressed by placing **y cuarto** and **y media** after the hour.

It's 6:15.	**Son las seis y cuarto.**	*sohn lahs sayss ee KWAHR-toh*
It's 7:30.	**Son las siete y media.**	*sohn lahs SYEH-tay ee MEH-dyah*

After passing the half-hour point on the clock, time is expressed in Spanish by *subtracting* the number of minutes from the next hour.

It's 7:35.	**Son las ocho menos veinticinco.**	*sohn lahs OH-choh meh-nohs bayn-tee-SEEN-koh*
It's 8:50.	**Son las nueve menos diez.**	*sohn lahs NWEH-bay meh-nohs dyehs*
At what time?	**¿A qué hora?**	*ah kay OH-rah*

At 1:00.	**A la una.** *ah lah OO-nah*
At 2:00 (3:00, etc.)	**A las dos (tres, etc.)** *ah lahs dohs (trehs)*
A.M.	**de la mañana (in the morning)** *day lah man-YAH-nah*
P.M.	**de la tarde (in the afternoon)** *day lah TAHR-day* **de la noche (at night)** *day lah NOH-chay*
It's noon.	**Es mediodía.** *ehs meh-dee-ohd-EE-ah*
It's midnight.	**Es medianoche.** *ehs MEH-dee-ah-NOH-chay*
It's early (late).	**Es temprano (tarde).** *ehs temp-RAH-noh (TAHR-day)*

Official time is based on the 24-hour clock. You will find train schedules and other such times expressed in terms of a point within a 24-hour sequence.

The train leaves at 15:30.	**El tren sale a las quince y media.** *ehl trehn SAH-lay ah lahs KEEN-say ee MEH-dee-ah*
The time is now 21:15.	**Son las veintiuna y cuarto.** *sohn lahs bayn-tee-OO-nah ee KWAHR-toh*

DAYS OF THE WEEK

What day is today?	**¿Qué día es hoy?** *kay DEE-ah ehs oy*

The days are *not* capitalized in Spanish.

Today is ____.	**Hoy es ____.** *oy ehs*
▪ Monday	**lunes** *LOO-nehs*
▪ Tuesday	**martes** *MAHR-tays*
▪ Wednesday	**miércoles** *MYEHR-kohl-ays*
▪ Thursday	**jueves** *HWEB-ays*
▪ Friday	**viernes** *bee-EHR-nays*
▪ Saturday	**sábado** *SAH-bah-doh*
▪ Sunday	**domingo** *doh-MEEN-goh*
yesterday	**ayer** *ah-YEHR*
the day before yesterday	**anteayer** *ANT-ay-ah-YEHR*
tomorrow	**mañana** *mahn-YAH-nah*
the day after tomorrow	**pasado mañana** *pah-SAH-doh mahn-YAH-nah*
last week	**la semana pasada** *lah seh-MAH-nah pah-SAH-dah*
next week	**la semana próxima** *lah seh-MAH-nah PROHK-see-mah*
tonight	**esta noche** *EHS-tah noh-chay*
last night	**anoche** *ahn-OH-chay*

MONTHS OF THE YEAR

The months are *not* capitalized in Spanish.

January	**enero**	*ay-NEHR-oh*
February	**febrero**	*fay-BREH-roh*
March	**marzo**	*MAHR-soh*
April	**abril**	*ah-BREEL*
May	**mayo**	*MAH-yoh*
June	**junio**	*HOO-nee-oh*
July	**julio**	*HOO-lee-oh*
August	**agosto**	*ah-GOHS-toh*
September	**septiembre**	*sep-tee-EHMB-ray*
October	**octubre**	*ohk-TOO-bray*
November	**noviembre**	*noh-bee-EHMB-ray*
December	**diciembre**	*dee-SYEHM-bray*

What's today's date? **¿Cuál es la fecha de hoy?** *kwahl ehs lah FAY-chah day oy*

The first of the month is *el primero* (an ordinal number). All other dates are expressed with *cardinal* numbers.

Today is August ____.	**Hoy es ____ de agosto.** *oy ehs ____ day ah-GOHS-toh*
first	**el primero** *ehl pree-MEHR-oh*
second	**el dos** *ehl dohs*
fourth	**el cuatro** *ehl KWAH-troh*
25th	**el veinticinco** *ehl bayn-tee-SEENK-oh*
this month	**este mes** *EHS-tay mehs*
last month	**el mes pasado** *ehl mehs pah-SAH-doh*

next month	**el mes próximo**	*ehl mehs PROHK-see-moh*
last year	**el año pasado**	*ehl AHN-yoh pah-SAH-doh*
next year	**el año que viene**	*ehl AHN-yoh kay bee-EN-ay*
May 1, 1876	**El primero de mayo de mil ochocientos setenta y seis.**	*ehl pree-MEHR-oh day MAH-ee-oh day meel oh-choh-SYEHN-tohs say-TEN-tah ee SAYSS*
July 4, 1984	**El cuatro de julio de mil novecientos ochenta y cuatro.**	*ehl KWAH-troh day HOOL-ee-oh day meel noh-bay-SYEHN-tohs oh-CHEN-tah ee KWAH-troh*

THE FOUR SEASONS

spring	**la primavera**	*lah pree-mah-BEHR-ah*
summer	**el verano**	*ehl behr-AH-noh*
fall	**el otoño**	*ehl oh-TOHN-yoh*
winter	**el invierno**	*ehl eem-BYEHR-noh*

THE WEATHER

How is the weather today?	**¿Qué tiempo hace hoy?**	*kay tyehm-poh ah-say oy*
It's nice (bad) weather.	**Hace buen (mal) tiempo.**	*ah-say bwehn (mahl) tyehm-poh*
It's raining.	**Llueve.**	*YWEHB-ay*

It's snowing.	**Nieva.** *NYEHB-ah*
It's ____.	**Hace ____.** *AH-say*
hot	**calor** *kah-LOHR*
cold	**frío** *FREE-oh*
cool	**fresco** *FREHS-koh*
windy	**viento** *BYEHN-toh*
sunny	**sol** *sohl*

TEMPERATURE CONVERSIONS

To change Fahrenheit to Centigrade, subtract 32 and multiply by 5/9.

To change Centigrade to Fahrenheit, multiply by 9/5 and add 32.

Grado
Centígrado   Fahrenheit

Termómetro

PUBLIC HOLIDAYS

January 1	**Año Nuevo**	New Year's Day
January 6	**Reyes Magos (Epifanía)**	Epiphany (Three Kings)
March 19	**San José**	St. Joseph's Day
	Viernes Santo	Good Friday
May 1	**Día del Trabajo**	Labor Day
	Corpus Christi	Corpus Christi
June 29	**San Pedro y San Pablo**	Saint Peter's & Saint Paul's Day
July 25	**Santiago**	Saint James' Day
August 15	**Asunción**	Assumption Day
October 12	**Día de la Raza**	Columbus Day
November 1	**Todos los Santos**	All Saints' Day
December 8	**Inmaculada Concepción**	Immaculate Conception
December 25	**Navidad**	Christmas

COUNTRIES AND NATIONALITIES

COUNTRY		NATIONALITY
Argentina	**la Argentina**	argentino
Bolivia	**Bolivia**	boliviano
Brazil	**el Brasil**	brasileño
Canada	**el Canadá**	canadiense
Chile	**Chile**	chileno
China	**China**	chino
Colombia	**Colombia**	colombiano
Costa Rica	**Costa Rica**	costarricense
Cuba	**Cuba**	cubano
Denmark	**Dinamarca**	danés
Dominican Republic	**la República Dominicana**	dominicano

COUNTRY		NATIONALITY
Ecuador	**el Ecuador**	ecuatoriano
Egypt	**Egipto**	egipcio
England	**Inglaterra**	inglés
Europe	**Europa**	europeo
Finland	**Finlandia**	finlandés
France	**Francia**	francés
Germany	**Alemania**	alemán
Great Britain	**Gran Bretaña**	inglés
Greece	**Grecia**	griego
Guatemala	**Guatemala**	guatemalteco
Holland	**Holanda**	holandés
Iceland	**Islandia**	islandés
Ireland	**Irlanda**	irlandés
Israel	**Israel**	israelí
Italy	**Italia**	italiano
Japan	**el Japón**	japonés
Mexico	**México or Méjico**	mexicano
Nicaragua	**Nicaragua**	nicaragüense
Norway	**Noruega**	noruego
Panama	**Panamá**	panameño
Paraguay	**el Paraguay**	paraguayo
Peru	**el Perú**	peruano
Poland	**Polonia**	polaco
Portugal	**Portugal**	portugués
Puerto Rico	**Puerto Rico**	puertorriqueño
Russia	**Rusia**	ruso
El Salvador	**El Salvador**	salvadoreño
Soviet Union	**La Unión Soviética**	ruso (soviético)

COUNTRY		NATIONALITY
Spain	**España**	español
Sweden	**Suecia**	sueco
Switzerland	**Suiza**	suizo
Turkey	**Turquía**	turco
United States	**Los Estados Unidos**	estadounidense (norteamericano)
Uruguay	**Uruguay**	uruguayo
Venezuela	**Venezuela**	venezolano

IMPORTANT SIGNS

Abajo	Down
Abierto	Open
Alto	Stop
Arriba	Up
Ascensor	Elevator
Caballeros	Men's room
Caja	Cashier
Caliente or "C"	Hot
Carretera particular	Private road
Cerrado	Closed
Completo	Filled up
Cuidado	Watch out, caution
Empuje	Push
Entrada	Entrance
Frío or "F"	Cold
Libre	Vacant
No obstruya la entrada	Don't block entrance
No pisar el césped	Keep off the grass
No tocar	Hands off, don't touch
Ocupado	Busy, occupied
¡Pase!	Walk, cross
Peligro	Danger
Prohibido	Forbidden, No _____
_____ **el paso**	No entrance, Keep out

_____ escupir	No spitting
_____ fumar	No smoking
_____ estacionarse	No parking
_____ bañarse	No bathing
Reservado	Reserved
Sala de espera	Waiting room
Salida	Exit
Se alquila	For rent
Señoras or Damas	Ladies room
Servicios	Toilets
Se vende	For sale
Tire	Pull
¡Veneno!	Poison!
Venta	Sale

COMMON ABBREVIATIONS

apdo.	**apartado de correos**	post office box
Av., Avda.	**avenida**	avenue
C., Cia	**compañía**	company
c.	**calle**	street
D.	**don**	title of respect used before a masculine first name: don Pedro
Da., Dª	**doña**	title of respect used before a feminine first name: doña María
EE.UU	**los Estados Unidos**	United States (U.S.)
F.C.	**ferrocarril**	railroad
Hnos.	**hermanos**	brothers
N°, num.	**número**	number
1°	**primero**	first
pta.	**peseta**	peseta (Spanish monetary unit)
RENFE	**Red Nacional de Ferrocarriles**	Spanish National Railroad System
2°	**segundo**	second
S., Sta	**San, Santa**	Saint

S.A.	**Sociedad Anónima**	Inc.
Sr.	**Señor**	Mr.
Sra.	**Señora**	Mrs.
Sres., Srs.	**Señores**	Gentlemen
Srta.	**Señorita**	Miss
Ud., Vd.	**Usted**	You (polite sing.)
Uds., Vds.	**Ustedes**	You (polite & familiar plural)

CENTIMETERS/INCHES

It is usually unnecessary to make exact conversions from your customary inches to the metric system, but to give you an approximate idea of how they compare, we give you the following guide.

1 **centímetro** (centimeter)	=	0.39 inches **(pulgadas)**
1 **metro**	=	39.37 inches
		3.28 feet **(pies)**
		1.09 yards **(yardas)**
1 inch	=	2.54 centimeters
1 foot	=	30.5 centimeters
		0.3 meters
1 yard	=	91.4 centimeters
		0.91 meters

To convert **centímetros** into inches, multiply by .39.
To convert inches into **centímetros,** multiply by 2.54.

Centímetros

Pulgadas

METERS/FEET

How tall are you in meters? See for yourself.

FEET, INCHES		METERS & CENTIMETERS
5		1.52
5	1	1.545
5	2	1.57
5	3	1.595
5	4	1.62
5	5	1.645
5	6	1.68
5	7	1.705
5	8	1.73
5	9	1.755
5	10	1.78
5	11	1.805
6		1.83
6	1	1.855

WHEN YOU WEIGH YOURSELF

1 _____ (kilogram) = 2.2 _____ (pounds)
1 pound   = .45 kilograms

KILOGRAMS	POUNDS
40	88
45	99
50	110
55	121
60	132
65	143
70	154
75	165

KILOGRAMS	POUNDS
80	176
85	187
90	198
95	209
100	220

LIQUID MEASUREMENTS

1 **litro** (liter) = 1.06 _____ (quarts)
4 liters = 1.06 _____ (gallons)

For quick approximate conversion, multiply the number of gallons by 4 to get liters. Divide the number of liters by 4 to get gallons.

NOTE: You'll find other conversion charts on pages 133, 176, and 190.

MINI-DICTIONARY FOR THE BUSINESS TRAVELER

amount (value)	**el importe**	*ehl eem-POHR-tay*
appraise (to)	**valuar**	*bahl-WAHR*
authorize (to)	**autorizar**	*ow-tohr-ee-SAHR*
authorized edition	**la edición autorizada**	*lah eh-dee-SYOHN ow-tohr-ee-SAH-dah*
bill (noun)	**la cuenta**	*lah KWEHN-tah*
▪ bill of exchange	**la letra de cambio**	*lah LEH-trah day KAHM-bee-oh*
▪ bill of lading	**el conocimiento de embarque**	*ehl koh-noh-see-MYEHN-toh day ehm-BAHR-kay*
▪ bill of sale	**la escritura de venta**	*lah ehs-kree-TOOR-ah day BEN-tah*

business operation	**la operación comercial** *lah oh-pehr-ah-SYOHN koh-mehr-SYAHL*
cash (money)	**el dinero contante** *ehl dee-NEHR-oh kohn-TAHN-tay*
▪ to buy for cash	**pagar al contado** *pa-GAHR ahl kon-TAH-doh*
▪ to sell for cash	**vender al contado** *ben-DEHR ah kon-TAH-doh*
▪ to cash a check	**cobrar un cheque** *koh-BRAHR oon CHEH-kay*
certified check	**el cheque certificado** *ehl CHEH-kay sehr-tee-fee-KAH-doh*
chamber of commerce	**la cámara de comercio** *lah KAH-mah-rah day koh-MEHR-see-oh*
compensation for damage	**la indemnización de daños y perjuicios** *lah een-dehm-nee-sah-SYOHN day DAHN-yohs ee pehr-WEE-see-ohs*
competition	**la competición** *la kohm-peh-tee-SYOHN*
▪ competitive price	**el precio competidor** *ehl PREH-see-oh kohm-peh-tee-DOHR*
contract	**el contrato** *ehl kohn-TRAH-toh*
▪ contractual obligations	**las obligaciones contractuales** *lahs oh-blee-gah-SYOHN-ays kohn-trah-TWAHL-ays*
controlling interest	**el interés predominante** *ehl een-tehr-AYS pray-doh-mee-NAHN-tay*
down payment	**el pago inicial** *ehl PAH-goh ee-nees-YAHL*
due	**vencido** *ben-SEE-doh*
enterprise	**la empresa** *lah ehm-PRAY-sah*
expedite (to) delivery (of goods)	**facilitar la entrega (de mercancía)** *fah-see-lee-TAHR lah ehn-tray-gah (day mehr-kahn-SEE-ah)*

◼expedite delivery (of letters)	**facilitar el reparto (de cartas)** *fah-seel-ee-TAHR ehl ray-PAHR-toh (day KAHR-tahs)*
expenses	**los gastos** *lohs GAHS-tohs*
goods	**las mercancías** *lahs mehr-kahn-SEE-ahs*
infringement of patent rights	**violación de derechos de patente** *bee-oh-lah-SYOHN day deh-RAY-chohs day pah-TEN-tay*
insurance against all risks	**seguros contra todo riesgo** *seh-GOOR-ohs kohn-trah TOH-doh ree-EHS-goh*
international law	**la ley internacional** *lah lay een-tehr-nah-syohn-AHL*
lawful possession	**la posesión legal** *lah poh-seh-SYOHN lay-GAHL*
lawsuit	**el pleito** *ehl PLAY-toh*
lawyer	**el abogado** *ehl ah-boh-GAH-doh*
letter of credit	**la carta de crédito** *lah KAHR-tah day KREH-dee-toh*
mail-order business	**el negocio de ventas por correo** *ehl neh-GOH-see-oh day BEN-tahs pohr kohr-AY-oh*
market-value	**el valor comercial** *ehl bah-LOHR koh-mehrs-YAHL*
manager	**el gerente** *ehl hehr-EN-tay*
owner	**el dueño** *ehl DWAYN-yoh*
partner	**el socio** *ehl SOH-see-oh*
payment	**el pago** *ehl PAH-goh*
◼partial payment	**el pago parcial** *ehl PAH-goh pahr-SYAHL*
past due	**vencido** *ben-SEE-doh*

post office box	**el apartado** *ehl ah-pahr-TAH-doh*
property	**la propiedad** *lah proh-pee-eh-DAHD*
purchasing agent	**el comprador** *ehl kohm-prah-DOHR*
put (to) on the American market	**poner en el mercado norteamericano** *poh-NEHR ehn ehl mehr-KAH-doh nohr-tay-ah-mehr-ee-KAH-noh*
sale	**la venta** *lah BEN-tah*
sell (to)	**vender** *ben-DEHR*
send (to)	**mandar** *mahn-DAHR*
▢ to send back	**devolver** *day-bohl-BEHR*
▢ to send C.O.D.	**mandar contra reembolso** *mahn-DAHR kohn-trah ray-ehm-BOHL-soh*
shipment	**el envío** *ehl ehm-BEE-oh*
tax	**el impuesto** *ehl eem-PWEHS-toh*
▢ tax-exempt	**libre de impuestos** *LEE-bray day eem-PWEHS-tohs*
▢ sales tax	**el impuesto sobre ventas** *ehl eem-PWEHS-toh soh-bray BEN-tahs*
▢ value added tax	**el impuesto sobre el valor añadido** *ehl eem-PWEHS-toh soh-bray ehl bah-LOHR ahn-yah-DEE-doh*
trade	**el comercio** *ehl koh-MEHR-see-oh*
transact business (to)	**hacer negocios** *ah-SEHR neh-GOH-see-ohs*
transfer (noun)	**la transferencia** *lah trahns-fehr-EHN-see-ah*
transportation charges	**gastos de transporte** *GAHS-tohs day trahns-POHR-tay*
via	**por vía** *pohr BEE-ah*
yield a profit (to)	**rendir una ganancia** *rehn-DEER oo-nah gah-NAHN-see-ah*

QUICK GRAMMAR GUIDE

Your facility with Spanish will be greatly enhanced if you know a little of its grammar. Here are a few simple rules governing the use of the various parts of speech.

NOUNS

In contrast with English, in which inanimate objects are considered neuter, Spanish nouns are designated either masculine or feminine. In addition, if a noun represents a male being, it is masculine; if it is for a female being, it is feminine.

Examples of some masculine nouns are:

el hombre (the man)
el hermano (the brother)
el padre (the father)

Some feminine nouns are:

la mujer (the woman)
la hermana (the sister)
la madre (the mother)

As a general rule, nouns ending in *o* are masculine while nouns ending in *a* are feminine.

el minuto (the minute)   **la joya** (the jewel)
el médico (the doctor)   **la manzana** (the apple)

But there are some exceptions, such as:

la mano (the hand)   **el día** (the day)
la foto (the photograph)   **el mapa** (the map)

To make singular nouns plural, add *s* to nouns that end in a vowel and *es* to those that end in a consonant.

el muchacho	**los muchachos**
la rosa	**las rosas**
el tren	**los trenes**
la mujer	**las mujeres**

ARTICLES

Articles (*the*, *a*, *an*) agree in gender (masculine or feminine) and in number (singular or plural) with the nouns they modify.

el libro (the book)	**los libros** (the books)
la casa (the house)	**las casas** (the houses)
un libro (a book)	**unos libros** (some books)
una casa (a house)	**unas casas** (some houses)

Two contractions are formed when **el** (*the*) combines with either **a** (*to*) or **de** (*of* or *from*).

a + el = al (to the)

Voy al cine (I'm going to the movies)

de + el = del (of or from the)

Es el principio del año (It's the beginning of the year)

ADJECTIVES

Adjectives agree in gender with the nouns they modify. Generally, descriptive adjectives follow the noun.

la casa blanca (the white house)
el hombre alto (the tall man)

Adjectives also agree in number with the nouns they modify. The plural of adjectives is formed in the same way as in the plural of nouns. For adjectives ending in a vowel, you add *s*; for adjectives ending in a consonant, add *es*.

el papel azul
(the blue paper)
la casa roja
(the red house)

los papeles azules
(the blue papers)
las casas rojas
(the red houses)

Limiting adjectives agree in number and gender with the nouns they modify, and usually precede the noun.

muchas cosas (many things)
pocos americanos (few Americans)

Demonstrative adjectives (*this*, *that*, *these*, *those*) are placed in front of the nouns they modify. They must agree in number and gender with the nouns, and in a series they are usually repeated before each noun. Use the following table to find the correct form of these demonstrative adjectives, then notice how they are used in context, agreeing with their nouns in gender and number.

SINGULAR (PLURAL)	MASCULINE	FEMININE
this (these)	este (estos)	esta (estas)
that (those)	esa (esos)	esa (esas)
that (those) (meaning far away)	aquel (aquellos)	aquella (aquellas)

Now, in context.

este zapato (this shoe)   **estos zapatos** (these shoes)

esa blusa (that blouse)   **esas blusas** (those blouses)

aquel edificio (that building—in the distance)   **aquellos edificios** (those buildings)

estos hombres y estas mujeres (these men and women)

Possessive adjectives must agree with the nouns they modify. Use the following table to locate the appropriate form to express what you mean.

	SINGULAR	PLURAL
my	mi	mis
your (familiar)	tu	tus
your (polite) his her its	su	sus
our	nuestro(a)	nuestros(as)
your (plural familiar)	vuestro(a)	vuestros(as)
your (plural polite) their	su	sus

Here are some examples of possessive adjectives, as they modify their nouns in number and gender.

mi amigo (my friend)	**mis amigos** (my friends)
nuestra casa (our house)	**nuestro coche** (our car)
nuestros libros (our books)	**tus zapatos** (your shoes)*

*This is the familiar form, used when talking to a friend, a child, or among members of the same family. **Sus zapatos** (your shoes) would be the polite form, always used when talking to strangers.

Since **su** and **sus** have six possible meanings, it is often necessary to use a prepositional phrase (**de usted, de ustedes, de él, de ellos, de ella, de ellas**) to avoid any possible ambiguity.

su casa (could mean your, her, his, its, or their house)
la casa de usted (your house)
la casa de ella (her house)

PRONOUNS

Subject pronouns (*I, you, he, she*, etc.) have both singular and plural forms.

SINGULAR		PLURAL	
I	yo	(we)	nosotros(as)
you	tú	you (familiar)	vosotros(as) (used in Spain)
you	usted	you (polite)	ustedes (used for both familiar and polite forms in Latin America)
he	él	they (m.)	ellos
she	ella	they (f.)	ellas

Direct object pronouns (*me, you, him, it, us, them*) are used as direct objects of verbs. They have both singular and plural forms, as the table below indicates.

SINGULAR		PLURAL	
me	me	us	nos
you	te	you (familiar)	vos (used in Spain)
you	le	you (polite)	los
him	lo		
her			
it	la	them (m.)	las
		them (f.)	

Object pronouns precede the verb unless the sentence is an affirmative command or the verb is an infinitive.

Yo te veo (I see you)
Ella me habla (She talks to me)

But in a command or with an infinitive,

Dígame la verdad (Tell me the truth)
Déme el paquete (Give me the package)
Yo quiero verla (I want to see her)
Usted no puede hacerlo (You can't do it)

Indirect object pronouns are pronouns serving as indirect objects. They take either singular or plural forms, as the table below indicates.

SINGULAR		PLURAL	
to me	me	to us	nos
to you	te	to you (familiar)	os (used in Spain)
to you			
him }			
her }	le	to you (polite)	
it }		to them	les

VERBS

In this phrase book, we limit the use of verbs to the present tense, since this is the most likely one for you to use as a tourist. All Spanish verbs in the infinitive end in either *ar*, *er*, or *ir*.

pasar (to pass)
beber (to drink)
vivir (to live)

In order to conjugate a verb this infinitive ending must be removed and replaced by the appropriate ending. The following are three typical regular verbs.

VERB WITH *AR* ENDING (HABLAR—TO SPEAK)			
yo	hablo	nosotros(as)	hablamos
tu	hablas	vosotros(as)	habláis (used in Spain)
usted el, ella	habla	ustedes ellos ellas	hablan

VERB WITH *ER* ENDING (COMER—TO EAT)			
yo	como	nosotros(as)	comemos
tu	comes	vosotros(as)	coméis (used in Spain)
usted el, ella	come	ustedes ellos ellas	comen

VERB WITH *IR* ENDING (ESCRIBIR—TO WRITE)			
yo	escribo	nosotros(as)	escribimos
tu	escribes	vosotros(as)	escribís (used in Spain)
usted el, ella	escribe	ustedes ellos ellas	escriben

Using the conjugation tables above, we give you some examples of verbs paired with the appropriate verb endings.

vender (to sell)   **Yo vendo** (I sell)
pasar (to pass)   **Ellos pasan** (They pass)
vivir (to live)   **Nosotros vivimos** (We live)

Many Spanish verbs are irregular. The following tables show the conjugations for commonly used irregular verbs.

DAR (TO GIVE)

doy	damos
das	dais
da	dan

DECIR (TO SAY, TO TELL)

digo	decimos
dices	decís
dice	dicen

HACER (TO DO, TO MAKE)

hago	
haces	
hace	

IR (TO GO)

voy	vamos
vas	vais
va	van

OÍR (TO HEAR)

oigo	oímos
oyes	oís
oye	oyen

PODER (TO BE ABLE)

puedo	podemos
puedes	podéis
puede	pueden

PONER (TO PUT, TO PLACE)

pongo	ponemos
pones	ponéis
pone	pones

QUERER (TO WISH, TO WANT)

quiero	queremos
quieres	queréis
quiere	quieren

SABER (TO KNOW)

sé	sabemos
sabes	sabéis
sabe	saben

SALIR (TO LEAVE, TO GO OUT)

salgo	salimos
sales	salís
sale	salen

TENER (TO HAVE)

tengo	tenemos
tienes	tenéis
tiene	tienen

TRAER (TO BRING)

traigo	traemos
traes	traéis
trae	traen

VENIR (TO COME)	
vengo	venimos
vienes	venís
viene	vienen

VER (TO SEE)	
veo	vemos
ves	veis
ve	ven

There are two verbs in Spanish which express the various forms of the verb to be.

SER (TO BE)	
soy	somos
eres	sois
es	son

ESTAR (TO BE)	
estoy	estamos
estás	estáis
está	están

The verb **estar** and its various forms are used in three major instances.

1. To tell about or inquire about location.
   Madrid está en España (Madrid is in Spain.)
   ¿Dónde está el policía? (Where is the policeman?)
2. To tell or ask about health.
   ¿Cómo está usted hoy? (How are you today?)
   Estoy bien, gracias. (I'm fine, thank you.)
3. To describe a temporary or changeable condition.
   La puerta está abierta. (The door is open.)
   El café está caliente. (The coffee is hot.)
   Nosotros estamos contentos. (We are happy.)
   Ella está cansada. (She is tired.)

At all other times, use the forms of ser.

   Yo soy norteamericano. (I am American.)
   El coche es grande. (The car is big.)
   El libro es importante. (The book is important.)
   Los anillos son de oro. [The rings are (made) of gold.]

The verb **tener** (*to have*) is used in a number of Spanish idiomatic expressions.

   tener frío (to be cold, literally to have cold)
   tener calor (to be hot)
   tener hambre (to be hungry)

tener sed (to be thirsty)
tener sueño (to be sleepy)
tener prisa (to be in a hurry)
tener miedo (to be afraid)
tener razón (to be right)
no tener razón (to be wrong)
tener _____ años (to be _____ years old)

And used in some examples,

No tengo calor. Tengo frío. (I'm not hot. I'm cold.)
¿Tiene usted hambre? (Are you hungry?)
No, tengo sed. (No, I am thirsty.)
Tenemos prisa. (We're in a hurry.)
Tengo razón. El tiene veinte años. (I'm right. He's 20 years old.)

PREPOSITIONS

The following is a listing of simple prepositions and their English equivalents.

a (to, at; with time)
con (with)
contra (against)
de (from, of, about)
en (in, on)
entre (between, among)
hacia (towards)
hasta (up to, until)
para (for, in order to, to)
por (for, by, through, because)
según (according to)
sin (without)
sobre (on, about)

And some compound prepositions.

además de (besides, in addition to)
al lado de (beside, at the side of)
antes de (before; references to time)

cerca de (near)
debajo de (under, underneath)
delante de (in front of)
dentro de (inside of, within)
después de (after)
detrás de (behind)
en vez de (instead of)
encima de (on top of)
enfrente de (facing, opposite, in front of)
fuera de (outside of)
lejos de (far from)

Used in some examples, here are some prepositions.

El policía está delante de la tienda. (The policeman is in front of the store.)
Voy con mi familia. (I'm going with my family.)
¿Está cerca de la estación? (It is near the station?)
Tomo el tren a las cinco. (I'm taking the train at 5:00.)

TO FORM QUESTIONS

Some common interrogative words in Spanish are the following.

¿Adónde (Where; to what place?)
¿Cómo? (How?)
¿Cuál? (Which?)
¿Cuándo? (When?)
¿Cuánto? (How much?)
¿Cuántos? (How many?)
¿Dónde? (Where?)
¿Para qué? (What for? Why?)
¿Por qué? (Why?)
¿Qué? (What?)
¿Quién? (Who?)
¿Quiénes? (who?)

Notice that all interrogative words have a written accent.

To form a question in Spanish, place the subject *after* the verb. For example

¿Habla usted español?	(Do you speak Spanish?)
¿Tiene María el billete?	Does María have the ticket?
¿Cuándo van ustedes al cine?	When are you going to the movies?

Note that in an interrogative sentence there is an inverted question mark before the sentence as well as the regular question mark after it.

TO FORM NEGATIVE WORDS

The most common negative word in Spanish is **no**. It always precedes the verb.

Yo no tengo dinero. (I have no money; I don't have any money.)

Other negative words are:

nadie (no one)
nada (nothing)
nunca (never)
ninguno (a) (none)
tampoco (neither)

Used in sentences, these would be:

Nadie viene. (No one is coming.)
No veo nada. (I don't see anything; I see nothing.)
Nunca comemos en casa. (We never eat at home.)
Ninguno me gusta. (I don't like any; I like none.)
Ella no tiene dinero, ni yo tampoco. (She has no money and neither do I.)

Any one of the negative words except **no** may be used either before or after the verb. If one is used after the verb, **no** is also used before the verb, making a double negative.

Nadie habla.	
No habla nadie.	(No body is speaking.)
Nada veo.	(I don't see anything; I see
No veo nada.	nothing.)

ENGLISH-SPANISH DICTIONARY

A

a, an un *oon*, una (f.) *oo-nah*

able (to be) poder *poh-DEHR*

about alrededor de *ahl-reh-deh-DOHR* day; . . . **two o'clock** a eso de las dos *Ah EH-soh day lahs dohs*

above arriba *ahr-REE-bah*, encima (de) *ehn-SEE-mah (day)*

abscess el absceso *ahbs-SEH-soh*

accelerator el acelerador *ah-seh-leh-rah-DOHR*

accept (v.) aceptar *ah-sehp-TAHR*

accident el accidente *ahk-see-DEHN-teh*

ache (head) el dolor de cabeza *doh-LOHR day kah-BEH-sah*; **(stomach)** el dolor de estómago *doh-LOHR day ehs-TOH-mah-goh*; **(tooth)** el dolor de muelas *doh-LOHR day MWEH-lahs*

across a través (de) *ah trah-BEHS (day)*

address la dirección *dee-rehk-SYOHN*

adhesive tape el esparadrapo *ehl ehs-pah-rah-DRAH-poh*

adjust (v.) ajustar *ah-hoos-TAHR*, arreglar *ahr-reh-GLAHR*

admittance (no) se prohibe la entrada *seh proh-EE-beh lah ehn-TRAH-dah*

afraid (to be) tener miedo *teh-NEHR MYEH-doh*

after después (de) *dehs-PWEHS (day)*

afternoon la tarde *TAHR-deh*

afterward después *dehs-PWEHS*, luego *LWEH-goh*

again otra vez *OH-trah behs*, de nuevo *deh NWEH-boh*

against contra *KOHN-trah*

ago hace *AH-seh*

agree (v.) estar de acuerdo *ehs-TAHR deh ah-KWEHR-doh*

ahead adelante *ah-deh-LAHN-teh*

aid la ayuda *ah-YOO-dah*; **first aid** primeros auxilios *pree-mehr-ohs ah-ook-SEEL-yohs*

air el aire *AHY-reh*; **air mail** el correo aéreo *kohr-REH-oh ah-EH-reh oh*

airline la línea aérea *LEE-neh-ah ah-EH-reh-ah*

airplane el avión *ah-BYOHN*

airport el aeropuerto *ah-eh-roh-PWEHR-toh*

alarm clock el despertador *dehs-pehr-tah-DOHR*

all todo *TOH-doh*; **all aboard!** ¡a bordo! *ah BOHR-doh*, ¡Señores viajeros al tren! *sehn-YOH-rehs byah-HEH-rohs ahl TREHN*

allow permitir *pehr-mee-TEER*

almond la almendra *ahl-MEHN-drah*

almost casi *KAH-see*

alone solo *SOH-loh*

already ya *yah*

also también *tahm-BYEHN*

always siempre *SYEHM-preh*

a.m. de (por) la mañana *deh (pohr) lah mahn-YAH-nah*

am soy *soy*, estoy *ehs-TOY*

American norteamericano *NOHR-teh-ah-meh-ree-KAH-noh*; **Ameri-**

can plan la pensión completa *pehn-SYOHN kohm-PLEH-tah*, cuarto y comida *KWAHR-toh ee koh-MEE-dah*

among entre *EHN-treh*

and y *ee*; e *eh* [before i or hi]

ankle el tobillo *toh-BEE-yoh*

annoy (v.) molestar *moh-lehs-TAHR*

another otro *OH-troh*

answer (response) la respuesta *rehs-PWEHS-tah*, la contestación *kohn-tehs-tah-SYOHN*

any algún *ahl-GOON*

anybody (anyone) alguien *AHL-gyehn*

anything algo *AHL-goh*; **anything else?** ¿algo más? *AHL-goh MAHS*

apartment el piso *PEE-soh*, el apartamento *ah-pahr-tah-MEHN-toh*

aperitif el aperitivo *ah-peh-ree-TEE-boh*

appetizers los entremeses *ehn-treh-MEH-sehs*

apple la manzana *mahn-SAH-nah*

apricot el albaricoque *ahl-bah-ree-KOH-keh*

April abril *ah-BREEL*

Arab árabe *AH-rah-beh*

are son *sohn*, están *ehs-TAHN*

Argentinian argentino *ahr-hehn-TEEN-oh*

arm el brazo *BRAH-soh*

armchair el sillón *see-YOHN*

around alrededor (de) *ahl-reh-deh-DOHR (deh)*

arrival la llegada *yeh-GAH-dah*

article el artículo *ahr-TEE-koo-loh*

as como *KOH-moh*

ash tray el cenicero *seh-nee-SEH-roh*

ask (a question) preguntar *preh-goon-TAHR*; **ask for** pedir *peh-DEER*

asparagus el espárrago *ehs-PAHR-ah-goh*

aspirin la aspirina *ahs-pee-REE-nah*

at en *ehn*, a *ah*, en casa de *ehn KAH-sah deh*; **at once** en seguida *ehn seh-GHEE-dah*

attention! ¡atención! *ah-tehn-SYOHN*, ¡cuidado! *kwee-DAH-doh*

August agosto (m.) *ah-GOHS-toh*

aunt la tía *lah TEE-ah*

Austrian austríaco *ows-TREE-ah-koh*

automobile el automóvil *ow-toh-MOH-beel*, el carro *KAHR-roh*, el coche *KOH-cheh*

autumn el otoño *oh-TOHN-yoh*

avoid evitar *eh-bee-TAHR*

awful terrible *tehr-REE-bleh*

B

baby el bebé *beh-BEH*, el nene *NEH-neh*, la nena *NEH-nah*

back (body part) la espalda *ehs-PAHL-dah*; **(behind)** detrás (de) *deh-TRAHS (deh)*; **(direction, movement)** atrás *ah-TRAHS*

bacon el tocino *toh-SEE-noh*

bad malo *MAH-loh*; **too . . . !** ¡es lástima! *ehs LAHS-tee-mah*

badly mal *mahl*

bag, handbag cartera *kahr-TEHR-ah*; **valise** la maleta *mah-LEH-tah*

baggage el equipaje *eh-kee-PAH-heh*; **. . . room** la sala de equipajes *SAH-lah deh eh-kee-PAH-hehs*

baked al horno *ahl OHR-noh*

balcony (theater) la galería *gah-leh-REE-ah*

ball la pelota *peh-LOH-tah*

banana el plátano *PLAH-tah-noh*

bandage (covering) la venda *BEHN-dah*; **to . . .** vendar *ben-DAHR*

bank el banco *BAHN-koh*

barber el peluquero *peh-loo-KEH-roh*, el barbero *bahr-BEH-roh*

barbershop la peluquería *peh-loo-keh-REE-ah*, la barbería *bahr-behr-EE-ah*

bargain la ganga *GAHN-gah*

basket la cesta *SEHS-tah*, la canasta *kah-NAHS-tah*

bath baño *BAHN-yoh*; **to bathe** bañarse *bahn-YAHR-seh*

bathing cap el gorro de baño *GOHR-roh deh BAHN-yoh*

bathing suit el traje de baño *TRAH-heh deh BAHN-yoh*

bathrobe el albornoz *ahl-bohr-NOHS*

bathroom el cuarto de baño *KWAHR-toh deh BAHN-yoh*

battery (automobile) el acumulador *ah-koo-moo-lah-DOHR*, la batería *bah-teh-REE-ah*

be ser *sehr*, estar *ehs-TAHR*; **be back** estar de vuelta *ehs-TAHR deh BWEHL-tah*

beach la playa *PLAH-yah*

beautiful bello *BEH-yoh*, hermoso *ehr-MOH-soh*

beauty salon el salón de belleza *sah-LOHN deh beh-YEH-sah*

because porque *POHR-keh*

bed la cama *KAH-mah*

bedroom la alcoba *ahl-KOH-bah*, el dormitorio *dohr-mee-TOH-ryoh*

beef la carne de vaca *KAHR-neh deh BAH-kah*; **roastbeef** el rosbif *rohs-BEEF*

beer la cerveza *sehr-BEH-sah*

beet la remolacha *reh-moh-LAH-chah*

before antes de *AHN-tehs deh*

begin comenzar *koh-mehn-SAHR*, empezar *ehm-peh-SAHR*

behind detrás de *deh-TRAHS deh*

Belgian belga *BEHL-gah*

believe creer *kreh-EHR*

bell (door) el timbre *TEEM-breh*

bellhop el botones *boh-TOH-nehs*

belong pertenecer *pehr-teh-neh-SEHR*

belt el cinturón *seen-too-ROHN*

best el mejor *ehl meh-HOHR*

bet (I'll . . .) apuesto a que *ah-PWEHS-toh ah keh*

better mejor *meh-HOHR*

between entre *EHN-treh*

bicarbonate of soda el bicarbonato de soda *bee-kahr-boh-NAH-toh deh SOH-dah*

big grande *GRAHN-deh*

bill (restaurant check) la cuenta *KWEHN-tah*

billion mil millones *meel mee-YOH-nehs*

bird el pájaro *PAH-hah-roh*

bite (get a . . .) tomar un bocado *toh-MAHR oon boh-KAH-doh*

bitter amargo *ah-MAHR-goh*

black negro *NEH-groh*

blade (razor) la hoja de afeitar *OH-hah deh ah-fey-TAHR*

blank (form) el formulario *fohr-moo-LAHR-ee-oh*

bleach (clothes) el blanqueador *blahn-keh-ah-DOHR*

block (city) la cuadra *KWAH-drah*, la manzana *mahn-SAH-nah*

blood la sangre *SAHN-greh*

blouse la blusa *BLOO-sah*

blue azul *ah-SOOL*

boardinghouse la casa de huéspedes *KAH-sah deh WEHS-peh-dehs*

boat   el barco *BAHR-koh*, el buque *BOO-keh*, el bote *BOH-teh*

body   el cuerpo *KWEHR-poh*

boiled   hervido *ehr-BEE-doh*

bolt (automobile)   el perno *PEHR-noh*

bone   el hueso *WEH-soh*

book   el libro *LEE-broh*; **guidebook** la guía *GHEE-ah*

bookstore   la librería *lee-breh-REE-ah*

booth (phone)   la cabina (telefónica) *kah-BEE-nah teh-leh-FOH-nee-kah*

boric acid   el ácido bórico *AH-see-doh BOH-ree-koh*

born (to be)   nacer *nah-SEHR*

borrow (v.)   pedir prestado *peh-DEER prehs-TAH-doh*; **(he borrowed $5 from me)** (me pidió cinco dólares prestados) *Meh pee-DYOH SEEN-koh DOH-lah-rehs prehs-TAH-dohs*

bother (v.)   molestar *moh-lehs-TAHR*; **don't . . .** no se moleste *noh seh moh-LEHS-teh*

bottle   la botella *boh-TEH-yah*

box   la caja *KAH-hah*

box office (theater)   la taquilla *tah-KEE-yah*

boy   el muchacho *moo-CHAH-choh*, el chico *CHEE-koh*

bra, brassiere   el sostén *sohs-TEHN*

bracelet   la pulsera *pool-SEHR-ah*

brakes (automobile)   los frenos *FREH-nohs*

Brazilian   brasileño *brah-see-LEH-nyoh*

bread   el pan *pahn*

break (v.)   romper *rohm-PEHR*

breakdown (auto)   la avería *ah-beh-REE-ah*

breakfast   el desayuno *deh-sah-YOO-noh*

breathe (v.)   respirar *rehs-pee-RAHR*

bridge   el puente *PWEHN-teh*

bring   traer *trah-EHR*

broiled   a la parrilla *ah lah pahr-REE-yah*

broken   roto *ROH-toh*, quebrado *keh-BRAH-doh*

brother   el hermano *ehr-MAH-noh*

brown   pardo *PAHR-doh*, castaño *kahs-TAH-nyoh*, moreno *moh-REH-noh*

bruise (injury)   la contusión *kohn-too-SYOHN*

brush (n.)   el cepillo *seh-PEE-yoh*; **shaving brush** la brocha de afeitar *broh-chah deh ah-fey-TAHR*; **to brush** cepillar *seh-pee-YAHR*

building   el edificio *eh-dee-FEE-syoh*

bulb (electric)   la bombilla *bohm-BEE-yah*

bull   el toro *TOH-roh*; **bull ring** la plaza de toros *PLAH-sah deh TOH-rohs*

bullfight   la corrida de toros *kohr-REE-dah deh TOH-rohs*

bumper (automobile)   el parachoques *pah-rah-CHOH-kehs*

burn (injury)   la quemadura *keh-mah-DOO-rah*; **to burn** quemar *keh-MAHR*

bus   el autobús *ow-toh-BOOS*

busy   ocupado *oh-koo-PAH-doh*

but   pero *PEH-roh*

butter   la mantequilla *mahn-teh-KEE-yah*

button   el botón *boh-TOHN*

buy (v.)   comprar *kohm-PRAHR*

by   de, por *deh, pohr*

C

cab el taxi *TAHK-see*

cabaret el cabaret *kah-bah-REHT*

cabbage la col *kohl*

cable (telegram) el cablegrama *kah-bleh-GRAH-mah*

cake la torta *TOHR-tah*

call (telephone call) la llamada *yah-MAH-dah*, la comunicación *koh-moo-nee-kah-SYOHN*; **to telephone** llamar por teléfono *yah-MAHR pohr teh-LEH-foh-noh*

camera la cámara *KAH-mah-rah*

can (container) la lata *LAH-tah*; **be able** poder *poh DEHR;* **can opener** el abrelatas *ah-breh-LAH-tahs*

Canadian canadiense *kah-nah-DYEHN-seh*

cancel (v.) cancelar *kahn-seh-LAHR*

candle la bujía *boo-HEE-ah*, la vela *BEH-lah*

candy los dulces *DOOL-sehs*, los bombones *bohm-BOH-nehs*

cap la gorra *GOHR-rah*

captain el capitán *kah-pee-TAHN*

car (automobile) el automóvil *ow-toh-MOH-beel*, el coche *KOH-cheh*; **railroad car** el vagón *bah-GOHN*; **streetcar** el tranvía *trahn-BEE-ah*

carbon paper el papel carbón *pah-PEHL kahr-BOHN*

carburetor el carburador *kahr-boo-rah-DOHR*

card (playing) la carta *KAHR-tah*, el naipe *NAH-ee-peh*

care (caution) el cuidado *kwee-DAH-doh*

careful (to be) tener cuidado *teh-NEHR kwee-DAH-doh*

carefully con cuidado *kohn kwee-DAH-doh*

carrot la zanahoria *sah-nah-OH-ryah*

carry (v.) llevar *yeh-BAHR*

case (cigarette) la pitillera *pee-tee-YEH-rah*; **in any . . .** en todo caso *ehn TOH-doh KAH-soh*

cash (money) el dinero contante *dee-NEH-roh kohn-TAHN-teh*; **to cash** cobrar *koh-BRAHR*, pagar *pah-GAHR*

cashier el cajero *kah-HEH-roh*

castle el castillo *kahs-TEE-yoh*

castor oil el aceite de ricino *ah-SAY-teh deh ree-SEE-noh*

cat el gato *GAH-toh*

catch (v.) coger *koh-hehr*

cathedral la catedral *kah-teh-DRAHL*

Catholic católico *kah-TOH-lee-koh*

cauliflower la coliflor *koh-lee-FLOHR*

caution el cuidado *kwee-DAH-doh*, la precaución *preh-kow-SYOHN*

ceiling el techo *TEH-choh*

celery el apio *AH-pyoh*

center el centro *SEHN-troh*

certainly ciertamente *syehr-tah-MEHN-teh*

certificate el certificado *sehr-tee-fee-KAH-doh*

chain la cadena *kah-DEH-nah*

chair la silla *SEE-lyah*

change (money) el cambio *KAHM-byoh*; **small . . .** la moneda suelta *moh-NEH-dah SWEHL-tah*, el suelto *SWEHL-toh*; **to change** cambiar *kahm-BYAHR*

charge (cover) el gasto mínimo *GAHS-toh MEE-nee-moh*; **to charge** cobrar *koh-BRAHR*

cheap barato *bah-RAH-toh*

check (baggage) el talón *tah-LOHN*; **traveler's check** el cheque de viajeros *CHEH-keh deh byah-HEH-rohs*; **to check (baggage)** facturar *fahk-too-RAHR*

checkroom la sala de equipajes *SAH-lah deh eh-kee-PAH-hehs*

cheek la mejilla *meh-HEE-yah*

cheese el queso *KEH-soh*

cherry la cereza *seh-REH-sah*

chest el pecho *PEH-choh*

chestnut la castaña *kahs-TAHN-yah*

chicken el pollo *POH-yoh*

child el niño *NEEN-yoh*, la niña *NEEN-yah*

Chilean chileno *chee-LEH-noh*

chill el escalofrío *ehs-kah-loh-FREE-oh*

chin la barba *BAHR-bah*

Chinese chino *CHEE-noh*

chiropodist el pedicuro *peh-dee-KOO-roh*

chocolate el chocolate *choh-koh-LAH-teh*; **chocolate candies** los bombones *bohm-BOH-nehs*

choose (v.) escoger *ehs-koh-HEHR*

chop, cutlet la chuleta *choo-LEH-tah*

Christmas la Navidad *nah-bee-DAHD*; **(Merry . . . !)** ¡Felices Pascuas! *feh-LEE-sehs PAHS-kwahs*, ¡Feliz Navidad! *feh-LEES nah-bee-DAHD*

church la iglesia *ee-GLEH-syah*

cigar el cigarro *see-GAHR-roh*, el puro *POO-roh*; **cigar store** la tabaquería *tah-bah-keh-REE-ah*, el estanco *ehs-TAHN-koh*

cigarette el cigarrillo *see-gahr-REE-yoh*, el pitillo *pee-TEE-yoh*; **cigarette case** la pitillera *pee-tee-YEH-rah*; **cigarette holder** la boquilla *boh-KEE-yah*

city la ciudad *syoo-DAHD*; **city hall** el ayuntamiento *ah-yoon-tah-MYEHN-toh*

class la clase *KLAH-seh*

clean (spotless) limpio *LEEM-pyoh*; **to clean** limpiar *leem-PYAHR*

cleaner's la tintorería *teen-toh-reh-REE-ah*

clear (transparent) claro *KLAH-roh*

climb (v.) trepar *treh-PAHR*

clipper (barber's) la maquinilla *mah-kee-NEE-yah*

clock el reloj *reh-LOH*

close (near) cerca *SEHR-kah*; **to close** cerrar *sehr-RAHR*; **closed** cerrado *sehr-RAH-doh*

cloth la tela *TEH-lah*, el paño *PAHN-yoh*

clothes, clothing la ropa *ROH-pah*, los vestidos *behs-TEE-dohs*; **evening . . .** el traje de etiqueta *TRAH-heh deh eh-tee-KEH-tah*; **. . . brush** el cepillo de ropa *seh-PEEL-yoh deh ROH-pah*

cloud la nube *NOO-beh*; **cloudy** nublado *noo-BLAH-doh*

club (night) el cabaret *kah-bah-REHT*

clutch (automobile) el embrague *ehm-BRAH-gheh*

coach (railroad) el coche *KOH-cheh*, el vagón *bah-GOHN*

coat el saco *SAH-koh*, la americana *ah-meh-ree-KAH-nah*; **coat hanger** el colgador *kohl-gah-DOHR*

cocktail el coctel *kohk-TEHL*

coffee el café *kah-FEH*

coin (money) la moneda *moh-NEH-dah*

cold (temperature) frío *FREE-oh*; **respiratory** el resfriado *rehs-FRYAH-doh*; **weather** hacer frío *ah-SEHR FREE-oh*

cold cuts   los fiambres (m. pl.) *FYAHM-brehs*

collar   el cuello *KWEHL-yoh*

collect (v.)   cobrar *koh-BRAHR*

cologne   el agua de colonia *AH-gwah deh koh-LOH-nyah*

color   el color *koh-LOHR*; **color film**   la película de color *peh-LEE-koo-lah deh koh-LOHR*

comb (n.)   el peine *PAY-neh*

come   venir *beh-NEER*; **to come in**   entrar *ehn-TRAHR*; **come in!**   ¡pase usted! *PAH-seh oo-STEHD*, ¡adelante! *ah-deh-LAHN-teh*

comedy   la comedia *koh-MEH-dyah*

comfortable   cómodo *KOH-moh-doh*

company   la compañía *kohm-pahn-YEE-ah*

compartment   el compartimiento *kohm-pahr-tee-MYEHN-toh*

complaint   la queja *KEH-hah*

concert   el concierto *kohn-SYEHR-toh*

conductor (train)   el revisor *reh-bee-SOHR*

congratulations   las felicitaciones *feh-lee-see-tah-SYOHN-ehs*, la enhorabuena *ehn-oh-rah-BWEH-nah*

connected (to be—telephone)   estar en comunicación *ehs-TAHR ehn koh-moo-nee-kah-SYOHN*

consul   el cónsul *KOHN-sool*

consulate   el consulado *kohn-soo-LAH-doh*

continue (v.)   continuar *kohn-tee-NWAHR*, seguir *seh-GHEER*

convent   el convento *kohn-BEHN-toh*

cooked   cocido *koh-see-doh*

cool   fresco *FREHS-koh*

corkscrew   el sacacorchos *sah-kah-KOHR-chohs*

corn   el maíz *mah-EES*

corner   la esquina *ehs-KEE-nah*

cost (amount)   el precio *PREH-syoh*, el costo *KOHS-toh*; **to cost**   costar (ue) *kohs-TAHR*

cotton   el algodón *ahl-goh-DOHN*

cough   toser *toh-SEHR*; **cough syrup**   el jarabe para la tos *hah-RAH-beh pah-rah lah TOHS*

count (v.)   contar (ue) *kohn-TAHR*

country (nation)   el país *pah-EES*; **countryside**   el campo *KAHM-poh*

course (in meal)   el plato *PLAH-toh*

cover charge   el gasto mínimo *GAHS-toh MEE-nee-moh*

crazy   loco *LOH-koh*

cream   la crema *KREH-mah*

crystal   el cristal *krees-TAHL*

Cuban   cubano *koo-BAH-noh*

cucumber   el pepino *peh-PEE-noh*

cuff links   los gemelos *heh-MEH-lohs*

cup   la taza *TAH-sah*

curtain   la cortina *kohr-TEE-nah*, el telon *teh-LOHN*

curve   la curva *KOOR-bah*

customs   la aduana *ah-DWAH-nah*

cut (to)   cortar *kohr-TAHR*; **cut it out!**   ¡Basta! *BAHS-tah*

cutlet   la chuleta *choo-LEH-tah*

Czech   checo *CHEH-koh*

D

daily (by the day)   por día *pohr DEE-ah*

damp   húmedo *OO-meh-doh*

dance (n.)   el baile *BAH-ee-lay*; **to dance**   bailar *bah-ee-LAHR*

danger   el peligro *peh-LEE-groh*; **dangerous**   peligroso *peh-lee-GROH-soh*

Danish danés *dah-NEHS*

dark obscuro, oscuro *ohs-KOO-roh*

darn it! ¡caramba! *kah-RAHM-bah*

date (today's) la fecha *FEH-chah*

daughter la hija *EE-hah*

day el día *DEE-ah*

dead muerto *MWEHR-toh*

death la muerte *MWEHR-teh*

December diciembre (m.) *dee-SYEHM-breh*

declaration la declaración *deh-klah-rah-SYOHN*

declare (v.) declarar *deh-klah-RAHR*

deep profundo *proh-FOON-doh*

deliver (v.) entregar *ehn-treh-GAHR*

delivery la entrega *ehn-TREH-gah*; **special delivery** el correo urgente *kohr-REH-oh oor-HEHN-teh*

dental dental *dehn-TAHL*

dentist el dentista *dehn-TEES-tah*

denture la dentadura *dehn-tah-DOO-rah*

deodorant el desodorante *deh-soh-doh-RAHN-teh*

department store el almacén *ahl-mah-SEHN*

desk (information) el despacho de informes (información) *dehs-PAH-choh deh een-FOHR-mehs (een-fohr-mah-SYOHN)*

dessert el postre *POHS-treh*

detour la desviación *dehs-byah-SYOHN*, el desvío *dehs-BEE-oh*

develop (film) (v.) revelar *reh-beh-LAHR*

devil el diablo *DYAH-bloh*, el demonio *deh-MOH-nyoh*

diapers los pañales *pah-NYAH-lehs*

dictionary el diccionario *deek-syoh-NAH-ryoh*

different diferente *dee-feh-REHN-teh*

difficult difícil *dee-FEE-seel*

difficulty la dificultad *dee-fee-kool-TAHD*, el apuro *ah-POO-roh*

dining car el coche comedor *KOH-cheh koh-meh-DOHR*

dining room el comedor *koh-meh-DOHR*

dinner la comida *koh-MEE-dah*

direct (v.) indicar *een-dee-KAHR*, dirigir *dee-ree-HEER*

direction la dirección *dee-rehk-SYOHN*

dirty sucio *soo-SYOH*

discount el descuento *dehs-KWEHN-toh*

dish el plato *PLAH-toh*

district el barrio *BAHR-ryoh*

disturb (v.) molestar *moh-lehs-TAHR*

dizzy (to feel) (v.) estar aturdido *ehs-TAHR ah-toor-DEE-doh*

do (v.) hacer *ah-SEHR*

dock el muelle *MWEH-yeh*

doctor el médico *MEH-dee-koh*, el doctor *dohk-TOHR*

document el documento *doh-koo-MEHN-toh*

dog el perro *PEHR-roh*

dollar el dólar *DOH-lahr*

domestic nacional *nah-syoh-NAHL*, del país *dehl-pah-EES*

door la puerta *PWEHR-tah*; **door handle** el tirador de puerta *tee-rah-DOHR deh PWEHR-tah*

doorman el portero *pohr-TEH-roh*

double room la habitación para dos personas *ah-bee-tah-SYOHN PAH-rah dohs pehr-SOH-nahs*

down abajo *ah-BAH-hoh*

dozen la docena *doh-SEH-nah*

draft (current of air) la corriente de aire *kohr-RYEHN-teh deh AH-ee-ray*

draw (v.) dibujar *dee-boo-HAHR*

drawer el cajón *kah-HOHN*

dress (garment) el vestido *behs-TEE-doh*; **to dress** vestirse *behs-TEER-seh*

dressing gown la bata *BAH-tah*

drink (beverage) la bebida *beh-BEE-dah*; **to drink** beber *beh-BEHR*

drinkable potable *poh-TAH-bleh*

drive (ride) el paseo en coche *pah-SEH-oh ehn KOH-cheh*; **to drive** guiar, conducir *ghee-AHR, kohn-doo-SEER* [first p. sing. (present), conduzco *(kohn-DOOS-koh)]*

driver el chófer *CHOH-fehr*

dropper (eye) el cuentagotas *kwehn-tah-GOH-tahs*

drugstore la farmacia *fahr-MAH-syah*

drunk borracho *bohr-RAH-choh*

dry seco *SEH-koh*; **dry cleaning** la limpieza en seco *leem-PYEH-sah ehn SEH-koh*

duck el pato *PAH-toh*

Dutch holandés *oh-lahn-DEHS*

dysentery la disentería *dee-sehn-teh-REE-ah*

E

each cada *KAH-dah*; **each one** cada uno *KAH-dah oo-noh*

ear la oreja *oh-REH-hah*

earache el dolor de oído *ehl doh-LOHR deh oh-EE-doh*

early temprano *tehm-PRAH-noh*

earring el arete *ah-REH-teh*, pendiente *pehn-DYEHN-teh*

east el este *EHS-teh*

easy fácil *FAH-seel*; **take it . . . !** ¡no se preocupe! *noh seh preh-oh-KOO-peh*, ¡tómelo con calma! *TOH-meh-loh kohn KAHL-mah*

eat (v.) comer *koh-MEHR*

egg el huevo *WEH-boh*

eight ocho *OH-choh*

eighteen diez y ocho *dyeh see OH-choh*

eighth octavo *ohk-TAH-boh*

eighty ochenta *oh-CHEHN-tah*

elbow el codo *KOH-doh*

electric eléctrico *eh-LEHK-tree-koh*

elevator el ascensor *ahs-sehn-SOHR*

eleven once *OHN-seh*

else (nothing . . .) nada más *NAH-dah mahs*; **what . . . ?** ¿qué más? *KEH MAHS*

empty vacío *bah-SEE-oh*

end (conclusion) el fin *feen*; **to end** terminar *tehr-mee-NAHR*

endorse endosar *ehn-doh-SAHR*

engine el motor *moh-TOHR*, la máquina *MAH-kee-nah*

English inglés *een-GLEHS*

enlargement la ampliación *ahm-plyah-SYOHN*

enough bastante *bahs-TAHN-teh*

evening la tarde *TAHR-deh*; **. . . clothes** el traje de etiqueta *TRAH-heh deh eh-tee-KEH-tah*

every cada *KAH-dah*

everybody, everyone todo el mundo *TOH-doh ehl MOON-doh*, todos *TOH-dohs*

everything todo *TOH-doh*

examine examinar *ehk-sah-mee-NAHR*

exchange (v.) cambiar *kahm-BYAHR*; **. . . office** la oficina de cambio *oh-fee-SEE-nah deh KAHM-byoh*

excursion la excursión *ehs-koor-SYOHN*

excuse (v.) perdonar *pehr-doh-NAHR*, dispensar *dees-pehn-SAHR*

exhaust (automobile) el escape *ehs-KAH-peh*

exit la salida *sah-LEE-dah*

expect (v.) esperar *ehs-peh-RAHR*, aguardar *ah-gwahr-DAHR*

expensive caro *KAH-roh*

express (train) el expreso *ehs-PREH-soh*

extra extra *EHS-trah*

extract sacar *sah-KAHR*

eye el ojo *OH-hoh*

eyebrow la ceja *SEH-hah*

eyeglasses las gafas *GAH-fahs*, los anteojos *ahn-teh-OH-hohs*

eyelash la pestaña *pehs-TAHN-yah*

eyelid el párpado *PAHR-pah-doh*

F

face (body part) la cara *KAH-rah*; **face powder** los polvos para la cara *POHL-bohs PAH-rah lah-KAH-rah*; **to face** dar a *dahr ah*

facecloth el paño de lavar *PAHN-yoh deh lah-BAHR*

facial el (masaje) facial *MAH-sah-heh fah-SYAHL*

fall (autumn) el otoño *oh-TOHN-yoh*; **(injury)** la caída *kah-EE-dah*; **to fall** caer *kah-EHR*

false falso *FAHL-soh*

family la familia *fah-MEEL-yah*; **family name** el apellido *ah-peh-YEE-doh*

fan (car or electric) el ventilador *behn-tee-lah-DOHR*; **(hand)** el abanico *ah-bah-NEE-koh*; **... belt** la correa de ventilador *kohr-REH-ah deh behn-tee-lah-DOHR*

far lejos *LEH-hohs*, lejano *leh-HAH-noh*

fare (fee) la tarifa *tah-REE-fah*

fast de prisa *deh PREE-sah*, pronto *PROHN-toh*; **the watch is ...**

el reloj va adelantado *reh-LOH bah ah-deh-lahn-TAH-doh*

faster más de prisa *mahs deh PREE-sah*

father el padre *PAH-dreh*

faucet el grifo *GREE-foh*

fear (dread) el miedo *MYEH-doh*; **to fear** tener miedo *teh-NEHR MYEH-doh*

February febrero (m.) *feh-BREH-roh*

feel (v.) sentirse *sehn-TEER-seh*; **... like** tener ganas de (+ infinitive) *teh-NEHR GAH-nahs deh*

felt (cloth) el fieltro *FYEHL-troh*

fender el guardabarro *gwahr-dah-BAHR-roh*

festival la fiesta *FYEHS-tah*

fever la fiebre *FYEH-breh*

few pocos *POH-kohs*; **a ...** unos cuantos *OO-nohs KWAHN-tohs*

fifteen quince *KEEN-seh*

fifth quinto *KEEN-toh*

fifty cincuenta *seen-KWEHN-tah*

fig el higo *EE-goh*

fill, fill out (v.) llenar *yeh-NAHR*; **fill a tooth (v.)** empastar *ehm-pahs-TAHR*; **fill it up!** ¡llénelo! *YEH-neh-loh*

filling el empaste *ehm-PAHS-teh*

film la película *peh-LEE-koo-lah*

find (v.) hallar *ah-YAHR*, encontrar *ehn-kohn-TRAHR*

fine (good) fino *FEE-noh*, bello *BEH-yoh*, bueno *BWEH-noh*

fine (fee) la multa *MOOL-tah*

finger el dedo *DEH-doh*

finish (v.) acabar *ah-kah-BAHR*, terminar *tehr-mee-NAHR*

fire el fuego *FWEH-goh*; **(destructive)** el incendio *een-SEHN-dyoh*

first primero *pree-MEH-roh*; **first aid** los primeros auxilios *pree-MEH-rohs ah-ook-SEEL-yohs*

fish (in water) el pez *pehs*; **(when caught)** el pescado *pehs-KAH-doh*

fit (v.) calzar *CAHL-sahr*, vestir *behs-TEER*

fix (v.) componer *kohm-poh-NEHR*, reparar *reh-pah-RAHR*, arreglar *ahr-reh-GLAHR*; **fixed-price meal** la comida corrida (completa) *koh-MEE-dah kohr-REE-dah (kohm-PLEH-tah)*

flashlight la linterna eléctrica *leen-TEHR-nah eh-LEHK-tree-kah*

flat (level) llano *YAH-noh*; **flat tire** el pinchazo *peen-CHAH-soh*

flight (plane) el vuelo *BWEH-loh*

flint el pedernal *peh-dehr-NAHL*

floor el piso *PEE-soh*, [in sense of "story"], el suelo *SWEH-loh*

flower la flor *flohr*

fluid (lighter) la bencina *behn-SEE-nah*

fog la niebla *NYEH-blah*

follow (v.) seguir *seh-GHEER*

foot el pie *pyeh*

for (purpose, destination) para *PAH-rah*; **(exchange)** por *pohr*

forbidden prohibido *proh-ee-BEE-doh*

forehead la frente *FREHN-teh*

foreign extranjero *ehs-trahn-HEH-roh*

forget (v.) olvidar *ohl-bee-DAHR*

fork el tenedor *teh-neh-DOHR*

form (document) el formulario *fohr-moo-LAH-ree-oh*

forty cuarenta *kwah-REHN-tah*

forward (direction) adelante *ah-deh-LAHN-teh*; **to forward** reexpedir *reh-ehs-peh-DEER*

fountain la fuente *FWEHN-teh*; **fountain pen** la pluma fuente *PLOO-mah FWEHN-teh*

four cuatro *KWAH-troh*

fourteen catorce *kah-TOHR-seh*

fourth cuarto *KWAHR-toh*

fracture (injury) la fractura *frahk-TOO-rah*

free (unattached) libre *LEE-breh*; **... of charge** gratis *GRAH-tees*

French francés *frahn-SEHS*

Friday el viernes *BYEHR-nehs*

fried frito *FREE-toh*

friend amigo *ah-MEE-goh*, amiga *ah-MEE-gah*

from de *deh*, desde *DEHS-deh*

front (position) delantero *deh-lahn-TEH-roh*, que da a la calle *keh dah ah lah KAH-yeh*

fruit la fruta *FROO-tah*

fuel pump la bomba de combustible *BOHM-bah deh kohm-boos-TEE-bleh*

full (as in bus) lleno *YEH-noh*; **(complete)** completo *kohm-PLEH-toh*

furnished amueblado *ah-mweh-BLAH-doh*

G

game el juego *HWEH-goh*, la partida *pahr-TEE-dah*

garage el garage *gah-RAH-heh*

garden el jardín *hahr-DEEN*

garlic el ajo *AH-hoh*

garter la liga *LEE-gah*

gas (fuel), petrol la gasolina *gah-soh-LEE-nah*; **gas station** la estación de gasolina *ehs-tah-SYOHN deh gah-soh-LEE-nah*

gate (railroad station) la barrera *bahr-REH-rah*

gauze la gasa *GAH-sah*

gear (car) el engranaje *ehn-grah-NAH-heh*

general delivery la lista de correos *LEES-tah deh kohr-REH-ohs*

gentleman el señor *sehn-YOHR*, el caballero *kah-bah-YEH-roh*

German alemán *ah-leh-MAHN*

get (obtain) (v.) conseguir *kohn-seh-GHEER*; **to get back (recover)** recobrar *reh-koh-BRAHR*; **to get dressed** vestirse *behs-TEER-seh*; **to get off** bajarse *bah-HAHR-seh*; **to get out** irse, salir *EER-seh, sah-LEER*; **to get up** levantarse *leh-bahn-TAHR-seh*; **get out!** ¡fuera!, ¡fuera de aquí! *FWEH-rah deh ah-KEE*

gift el regalo *reh-GAH-loh*

gin la ginebra *hee-NEH-brah*

girdle la faja *FAH-hah*

girl la muchacha *moo-CHAH-chah*, la chica *CHEE-kah*

give (v.) dar *dahr*; **to give back** devolver *deh-bohl-BEHR*

glad contento *kohn-TEHN-toh*, alegre *ah-LEH-greh*

gladly con mucho gusto *kohn MOO-choh GOOS-toh*

glass (drinking) el vaso *BAH-soh*; **(material)** el vidrio *BEE-dryoh*

glasses (eye) las gafas (f. pl.) *GAH-fahs*, los anteojos (m. pl.) *ahn-teh-OH-hohs*

glove el guante *GWAHN-teh*

go (v.) ir *eer*; **to go away** irse *EER-seh*, marcharse *mahr-CHAR-seh*; **to go shopping** ir de compras (de tiendas) *eer deh KOHM-prahs (deh TYEHN-dahs)*; **to go down** bajar *bah-HAHR*; **to go home** ir a casa *eer ah KAH-sah*; **to go in** entrar *ehn-TRAHR*; **to go out** salir *sah-LEER*; **to go to bed** acostarse *ah-kohs-TAHR-seh*; **to go up** subir *soo-BEER*

gold el oro *OH-roh*

good bueno *BWEH-noh*; **good-by** hasta la vista *AHS-tah lah BEES-tah*, adiós *ah-DYOHS*

goose el ganso *GAHN-soh*

grade (on road) la cuesta *KWEHS-tah*; **grade crossing** el paso a nivel *PAH-soh ah nee-BEHL*

gram el gramo *GRAH-moh*

grapefruit la toronja *toh-ROHN-hah*, el pomelo *poh-MEHL-oh*

grapes las uvas *OO-bahs*

grass la hierba *YEHR-bah*

grateful agradecido *ah-grah-deh-SEE-doh*

gravy, sauce la salsa *SAHL-sah*

gray gris *grees*

grease (lubricate) (v.) engrasar *ehn-grah-SAHR*

Greek griego *GRYEH-goh*

green verde *BEHR-deh*

greeting el saludo *sah-LOO-doh*

guide el guía *GHEE-ah*; **guidebook** la guía *GHEE-ah*

gum (chewing) el chicle *CHEE-kleh*

gums las encías *ehn-SEE-ahs*

guy el tipo *TEE-poh*

H

hair el pelo *PEH-loh*, el cabello *kah-BEH-yoh*; . . . **bleach** el descolorante *dehs-koh-loh-RAHN-teh*; . . . **lotion** la loción para el pelo *loh-SYOHN PAH-rah ehl PEH-loh*; . . . **net** la redecilla *reh-deh-SEEL-yah*; . . . **tonic** el tónico para el pelo *TOH-nee-koh PAH-rah ehl PEH-loh*; . . . **wash** el enjuague *ehn-HWAH-gheh*

hairbrush el cepillo de cabeza *seh-PEE-yoh deh kah-BEH-sah*

haircut el corte de pelo *KOHR-teh deh PEH-loh*

hairpin el gancho *GAHN-choh*, la horquilla *ohr-KEE-yah*

half (adj.) medio *MEH-dyoh*; **(n.)** la mitad *mee-TAHD*

halt! ¡alto! *AHL-toh*

ham el jamón *hah-MOHN*

hammer el martillo *mahr-TEE-yoh*

hand la mano *MAH-noh*; **hand lotion** la loción para las manos *loh-SYOHN PAH-rah lahs MAH-nohs*

handbag la bolsa *BOHL-sah*

handkerchief el pañuelo *pah-NY-WEH-loh*

handmade hecho a mano *EH-choh ah MAH-noh*

hanger (coat) el colgador *kohl-gah-DOHR*

happen (v.) pasar *pah-SAHR*, suceder *soo-seh-DEHR*, ocurrir *oh-koor-REER*, resultar *reh-sool-TAHR*

happy feliz *feh-LEES*

Happy New Year! ¡Feliz Año Nuevo! *Feh-LEES AHN-yoh NWEH-boh*

harbor el puerto *PWEHR-toh*

hard (difficult) difícil *dee-FEE-seel*; **(tough)** duro *DOO-roh*

hard-cooked egg el huevo duro *WEH-boh DOO-roh*

hat el sombrero *sohm-BREH-roh*; **hat shop** la sombrería *sohm-breh-REE-ah*

have (v.) tener *teh-NEHR*; **to have to** deber *deh-BEHR*, tener que *teh-NEHR keh*

hazelnut la avellana *ah-beh-YAH-nah*

he el *ehl*

head la cabeza *kah-BEH-sah*

headache el dolor de cabeza *doh-LOHR deh kah-BEH-sah*

headlight el farol *fah-ROHL*

headwaiter el jefe de comedor *HEH-feh deh koh-meh-DOHR*

health la salud *sah-LOOD*; . . . **certificate** el certificado de sanidad *sehr-tee-fee-KAH-doh deh sah-nee-DAHD*

hear (v.) oír *oh-EER*; **to hear from** tener (recibir) noticias de *teh-NEHR (reh-see-BEER) noh-TEE-syahs deh*

heart el corazón *koh-rah-SOHN*

heat el calor *kah-LOHR*

heaven el cielo *SYEH-loh*

heavy pesado *peh-SAH-doh*

Hebrew hebreo *eh-BREH-oh*

heel (of foot) el talón *tah-LOHN*; **(of shoe)** el tacón *tah-KOHN*

hell el infierno *een-FYEHR-noh*

hello! ¡hola! *OH-lah*, ¡qué tal! *KEH TAHL*; **(on phone)** ¡diga!

help (v.) ayudar *ah-yoo-DAHR*; **may I . . . you?** ¿qué desea? *KEH deh-SEH-ah* ¿en qué puedo servirle? *EHN KEH PWEH-doh sehr-BEER-leh*; . . . **yourself** sírvase usted *SEER-bah-seh oo-STEHD*

here aquí *ah-KEE*

high alto *AHL-toh*; **high mass** la misa cantada *MEE-sah kahn-TAH-dah*

highway (auto) la carretera *kahr-reh-TEH-rah*

hip la cadera *kah-DEH-rah*

hire (v.) alquilar *ahl-kee-LAHR*

his su *soo*

hold the wire no cuelgue *noh KWEHL-geh*

holder (cigarette) la boquilla *boh-KEEL-yah*

home la casa *KAH-sah*, el hogar *oh-GAHR*; **to go . . .** ir a casa *eer ah KAH-sah*; **to be at . . .** estar en casa *ehs-TAHR ehn KAH-sah*

hood (car) el capó *kah-POH*

hook el gancho *GAHN-choh*

hope (v.) esperar *ehs-peh-RAHR*

horn (car) la bocina *boh-SEE-nah*

hors d'oeuvre los entremeses *ehn-treh-MEH-sehs*

horse el caballo *kah-BAH-yoh*

hospital el hospital *ohs-pee-TAHL*

hostel (youth) albergue de jóvenes *ahl-BEHR-ghe deh HOH-ben-ehs*

hostess (plane) la azafata *ah-sah-FAH-tah*

hot caliente *kah-LYEHN-teh*

hotel el hotel *oh-TEL*

hour la hora *OH-rah*; **by the . . .** por hora *pohr OH-rah*

house la casa *KAH-sah*

how cómo *KOH-moh*; **how far?** ¿a qué distancia? *ah KEH dees-TAHN-syah*; **how long?** ¿cuánto tiempo? *KWAHN-toh TYEHM-poh*, desde cuándo *DEHS-deh KWAHN-doh*; **how many?** ¿cuántos? *KWAHN-tohs*; **how much?** ¿cuánto? *KWAHN-toh*

hundred ciento *SYEHN-toh* [*Cien* is used immediately before the noun: $100, cien dólares *(syehn DOH-lah-rehs)*, but: $160, ciento sesenta dólares *(SYEHN-toh seh-SEHN-tah DOH-lah-rehs)*

Hungarian húngaro *OON-gah-roh*

hungry (to be) tener hambre *teh-NEHR AHM-breh*

hurry (v.) darse prisa *DAHR-seh PREE-sah*; **to be in a . . .** tener prisa *teh-NEHR PREE-sah*

hurt (v.) lastimar *lahs-tee-MAHR*, hacer(se) daño *ah-SEHR-(seh) DAHN-yoh*

husband el marido *mah-REE-doh*

I

I yo *yoh*

ice el hielo *YEH-loh*; **ice cream** el helado *eh-LAH-doh*; **ice water** el agua helada *AH-gwah eh-LAH-dah*

identification la identificación *ee-dehn-tee-fee-kah-SYOHN*

if si *see*

ignition (car) el encendido *ehn-sehn-DEE-doh*

ill enfermo *ehn-FEHR-moh*

illness la enfermedad *ehn-fehr-meh-DAHD*

imported importado *eem-pohr-TAH-doh*

in en *ehn*

included incluído *een-kloo-EE-doh*

indigestion indigestión *een-dee-hes-TYOHN*

indisposed indispuesto *een-dees-PWEHS-toh*

information los informes (m. pl.) *een-FOHR-mehs*; **. . . desk** la oficina de informes *oh-fee-SEE-nah deh een-FOHR-mehs*

injection la inyección *een-yehk-SYOHN*

ink la tinta *TEEN-tah*

inner tube la cámara de aire *KAH-mah-rah deh AHY-reh*

inquire preguntar *preh-goon-TAHR*, averiguar *ah-beh-ree-GWAHR*

insect el insecto *een-SEHK-toh*

insecticide el insecticida *een-sehk-tee-SEE-dah*

inside dentro (de) *DEHN-troh (deh)*

instead en vez *ehn BEHS*

insurance el seguro *seh-GOO-roh*

insure (v.) asegurar *ah-seh-goo-RAHR*

interest el interés *een-teh-REHS*

interpreter el intérprete *een-TEHR-preh-teh*

intersection la bocacalle *boh-kah-KAH-yeh*, el cruce *KROO-seh*

into en *ehn*, dentro de *DEHN-troh deh*

introduce (v.) presentar *preh-sehn-TAHR*

iodine el yodo *YOH-doh*

iron (metal) el hierro *YEHR-roh*; **flat . . .** la plancha *PLAHN-chah*; **to iron** planchar *plahn-CHAHR*

is es *ehs*, está *ehs-TAH*

Italian italiano *ee-tah-LYAH-noh*

J

jack (for car) el gato *GAH-toh*; **to jack up (car)** alzar (levantar) con el gato *ahl-SAHR (leh-bahn-TAHR) kohn ehl GAH-toh*

jam (fruit) la mermelada

January enero (m.) *eh-NEH-roh*

Japanese japonés *hah-poh-NEHS*

jaw la quijada *kee-HAH-dah*

jeweler el joyero *hoh-YEH-roh*

jewelry las joyas *HOH-yahs*, las alhajas *ahl-AH-has*; **jewelry store** la joyería *hoh-yeh-REE-ah*

Jewish judío *hoo-DEE-oh*

journey (trip) el viaje *BYAH-heh*

juice el jugo *HOO-goh*, el zumo *SOO-moh*

July julio (m.) *HOO-lyoh*

June junio (m.) *HOO-nyoh*

K

keep (v.) guardar *gwahr-DAHR*, quedarse con *keh-DAHR-seh kohn*;

to . . . right seguir la derecha *seh-GHEER lah deh-REH-chah*

key la llave *YAH-beh*

kilogram el kilogramo *kee-loh-GRAH-moh*

kilometer el kilómetro *kee-LOH-meh-troh*

kind (nice) bueno *BWEH-noh*, amable *ah-MAH-bleh*; **(type)** la clase *KLAH-seh*, el género *HEH-neh-roh*

kiss (buss) el beso *BEH-soh*; **to kiss** besar *beh-SAHR*

kitchen la cocina *koh-SEE-nah*

knee la rodilla *roh-DEE-yah*

knife el cuchillo *koo-CHEE-yoh*

knock (v.) llamar *yah-MAHR*

know (v.) (fact, know-how) saber *sah-BEHR*; **(person or thing)** conocer *koh-noh-SEHR*

L

label la etiqueta *eh-tee-KEH-tah*

lace el encaje *ehn-KAH-heh*

laces (shoe) los cordones para los zapatos (m. pl.) *lohs kohr-DOH-nehs PAH-rah lohs sah-PAH-tohs*

ladies' room el tocador de señoras *toh-kah-DOHR deh sehn-YOH-rahs*

lady la señora *sehn-YOH-rah*

lamb la carne de cordero *KAHR-neh deh kohr-DEH-roh*

lamp la lámpara *LAHM-pah-rah*

land (ground) la tierra *TYEHR-rah*; **to land** desembarcar *deh-sehm-bahr-KAHR*

language el idioma *ee-DYOH-mah*, la lengua *LEHN-gwah*

large grande *GRAHN-deh*

last (final) pasado *pah-SAH-doh*, último *OOL-tee-moh*; **to last** durar *doo-RAHR*

late tarde *TAHR-deh*

latest (at the . . .) a más tardar *ah mahs tahr-DAHR*

laugh (v.) reír *reh-EER*, reírse *reh-EER-seh*

laundress la lavandera *lah-bahn-DEH-rah*

laundry la lavandería *lah-bahn-deh-REE-ah*

lavatory el lavabo *lah-BAH-boh*, el retrete *reh-TREH-teh*

laxative el laxante *lahk-SAHN-teh*

leak (drip) el escape *ehs-KAH-peh*; **to leak** escapar *ehs-kah-PAHR*

lean (v.) apoyarse en *ah-poh-YAHR-seh ehn*; **to lean out** asomarse a *ah-soh-MAHR-seh ah*

learn (v.) aprender *ah-prehn-DEHR*

least (at . . .) al (por lo) (a lo) menos *ahl (pohr loh) (ah loh) MEH-nohs*

leather el cuero *KWEH-roh*

leave (behind) (v.) dejar *deh-HAHR*; **to depart** salir *sah-LEER*

left (opposite of right) izquierdo *ees-KYEHR-doh*

leg la pierna *PYEHR-nah*

lemon el limón *lee-MOHN*

lemonade la limonada *lee-moh-NAH-dah*

lend (v.) prestar *prehs-TAHR*

length el largo *LAHR-goh*

lens el cristal *krees-TAHL*

less menos *MEH-nohs*

let (v.) dejar *deh-HAHR*, permitir *pehr-mee-TEER*

letter la carta *KAHR-tah*

letterbox el buzón *boo-SOHN*

lettuce la lechuga *leh-CHOO-gah*

library la biblioteca *bee-blyoh-TEH-kah*

lie (down) (v.) acostarse (ue) *ah-kohs-TAHR-seh*

life la vida *BEE-dah*; **life preserver** el salvavidas *sahl-bah-BEE-dahs*

lifeboat el bote salvavidas *boh-teh sahl-bah-BEE-dahs*

lift (of shoe) la tapa *TAH-pah*; **to lift** levantar *leh-behn-TAHR*, alzar *ahl-SAHR*

light (color) claro *KLAH-roh*; **(brightness)** la luz *loos*; **tail . . .** el farol de cola *fah-ROHL deh KOH-lah*; **(weight)** ligero *lee-HEH-roh*; **give me a light** déme usted fuego *DEH-meh oo-STEHD FUEH-goh*; **to light** encender *ehn-sehn-DEHR*

lighter (cigarette) el encendedor *ehn-sehn-deh-DOHR*

lightning el relámpago *reh-LAHM-pah-goh*

like (as) como *KOH-moh*; **to like** gustar *goos-TAHR*

limit (speed) la velocidad máxima *beh-loh-see-DAHD MAHK-see-mah*

line la línea *LEE-neh-ah*

linen el lino *LEE-noh*, la ropa blanca *ROH-pah BLAHN-kah*

lip el labio *LAH-byoh*

lipstick el lápiz de labios *LAH-pees deh LAH-byohs*

liqueur licor *lee-KOHR*

liquor la bebida alcohólica *beh-BEE-dah ahl-koh-OH-lee-kah*

list (wine, food) la lista *LEES-tah*

listen, listen to (v.) escuchar *ehs-koo-CHAHR*

liter el litro *LEE-troh*

little pequeño *peh-KEHN-yoh*; **a . . .** un poco *oon poh-koh*

live (v.) vivir *bee-BEER*

liver el hígado *EE-gah-doh*

living room la sala *SAH-lah*

lobby el vestíbulo *behs-TEE-boo-loh*, el salón de entrada *sah-LOHN deh ehn-TRAH-dah*

lobster la langosta *lahn-GOHS-tah*

local (train) el tren ómnibus *trehn OHM-nee-boos*; **(phone call)** la llamada local *yah-MAH-dah loh-KAHL*

lock (fastening) la cerradura *sehr-rah-DOO-rah*

long largo *LAHR-goh*; **how . . . ?** ¿cuánto tiempo? *KWAHN-toh TYEHM-poh*, desde cuándo *dehs-deh KWAHN-doh*; **long-distance call** la llamada a larga distancia *yah-MAH-dah ah LAHR-gah dees-TAHN-syah*, la conferencia interurbana *kohn-feh-REHN-syah een-tehr-oor-BAH-nah*

look, look at (v.) mirar *mee-RAHR*; **to look for** buscar *boos-KAHR*; **look out!** ¡cuidado! *kwee-DAH-doh*

lose (v.) perder *pehr-DEHR*

lost and found la oficina de objetos perdidos *oh-fee-SEE-nah deh ohb-HEH-tohs pehr-DEE-dohs*

lotion la loción *loh-SYOHN*

lots (of), many mucho *MOO-choh*, muchos *MOO-chohs*

lounge el salón *sah-LOHN*

low bajo *BAH-hoh*

lower berth la litera baja *lee-TEH-rah BAH-hah*

luck la suerte *SWEHR-teh*

lunch el almuerzo *ahl-MWEHR-soh*; **to lunch** almorzar *ahl-mohr-SAHR*

lung el pulmón *pool-MOHN*

M

maid (chamber) la camarera *kah-mah-REH-rah*

mail el correo *kohr-REH-oh*

mailbox el buzón *boo-SOHN*

magazine la revista *reh-BEES-tah*

make (v.) hacer *ah-SEHR*

man el hombre *OHM-breh*

manager el director *dee-rehk-TOHR*, el gerente *heh-REHN-teh*, el administrador *ahd-mee-nees-trah-DOHR*

manicure la manicura *mah-nee-KOO-rah*

many muchos *MOO-chohs*

map (road) el mapa de carreteras *MAH-pah deh kahr-reh-TEHR-ahs*, el mapa itinerario *mah-pah ee-tee-neh-RAH-ryoh*

March marzo (m.) *MAHR-soh*

market el mercado *mehr-KAH-doh*

mashed majado *mah-HAH-doh*

mass la misa *MEE-sah*; **high . . .** la misa cantada (mayor) *MEE-sah kahn-TAH-dah (mah-YOHR)*

massage el masaje *mah-SAH-heh*

match el fósforo *FOHS-foh-roh*

matter (it doesn't matter) no importa *noh eem-POHR-tah*; **what's the . . . ?** ¿qué pasa? *keh PAH-sah*, ¿qué hay? *key-AH-ee*

mattress el colchón *kohl-CHOHN*

May mayo (m.) *MAH-yoh*

maybe quizá *kee-SAH*, quizás *kee-SAHS*, tal vez *tahl BEHS*, acaso *ah-KAH-soh*

meal la comida *koh-MEE-dah*

mean (v.) significar *seeg-nee-fee-KAHR*, querer decir *keh-REHR deh-SEER*

measurement la medida *meh-DEE-dah*

meat la carne *KAHR-neh*

mechanic el mecánico *meh-KAH-nee-koh*

medical médico *MEH-dee-koh*

medicine la medicina *meh-dee-SEE-nah*

meet (v.) encontrar *ehn-kohn-TRAHR;* **(socially) (v.)** conocer *koh-noh-SEHR*

melon el melón *meh-LOHN*

mend remendar *reh-mehn-DAHR*

men's room el lavabo de señores *lah-BAH-boh deh sehn-YOH-rehs*

mention (don't . . . it) no hay de qué *noh ah-ee deh keh*

menu el menú *meh-NOO,* la lista de platos *LEES-tah deh plah-tohs*

merry alegre *ah-LEH-greh*

Merry Christmas! ¡Felices Pascuas! *feh-LEE-sehs pahs-kwahs,* ¡Feliz Navidad! *feh-LEES nah-bee-DAHD*

message el mensaje *mehn-SAH-heh,* el recado *reh-KAH-doh*

meter (length) el metro *MEH-troh*

meter (taxi) el taxímetro *tahk-SEE-meh-troh*

Mexican mexicano, mejicano *meh-hee-KAH-noh*

middle (center) el medio *MEH-dyoh,* el centro *SEHN-troh*

midnight la medianoche *meh-dyah-NOH-cheh*

mild ligero *lee-HEH-roh,* suave *SWAH-beh*

milk la leche *LEH-cheh*

million el millón *mee-YOHN*

mind (understanding) la mente *MEHN-teh;* **never . . .** no importa *noh eem-POHR-tah*

mine mío *MEE-oh,* los míos (pl.) *MEE-ohs*

mineral water el agua mineral *AH-gwah mee-neh-RAHL*

minister el ministro *mee-NEES-troh*

minute el minuto *mee-NOO-toh*

mirror el espejo *ehs-PEH-hoh*

Miss (woman) la señorita *sehn-yoh-REE-tah*

miss (a train) perder *pehr-DEHR*

missing (to be) faltar *fahl-TAHR*

mistake el error *ehr-ROHR,* la falta *FAHL-tah*

monastery el monasterio *moh-nahs-TEH-ryoh*

Monday el lunes *LOO-nehs*

money el dinero *dee-NEH-roh;* **money order** el giro (postal) *HEE-roh (pohs-TAHL)*

month el mes *mehs*

monument el monumento *moh-noo-MEHN-toh*

moon la luna *LOO-nah*

more más *mahs*

morning la mañana *mahn-YAH-nah*

mosquito el mosquito *mohs-KEE-toh;* **mosquito netting** el mosquitero *mohs-kee-TEH-roh*

mother la madre *MAH-dreh*

motion picture el cine *SEE-neh*

motor (car) el motor *moh-TOHR*

mouth la boca *BOH-kah;* **mouth wash** el enjuague *ehn-HWAH-gheh*

move (v.) mover *moh-BEHR;* **(change residence)** mudarse de casa *moo-DAHR-seh deh KAH-sah*

movie film la película *peh-LEE-koo-lah*

Mr. el señor *sehn-YOHR;* **(with first name only)** don *dohn*

Mrs. la señora *sehn-YOH-rah;* **(with first name only)** doña *DOHN-yah*

much mucho *MOO-choh*

museum el museo *moo-SEH-oh*

mushroom la seta *SEH-tah,* el hongo *OHN-goh*

must deber *deh-BEHR,* tener que *teh-NEHR keh*

my mi *mee,* mis *mees*

N

nail (finger or toe) la uña *OON-yah*; **nail file** la lima de uñas *lee-mah deh OON-yahs*; **nail polish** el esmalte *ehs-MAHL-teh*

name el nombre *NOHM-breh*; **family . . .** el apellido *ah-peh-YEE-doh*

napkin la servilleta *sehr-bee-YEH-tah*

narrow estrecho *ehs-TREH-choh*, angosto *ahn-GOHS-toh*

nationality la nacionalidad *nah-syoh-nah-lee-DAHD*

nauseated tener náuseas *teh-nehr NOW-seh-ahs*

near (adj.) cercano *sehr-KAH-noh*; **(prep.)** cerca de *SEHR-kah deh*

nearly casi *KAH-see*

necessary necesario *neh-seh-SAH-ryoh*

neck el cuello *KWEHL-yoh*

necklace el collar *koh-YAHR*

necktie la corbata *kohr-BAH-tah*

need (v.) necesitar *neh-seh-see-TAHR*

needle la aguja *ah-GOO-hah*

nerve el nervio *NEHR-byoh*

net (hair) la redecilla *reh-deh-SEE-yah*; **mosquito . . .** el mosquitero *mohs-kee-TEH-roh*

never nunca *NOON-kah*

new nuevo *NWEH-boh*

New Year el día de año nuevo *ehl DEE-ah deh ahn-yoh NWEH-boh*; **Happy . . . !** ¡Feliz Año Nuevo! *feh-LEES ahn-yoh NWEH-boh*

newspaper el periódico *peh-RYOH-dee-koh*

newsstand el quiosco *KYOHS-koh*

next próximo *PROHK-see-moh*, siguiente *see-GYEHN-teh*

night la noche *NOH-cheh*

night rate la tarifa nocturna *tah-REE-fah nohk-TOOR-nah*

nightclub el cabaret *kah-bah-REHT*, la sala de fiestas *SAH-lah deh FYEHS-tas*

nightgown el camisón *kah-mee-SOHN*

nightlife la vida nocturna *bee-dah nohk-TOOR-nah*

nine nueve *NWEH-beh*

nineteen diez y nueve *dyeh see NWEH-beh*

ninety noventa *noh-BEHN-tah*

ninth noveno *noh-BEH-noh*

no (adj.) ninguno *neen-GOO-noh*, ningún *neen-GOON* [before m. sing. noun]; **(adv.)** no *noh*; **no one** nadie *NAH-dyeh*

noise el ruido *RWEE-doh*

noisy ruidoso *rwee-DOH-soh*

none ninguno *neen-GOO-noh*

noon el mediodía *meh-dyoh-DEE-ah*

north el norte *NOHR-teh*

Norwegian noruego *noh-RWEH-goh*

nose la nariz *nah-REES*

not no *noh*

nothing nada *NAH-dah*; **. . . else** nada más *nah-dah MAHS*

notice (announcement) el aviso *ah-BEE-soh*

novel (book) la novela *noh-BEH-lah*

November noviembre *noh-BYEHM-breh*

now ahora *ah-OHR-ah*

number el número *NOO-meh-roh*

nurse la enfermera *ehn-fehr-MEH-rah*

nut (walnut) la nuez *nwehs*; **(mechanical)** la tuerca *TWEHR-kah*

O

occupied ocupado *oh-koo-PAH-doh*

October octubre (m.) *ohk-TOO-breh*

oculist el oculista *oh-koo-LEES-tah*

of de *deh*

of course naturalmente *nah-too-rahl-MEHN-teh*, desde luego *dehs-deh-LWEH-goh*, por supuesto *pohr soo-PWEHS-toh*

office la oficina *oh-fee-SEE-nah*; **box . . .** la taquilla *tah-KEE-yah*; **exchange . . .** la oficina de cambio *oh-fee-SEE-nah deh KAHM-byoh*; **post . . .** el correo *kohr-REH-oh*

often a menudo *ah meh-NOO-doh*

oil el aceite *ah-SEY-teh*; **castor . . .** el aceite de ricino *ah-SEY-teh deh ree-SEE-noh*; **olive . . .** el aceite de oliva *ah-SEY-teh deh oh-LEE-bah*

okay (it's) está bien *ehs-tah BYEHN*, conforme *kohn-FOHR-meh*

old viejo *BYEH-hoh*, anciano *ahn-SYAH-noh*; **how . . . are you?** ¿qué edad tiene usted? *keh eh-DAHD TYEH-neh oo-STEHD*, ¿cuántos años tiene usted? *KWAHN-tohs AHN-yohs TYEH-neh oo-STEHD*; **I am 20 years . . .** tengo veinte años *TEHN-goh BEYN-teh AHN-yohs*

olive la aceituna *ah-sey-TOO-nah*

omelet la tortilla *tohr-TEEL-yah*

on en *en*, sobre *SOH-breh*

once una vez *OO-nah behs*; **at . . .** en seguida *ehn seh-GHEE-dah*

one un *oon*, uno *oo-noh*, una *oo-nah*; **one-way traffic** la dirección única *dee-rehk-SYOHN OO-nee-kah*

onion la cebolla *seh-BOH-yah*

only sólo *SOH-loh*, solamente *soh-lah-MEHN-teh*

open (adj.) abierto *ah-BYEHR-toh*; **to open** abrir *ah-BREER*

opera la ópera *OH-peh-rah*; **opera glasses** los gemelos de teatro *heh-MEH-lohs deh teh-AH-troh*

operator (phone) la telefonista *teh-leh-foh-NEES-tah*

optician el óptico *OHP-tee-koh*

or o *oh*, u *oo* [before word beginning with vowel sound o]

orange la naranja *nah-RAHN-hah*

orangeade la naranjada *nah-rahn-HAH-dah*

orchestra (band) la orquesta *ohr-KEHS-tah*; **. . . section** la platea *plah-TEH-ah*; **. . . seat** la butaca *boo-TAH-kah*

order el encargo *ehn-KAHR-goh*; **to order** encargar *ehn-kahr-GAHR*

other otro *OH-troh*

ouch! ¡ay! *AH-ee*

our, ours nuestro *NWEHS-troh*

out afuera *ah-FWEH-rah*

outlet (electric) el toma-corriente *TOH-mah kohr-RYEHN-teh*, el enchufe *ehn-CHOO-feh*

outside fuera *FWEH-rah*, afuera *ah-FWEH-rah*

over (above) encima (de) *ehn-SEE-mah (deh)*; **(finished)** acabado *ah-kah-BAH-doh*

overcoat el abrigo *ah-BREE-goh*, el sobretodo *soh-breh-TOH-doh*, el gabán *gah-BAHN*

overdone requemado *reh-keh-MAH-doh*

overheat (motor) (v.) recalentar *reh-kah-lehn-TAHR*

overnight por la noche *pohr lah NOH-cheh*

owe (v.) deber *deh-BEHR*

own (v.) poseer *poh-seh-EHR*

oyster la ostra *OHS-trah*

P

pack (luggage) (v.) hacer las maletas *(ah-SEHR lahs mah-LEH-tahs*

package el bulto *BOOL-toh*

packet el paquete *pah-KEH-teh*

page (of book) la página *PAH-hee-nah;* **to page** llamar *yah-MAHR*

pain el dolor *doh-LOHR*

paint (wet) recién pintado *reh-SYEHN peen-TAH-doh*

pair el par *pahr*

pajamas el pijama *pee-HAH-mah*

palace el palacio *pah-LAH-syoh*

panties las bragas *BRAH-ghahs*

pants los pantalones *pahn-tah-LOH-nehs*

paper el papel *pah-PEHL;* **toilet . . .** el papel higiénico *pah-PEHL ee-HYEH-nee-koh;* **wrapping . . .** el papel de envolver *pah-PEHL deh ehn-bohl-BEHR;* **writing . . .** el papel de cartas *pah-PEHL deh KAHR-tahs*

parasol el quitasol *kee-tah-SOHL*

parcel el paquete *pah-KEH-teh;* **parcel post** el paquete postal *pah-KEH-teh pohs-TAHL*

pardon (v.) perdonar *pehr-doh-NAHR,* dispensar *dees-pehn-SAHR;* **pardon me!** ¡Perdón! *pehr-DOHN,* ¡dispénseme usted! *dees-PEHN-seh-meh oo-STEHD*

park (car) parquear *pahr-keh-AHR,* estacionar *ehs-tah-syohn-AHR;* **(garden)** el parque *PAHR-keh*

parking (no) prohibido estacionar *proh-ee-BEE-doh ehs-tah-syoh-NAHR*

part (section) la parte *PAHR-teh;* **to part hair** hacer la raya *ah-SEHR lah RAH-yah;* **to separate** separar *seh-pah-RAHR,* dividir *dee-bee-DEER*

parts (spare) las piezas de repuesto (f. pl.) *PYEH-sahs deh reh-PWEHS-toh*

pass (permit) el permiso *pehr-MEE-soh;* **to pass** pasar *pah-SAHR*

passenger el pasajero *pah-sah-HEH-roh*

passport el pasaporte *pah-sah-POHR-teh*

past el pasado *pah-SAH-doh*

pastry los pasteles *lohs pahs-TEH-lehs*

pay (v.) pagar *pah-GAHR*

pea el guisante *ghee-SAHN-teh*

peach el melocotón *meh-loh-koh-TOHN,* el durazno *doo-RAHS-noh*

pear la pera *PEH-rah*

pedestrian el peatón *peh-ah-TOHN*

pen la pluma *PLOO-mah;* **fountain . . .** la pluma fuente *ploo-mah FWEHN-teh*

pencil el lápiz *LAH-pees*

people la gente *HEN-teh*

pepper (black) la pimienta *pee-MYEHN-tah*

peppers los pimientos *pee-MYEHN-tohs*

per por *pohr*

performance la función *foon-SYOHN*

perfume el perfume *pehr-FOO-meh;* **perfume shop** la perfumería *pehr-foo-meh-REE-ah*

perhaps quizá *kee-SAH,* tal vez *tahl BEHS*

permanent (wave) la permanente *pehr-mah-NEHN-teh*

permit (pass) el permiso *pehr-MEE-soh;* **to permit** permitir *pehr-mee-TEER*

Persian persa *PEHR-sah*

personal personal *pehr-soh-NAHL*

phone el teléfono *teh-LEH-foh-noh*; **to phone** telefonear *teh-leh-foh-neh-AHR*

photograph la fotografía *foh-toh-grah-FEE-ah*; **to photograph** fotografiar *foh-toh-grah-fee-AHR*

pickle el encurtido *ehn-koor-TEE-doh*

picnic la jira *HEE-rah*, la comida campestre *koh-MEE-dah kahm-PEHS-treh*

picture (art) el cuadro *KWAH-droh*, la pintura *peen-TOO-rah*; **(motion)** la película *peh-LEE-koo-lah*, el cine *SEE-neh*

pie el pastel *pahs-TEHL*

piece el pedazo *peh-DAH-soh*

pier el muelle *MWEH-yeh*

pill la píldora *PEEL-doh-rah*

pillow la almohada *ahl-moh-AH-dah*

pillowcase la funda *FOON-dah*

pilot el piloto *pee-LOH-toh*

pin el alfiler *ahl-fee-LEHR*; **safety . . .** el imperdible *eem-pehr-DEE-bleh*

pineapple la piña *PEEN-yah*

pink rosado *roh-SAH-doh*, color de rosa *koh-LOHR deh ROH-sah*

pipe (smoking) la pipa *PEE-pah*

pitcher el jarro *HAHR-roh*, el cántaro *KAHN-tah-roh*

pity (what a . . . !) ¡qué lástima! *keh LAHS-tee-mah*

place (site) el sitio *SEE-tyoh*, el lugar *loo-GAHR*; **to place** lugar *loo-GAHR*

plane (air) el avión *ah-BYOHN*

plate el plato *PLAH-toh*

platform el andén *ahn-DEHN*, la plataforma *plah-tah-FOHR-mah*

play el drama *DRAH-mah*, la pieza *PYEH-sah*; **to play (game)** jugar (ue) *hoo-GAHR*; **to play (instrument)** tocar *toh-KAHR*

playing cards los naipes *NAH-ees*, las cartas *KAHR-tahs*

pleasant agradable *ah-grah-DAH-bleh*; **(referring to a person)** simpático *seem-PAH-tee-koh*

please por favor *pohr fah-BOHR*, haga el favor (de) (+ infinitive) *AH-gah ehl fah-BOHR (deh)*

pleasure el gusto *GOOS-toh*, el placer *plah-SEHR*

pliers los alicates *ah-lee-KAH-tehs*, las tenazas *teh-NAH-sahs*

plug (spark) la bujía *boo-HEE-ah*

plum la ciruela *see-RWEH-lah*

p.m. de la tarde *deh lah TAHR-deh*, de la noche *deh lah NOH-cheh*

pocket (n.) el bolsillo *bohl-SEE-yoh*; **(adj.)** de bolsillo *deh bohl-SEE-yoh*

pocketbook la bolsa *BOHL-sah*

point (place) el punto *POON-toh*, el lugar *loo-GAHR*; **(sharp end)** la punta *POON-tah*

poison el veneno *beh-NEH-noh*

police la policía *poh-lee-SEE-ah*; **police station** la comisaría *koh-mee-sah-REE-ah*

policeman el policía *poh-lee-SEE-ah*, el agente de policía *ehl ah-HEHN-teh deh poh-lee-SEE-ah*

Polish polaco *poh-LAH-koh*

polish (nail) el esmalte *ehs-MAHL-teh*; **polish remover** el acetón *ah-seh-TOHN*

polite cortés *kohr-TEHS*

politeness la cortesía *kohr-teh-SEE-ah*

pomade la pomada *poh-MAH-dah*

poor pobre *POH-breh*

pork la carne de cerdo *KAHR-neh deh SEHR-doh*

port (harbor) el puerto *PWEHR-toh*

porter el mozo *MOH-soh*

portion   la porción *pohr-SYOHN*, la ración *rah-SYOHN*

Portuguese   portugués *pohr-too-GHEHS*

possible   posible *poh-SEE-bleh*

post card   la tarjeta postal *tahr-HEH-tah pohs-TAHL*; **picture . . . la tarjeta postal ilustrada** *tahr-HEH-tah pohs-TAHL ee-loos-TRAH-dah*; **. . . office**   la casa de correos *KAH-sah deh kohr-REH-ohs*, el correo *kohr-REH-oh*

postage   el porte *POHR-teh*, el franqueo *frahn-KEH-oh*

potato   la patata *pah-TAH-tah*, la papa *PAH-pah*

pouch (tobacco)   la petaca *peh-TAH-kah*

pour (rain) (v.)   llover a cántaros *lyoh-BEHR ah KAHN-tah-rohs*

powder   el polvo *POHL-boh*; **face . . .** los polvos para la cara *POHL-bohs pah-rah lah KAH-rah*; **powder puff** la borla *BOHR-lah*; **powder room** el (cuarto) tocador *(KWAHR-toh) toh-kah-DOHR*

prefer (v.)   preferir *preh-feh-REER*

prepare (v.)   preparar *preh-pah-RAHR*

prescription   la receta *reh-SEH-tah*

press (iron) (v.)   planchar *plahn-CHAHR*

pretty   bonito *boh-NEE-toh*, lindo *LEEN-doh*

price   el precio *PREH-syoh*

priest   el cura *KOO-rah*

print (photo)   la copia *KOH-pyah*

program   el programa *proh-GRAH-mah*

promise (v.)   prometer *proh-meh-TEHR*

Protestant   protestante *proh-tehs-TAHN-teh*

provide (v.)   proveer *proh-beh-EHR*

prune   la ciruela pasa *see-RWEH-lah PAH-sah*

pudding   el budín *boo-DEEN*

pump (fuel)   la bomba de combustible *BOHM-bah deh kohm-boos-TEE-bleh*

puncture (tire)   el pinchazo *peen-CHAH-soh*

purchase (item)   la compra *KOHM-prah*; **to purchase**   comprar *kohm-PRAHR*

purple   morado *moh-RAH-doh*

purse   la bolsa *BOHL-sah*

purser   el sobrecargo *soh-breh-KAHR-goh*

push (v.)   empujar *ehm-poo-HAHR*

put (v.)   poner *poh-NEHR*; **put in** meter en *meh-TEHR ehn*; **put on** ponerse *pon-NEHR-seh*

Q

quarter   el cuarto *KWAHR-toh*

quick, quickly   pronto *PROHN-toh*

quiet   quieto *KYEH-toh*, tranquilo *trahn-KEE-loh*

quinine   la quinina *kee-NEE-nah*

quite   bastante *bahs-TAHN-teh*

R

rabbi   el rabino *rah-BEE-noh*

rack (train)   la red, la rejilla *rehd, reh-HEE-yah*

radiator   el radiador *rah-dyah-DOHR*

radio   la radio *RAH-dyoh*

radish   el rábano *RAH-bah-noh*

railroad   el ferrocarril *fehr-roh-kahr-REEL*

rain la lluvia *LYOO-byah*; **to rain** llover *lyoh-BEHR*

raincoat el impermeable *eem-pehr-meh-AH-bleh*

rare (meat) poco asado (hecho) *poh-koh ah-SAH-doh (EH-choh)*

rate of exchange el tipo de cambio *TEE-poh deh KAHM-byoh*; **hourly . . .** la tarifa por hora *tah-REE-fah pohr OH-rah*

rather (have) (v.) preferir *preh-feh-REER*

razor la navaja de afeitar *nah-BAH-hah deh ah-fey-TAHR*; **safety . . .** la maquinilla de afeitar *mah-kee-NEE-yah deh ah-fey-TAHR*; **. . . blade** la hojita de afeitar *oh-HEE-tah deh ah-fey-TAHR*

read (v.) leer *leh-EHR*

ready (to be) estar listo *ehs-TAHR LEES-toh*

real verdadero *behr-dah-DEH-roh*

really de veras, verdaderamente *deh BEH-rahs, behr-dah-DEH-rah-mehn-teh*

reasonable (price) razonable *rah-soh-NAH-bleh*

receipt el recibo *reh-SEE-boh*

receiver (on packages) el destinatario *dehs-tee-nah-TAH-ryoh*

recommend (v.) recomendar *reh-koh-mehn-DAHR*

record (phonograph) el disco *DEES-koh*

recover (v.) (get back) recobrar *reh-koh-BRAHR*; **(health)** reponerse *reh-poh-NEHR-seh*

red rojo *ROH-hoh*

refund (payment) el reembolso *reh-ehm-BOHL-soh*; **to refund** reembolsar *reh-ehm-bohl-SAHR*

refuse (v.) rehusar *reh-oo-SAHR*, rechazar *reh-chah-SAHR*

regards recuerdos *reh-KWEHR-dohs*, saludos *sah-LOO-dohs*

registered mail certificado *sehr-tee-fee-KAH-doh*

registry window la ventanilla de los certificados *behn-tah-NEE-yah deh lohs sehr-tee-fee-KAH-dohs*

regular (ordinary) ordinario *ohr-dee-NAH-ryoh*

remedy el remedio *reh-MEH-dyoh*

remember (v.) recordar *reh-kohr-DAHR*, acordarse de *ah-kohr-DAHR-seh deh*

rent el alquiler *ahl-kee-LEHR*; **to rent** alquilar *ahl-kee-LAHR*; **for . . .** se alquila *seh ahl-KEE-lah*

repair la reparación *reh-pah-rah-SYOHN*, la compostura *kohm-pohs-TOO-rah*; **to repair** reparar *reh-pah-RAHR*, componer *kohm-poh-NEHR*

repeat (v.) repetir *reh-peh-TEER*

reply (v.) responder *rehs-pohn-DEHR*, contestar *kohn-tehs-TAHR*

reservation la reservación *reh-sehr-bah-SYOHN*, la reserva *reh-SEHR-bah*

reserve (v.) reservar *reh-sehr-BAHR*

reserved seat el asiento reservado *ah-SYEHN-toh reh-sehr-BAH-doh*

rest (v.) descansar *dehs-kahn-SAHR*

rest room el labavo *lah-BAH-boh*, el retrete *reh-TREH-teh*

restaurant el restaurante *rehs-tow-RAHN-teh*

return (v.) (give back) devolver *deh-bohl-BEHR*; **(go back)** volver *bohl-BEHR*

rib la costilla *kohs-TEE-yah*

ribbon la cinta *SEEN-tah*

rice el arroz *ahr-ROHS*

rich rico *REE-koh*

ride el paseo *pah-SEH-oh*; **to ride** pasear en *pah-seh-AHR ehn*, ir en *EER ehn*

right (opposite of left) derecho *deh-REH-choh*; **to be . . .** tener razón *teh-NEHR rah-SOHN*; **all . . .** está bien *ehs-TAH byehn*; **right now** ahora mismo *ah-OH-rah MEES-moh*

ring (on finger) el anillo *ah-NEE-yoh*, la sortija *sohr-TEE-hah*; **to ring (call)** llamar *yah-MAHR*

rinse el enjuague *ehn-HWAH-gheh*

river el río *REE-oh*

road el camino *kah-MEE-noh*, la carretera *kahr-reh-TEH-rah*, la vía *BEE-ah*; **road map** el mapa de carretera *MAH-pah deh kahr-reh-TEH-rah*, el mapa itinerario *MAH-pah ee-tee-neh-RAH-ryoh*

roast asado *ah-SAH-doh*; **roast beef** el rosbif *rohs-BEEF*

rob (v.) robar *roh-BAHR*

robe la bata *BAH-tah*

roll (bread) el panecillo *pah-neh-SEE-yoh*, el bollito *boh-YEE-toh*; **(film)** el rollo *ROH-yoh*, el carrete *kah-REH-teh*

room el cuarto *KWAHR-toh*, la habitación *ah-bee-tah-SYOHN*

root la raíz *rah-EES*

rope la cuerda *KWEHR-dah*

rouge el colorete *koh-loh-REH-teh*

round redondo *reh-DOHN-doh*; **round trip** el viaje de ida y vuelta *BYAH-heh deh EE-dah ee BWEHL-tah*

royal real *reh-AHL*

row (theater) la fila *FEE-lah*

rubber el caucho *KOW-choh*, la goma *GOH-mah*; **. . . band** el elástico *eh-LAHS-tee-koh*, la liga de goma *LEE-gah deh goh-mah*; **. . . heels** los tacones de goma *tah-KOH-nehs deh goh-mah*

rubbers los chanclos *CHAHN-klohs*

rug la alfombra *ahl-FOHM-brah*

Rumanian rumano *roo-MAH-noh*

run (v.) correr *kohr-REHR*

running water el agua corriente *AH-gwah kohr-RYEHN-teh*

runway (plane) la pista *PEES-tah*

Russian ruso *ROO-soh*

S

safe (strongbox) la caja fuerte *kah-hah FWEHR-teh*

safety pin el imperdible *eem-pehr-DEE-bleh*; **. . . razor** la maquinilla de afeitar *mah-kee-NEE-yah deh ah-fey-TAHR*

sake (for heaven's . . .!) ¡por Dios! *pohr-DYOHS*

salad la ensalada *ehn-sah-LAH-dah*

salami el salchichón *sahl-chee-CHOHN*

sale la venta *BEHN-tah*

salon (beauty) el salón de belleza *sah-LOHN deh beh-YEH-sah*

saloon la cantina *kahn-TEE-nah*, la taberna *tah-BEHR-nah*

salt la sal *sahl*

salty salado *sah-LAH-doh*

same mismo *MEES-moh*

sand la arena *ah-REH-nah*

sandal la sandalia *sahn-DAH-lyah*

sandwich el emparedado *ehm-pah-reh-DAH-doh*

sardine la sardina *sahr-DEE-nah*

Saturday el sábado *SAH-bah-doh*

sauce la salsa *SAHL-sah*

saucer el platillo *plah-TEE-yoh*

sausage la salchicha *sahl-CHEE-chah*, el chorizo *choh-REE-soh*

say (v.) decir *deh-SEER*

scalp massage el masaje de cabeza *mah-SAH-heh deh kah-BEH-sah*

scarf la bufanda *boo-FAHN-dah*

school la escuela *ehs-KWEH-lah*

scissors las tijeras *tee-HEH-rahs*

scram! ¡váyase! *BAH-yah-seh*, ¡fuera de aquí! *FWEH-rah deh ah-KEE*

screwdriver el destornillador *dehs-tohr-nee-yah-DOHR*

sea el mar *mahr*

seafood los mariscos *mah-REES-kohs*

seasickness el mareo *mah-REH-oh*

season la estación *ehs-tah-SYOHN*

seasoned sazonado *sah-soh-NAH-doh*

seat (in conveyance) el asiento *ah-SYEHN-toh*

second segundo *seh-GOON-doh*

secretary el secretario *seh-kreh-TAH-ryoh*, la secretaria *seh-kreh-TAH-ryah*

see (v.) ver *behr*

seem (v.) parecer *pah-reh-SEHR*; **it seems to me** me parece *Meh pah-REH-seh*

select (v.) escoger *ehs-koh-HEHR*

sell (v.) vender *behn-DEHR*

send (v.) mandar, enviar *mahn-DAHR*, *ehn-BYAHR*; **to send for** enviar por *ehn-BYAHR pohr*

sender (on mail) el remitente *reh-mee-TEHN-teh*

September septiembre, setiembre (m.) *seh-TYEHM-breh*

serve (v.) servir *sehr-BEER*

service el servicio *sehr-BEE-syoh*; **at your . . .** a sus órdenes *ah soos OHR-deh-nehs*

set (hair) (v.) arreglarse *ahr-reh-GLAHR-seh*

seven siete *SYEH-teh*

seventeen diez y siete *dyeh see SYEH-teh*

seventh séptimo *SEHP-tee-moh*

seventy setenta *seh-TEHN-tah*

several varios *BAH-ryohs*

shade (in the . . .) a la sombra *ah lah SOHM-brah*; **window. . .** persianas *pehr-SYAH-nahs*

shampoo el champú *chahm-POO*

shave (v.) afeitar *ah-fay-TAHR*

shaving brush la brocha de afeitar *BROH-chah deh ah-fey-TAHR*; **. . . cream** la crema de afeitar *KREH-mah deh ah-fey-TAHR*

shawl el chal *chahl*

she ella *EH-yah*

sheet la sábana *SAH-bah-nah*

shine (v.) (shoes) lustrar *loos-TRAHR*; **(stars)** brillar *bree-YAHR*

ship el buque *BOO-keh*, el barco *BAHR-koh*, el vapor *bah-POHR*; **to ship** enviar *ehn-BYAHR*

shirt la camisa *kah-MEE-sah*

shoe el zapato *sah-PAH-toh*; **shoe store** la zapatería *sah-pah-teh-REE-ah*

shoelaces los cordones de zapato *kohr-DOH-nehs deh sah-PAH-toh*

shop la tienda *TYEHN-dah*

shopping (to go) (v.) ir de compras *eer deh KOHM-prahs*, ir de tiendas *TYEHN-dahs*

short corto *KOHR-toh*

shorts (underwear) los calzoncillos *kahl-sohn-SEE-yohs*

shoulder el hombro *ohm-broh*

show (v.) mostrar *mohs-trahr*, enseñar *ehn-sehn-YAHR*

showcase la vitrina *bee-TREE-nah*

shower la ducha *DOO-chah*

shrimp el camarón *kah-mah-ROHN*, la gamba *GAHM-bah*

shrine el santuario *sahn-TWAH-ryoh*

shut (v.) cerrar *sehr-RAHR*

shutter la contraventana *kohn-trah-behn-TAH-nah*

sick enfermo *ehn-FEHR-moh*

sickness la enfermedad *ehn-fehr-meh-DAHD*

side el lado *LAH-doh*

sidewalk la acera *ah-SEH-rah*

sightseeing el turismo *too-REES-moh*

sign (display) el letrero *leh-TREH-roh*, el aviso *ah-BEE-soh*; **to sign (a letter)** (v.) firmar *feer-MAHR*

silk la seda *SEH-dah*

silver la plata *PLAH-tah*

since desde *DEHS-deh*

sing (v.) cantar *kahn-TAHR*

single room la habitación para uno (habitación individual) *ah-bee-tah-SYOHN pah-rah OO-noh (ah-bee-tah-SYOHN een-dee-bee-DWAHL)*

sink (basin) el lavabo *lah-BAH-boh)*

sir el señor *sehn-YOHR*

sister la hermana *ehr-MAH-nah*

sit (down) (v.) sentarse *sehn-TAHR-seh*

six seis *seys*

sixteen diez y seis *dyeh see SEYS*

sixth sexto *SEHS-toh*

sixty sesenta *seh-SEHN-tah*

size el tamaño *tah-MAHN-yoh*

skin la piel *pyehl*

skirt la falda *FAHL-dah*

sky el cielo *SYEH-loh*

sleep (v.) dormir *dohr-MEER*

sleeping car el coche-cama *KOH-cheh-KAH-mah*

sleepy (to be) (v.) tener sueño *teh-nehr SWEHN-yoh*

sleeve la manga *MAHN-gah*

slip (garment) la combinación *kohm-bee-nah-SYOHN*

slippers las zapatillas *sah-pah-TEE-yahs*

slow lento *LEHN-toh*; **the watch is . . .** el reloj va atrasado *reh-LOH bah ah-trah-SAH-doh*

slowly despacio *dehs-PAH-syoh*, lentamente *lehn-tah-MEHN-teh*

small pequeño *peh-KEHN-yoh*, chiquito *chee-KEE-toh*

smelling salts las sales aromáticas *SAH-lehs ah-roh-MAH-tee-kahs*

smoke (v.) fumar *foo-MAHR*

smoking car el (coche) fumador *(KOH-cheh) foo-mah-DOHR*

snow la nieve *NYEH-beh*; **to snow** nevar *neh-BAHR*

so así *ah-SEE*

soap el jabón *hah-BOHN*; **soap flakes** los copos de jabón *KOH-pohs deh hah-BOHN*

soccer el fútbol *FOOT-bohl*

socks los calcetines *kahl-seh-TEE-nehs*

soda (bicarbonate) el bicarbonato (de soda) *bee-kahr-boh-NAH-toh (deh-SOH-dah)*

sofa el sofá *soh-FAH*

soft blando *BLAHN-doh*, suave *SWAH-beh*; **soft drink** el refresco *reh-FREHS-koh*, la bebida no alcohólica *beh-BEE-dah noh ahl-koh-OH-lee-kah*

sole (shoe) la suela *SWEH-lah*

some algún *ahl-GOON*

someone alguien *AHL-gyehn*

something algo *AHL-goh*

sometimes a veces *ah BEH-sehs*, algunas veces *ahl-goo-nahs BEH-sehs*

son el hijo *EE-hoh*

song la canción *kahn-SYOHN*

soon pronto *PROHN-toh*

sore throat el dolor de garganta *doh-LOHR deh gahr-GAHN-tah*

sorry (to be) sentir *sehn-TEER*; **I am . . .** lo siento *loh-SYEHN-toh*

soup la sopa *SOH-pah*; **soup dish** el plato sopero *PLAH-toh soh-PEH-roh*

sour agrio *AH-gryoh*

south el sur *soor*, el sud *sood*

souvenir el recuerdo *reh-KWEHR-doh*

Spanish español *ehs-pahn-YOHL*

spare tire el neumático de repuesto *neh-oo-MAH-tee-koh deh reh-PWEHS-toh*, la goma de recambio *GOH-mah deh reh-KAHM-byoh*

spark plug la bujía *boo-HEE-ah*

sparkling wine el vino espumante (espumoso) *BEE-noh ehs-poo-MAHN-teh (ehs-poo-MOH-soh)*

speak (v.) hablar *ah-BLAHR*

special especial *ehs-peh-SYAHL*; **. . . delivery** el correo urgente *kohr-REH-oh oor-HEHN-teh*; **today's . . .** el plato del día *ehl-plah-toh dehl DEE-ah*

speed limit la velocidad máxima *beh-loh-see-DAHD MAHK-see-mah*

spend (v.) (money) gastar *gahs-TAHR*; **(time)** pasar *pah-SAHR*

spinach las espinacas *ehs-pee-NAH-kahs*

spitting forbidden prohibido escupir *proh-ee-BEE-doh ehs-koo-PEER*

spoon la cuchara *koo-CHAH-rah*

sprain la torcedura *tohr-seh-DOO-rah*

spring (mechanical) el muelle *MWEH-yeh*, el resorte *reh-SOHR-teh*; **(season)** la primavera *pree-mah-BEH-rah*

square (adj.) cuadrado *kwah-DRAH-doh*; **plaza** la plaza *PLAH-sah*

stairs la escalera *ehs-kah-LEH-rah*

stall (car) (v.) parar *pah-RAHR*

stamp (postage) el sello *SEH-yoh*

stand (v.) estar de pie *ehs-TAHR deh pyeh*; **stand in line** hacer cola *ah-SEHR KOH-lah*

star la estrella *ehs-TREH-yah*, el astro *AHS-troh*

starch (laundry) el almidón *ahl-mee-DOHN*; **to starch** almidonar *ahl-mee-doh-NAHR*

start (v.) empezar *ehm-peh-SAHR*, comenzar *koh-mehn-SAHR*, principiar *preen-see-PYAHR*

starter (car) el arranque *ahr-RAHN-keh*

stateroom el camarote *kah-mah-ROH-teh*

station (gasoline) la estación de gasolina *ehs-tah-SYOHN deh gah-soh-LEE-nah*, la gasolinera *gah-soh-lee-NEH-rah*; **(railroad)** la estación de ferrocarril *ehs-tah-SYOHN deh fehr-roh-kahr-REEL*

stationery store la papelería *pah-peh-leh-REE-ah*

stationmaster el jefe de estación *heh-feh-deh ehs-tah-SYOHN*

stay (a visit) la estancia *ehs-TAHN-syah*, la morada *moh-RAH-dah*, la permanencia *pehr-mah-NEHN-syah*; **to stay** quedar(se) *keh-DAHR-(seh)*

steak el bistec *bees-TEHK*, el biftec *beef-TEHK*

steal (v.) robar *roh-BAHR*

steel el acero *ah-SEH-roh*

steep grade la cuesta *KWEHS-tah*

steering wheel el volante *boh-LAHN-teh*

stew el guisado *ghee-SAH-doh*, el estofado *ehs-toh-FAH-doh*

steward (deck) el camarero (de cubierta) *kah-mah-REH-roh (deh koo-BYEHR-tah)*

stewardess (airplane) la azafata *ah-sah-FAH-tah*

stockings las medias *MEH-dyahs*

stomach el estómago *ehs-TOH-mah-goh*; . . . **ache** el dolor de estómago *doh-lohr deh ehs-TOH-mah-goh*

stop (bus) la parada *pah-RAH-dah*;

stoplight la luz de parada *loos deh pah-RAH-dah*, el semáforo de circulación *seh-MAH-foh-roh deh seer-koo-lah-SYOHN*

store la tienda *TYEHN-dah*

straight derecho *deh-REH-choh*, seguido *seh-GHEE-doh*

strap la correa *kohr-REH-ah*

straw la paja *PAH-hah*

strawberry la fresa *FREH-sah*

street la calle *KAH-yeh*

streetcar el tranvía *trahn-BEE-ah*

string la cuerda *KWEHR-dah*

string (green) bean la habichuela verde *ah-bee-CHWEH-lah BEHR-deh*

strong fuerte *FWEHR-teh*

style el estilo *ehs-TEE-loh*; **(fashion)** la moda *MOH-dah*

sudden repentino *reh-pehn-TEE-noh*, súbito *SOO-bee-toh*

suddenly de repente *deh-reh-PEHN-teh*

sugar el azúcar *ah-SOO-kahr*

suit el traje *TRAH-heh*

suitcase la maleta *mah-LEH-tah*

summer el verano *beh-RAH-noh*

sun el sol *sohl*

sunglasses las gafas contra el sol *GAH-fahs kohn-trah ehl SOHL*

suntan ointment el ungüento contra quemadura de sol *oon-GWEHN-toh kohn-trah keh-mah-DOO-rah deh SOHL*

Sunday el domingo *doh-MEEN-goh*

sunny asoleado *ah-soh-leh-AH-doh*, de sol *deh SOHL*

supper la cena *SEH-nah*

surgeon el cirujano *see-roo-HAH-noh*

sweater el suéter *SWEH-tehr*

Swedish sueco *SWEH-koh*

sweet dulce *DOOL-seh*; **sweet wine** vino dulce *BEE-noh DOOL-seh*

swell (v.) hinchar *een-CHAHR*

swim (v.) nadar *nah-DAHR*

swimming pool la piscina *pees-SEE-nah*

Swiss suizo *SWEE-soh*

switch (electric) el interruptor *een-tehr-roop-TOHR*, el conmutador *kohn-moo-tah-DOHR*

swollen hinchado *een-CHAH-doh*, inflamado *een-flah-MAH-doh*

synagogue la sinagoga *see-nah-GOH-gah*

syrup (cough) el jarabe para la tos *hah-RAH-beh pah-rah lah TOHS*

T

table la mesa *MEH-sah*; **table d'hôte** la comida a precio fijo *koh-MEE-dah ah PREH-syoh FEE-hoh*, la comida corrida (completa) *kohr-REE-dah (kohm-PLEH-tah)*

tablecloth el mantel *mahn-TEHL*

tablespoon la cuchara *coo-CHAH-rah*

tablespoonful la cucharada *koo-chah-RAH-dah*

tablet la pastilla *pahs-TEE-yah*

tail light (car) el farol de cola *fah-ROHL-deh KOH-lah*, el farol trasero *fah-ROHL trah-SEH-roh*

tailor el sastre *SAHS-treh*

take (v.) (carry) llevar *yeh-BAHR*; **(person)** conducir *kohn-doo-SEER*, llevar *yeh-BAHR*; **(thing)** tomar *toh-MAHR*; **will . . . time** tomará (llevará) tiempo *toh-mah-RAH TYEHM-poh (yeh-bah-RAH) TYEHM-poh*

take off (garment) (v.) quitarse *kee-TAHR-seh*

taken (occupied) ocupado *oh-koo-PAH-doh*

talcum powder el polvo de talco *POHL-boh deh TAHL-koh*

tall alto *AHL-toh*

tan (color) el color de canela *koh-LOHR deh kah-NEH-lah*, café claro *kah-FEH KLAH-roh*

tangerine la mandarina *mahn-dah-REE-nah*

tank (car) el depósito *deh-POH-see-toh*

tap el grifo *GREE-foh*

tape (adhesive) el esparadrapo *ehs-pah-rah-DRAH-poh*

tasty sabroso *sah-BROH-soh*, rico *REE-koh*

tax el impuesto *eem-PWEHS-toh*

taxi el taxi *TAHK-see*

tea el té *teh*

teaspoon la cucharita *koo-chah-REE-tah*, la cucharilla *koo-chah-REE-yah*

teaspoonful la cucharadita *koo-chah-rah-DEE-tah*

telegram el telegrama *teh-leh-GRAH-mah*

telegraph (cable) el telégrafo *teh-LEH-grah-foh*; **to telegraph** telegrafiar *teh-leh-grah-FYAHR*

telephone el teléfono *teh-LEH-foh-noh*; **to telephone** telefonear *teh-leh-foh-neh-AHR*

tell decir *deh-SEER*

teller (bank) el cajero *kah-HEH-roh*

temporarily temporalmente *tehm-poh-rahl-MEHN-teh*, provisionalmente *proh-bee-syoh-nahl-MEHN-teh*

ten diez *dyes*

tension (high . . . wires) los cables de alta tensión *KAH-blehs deh AHL-tah tehn-SYOHN*

tenth décimo *DEH-see-moh*

terminal (bus, plane) la terminal *tehr-mee-NAHL*

thank (v.) dar las gracias a *dahr lahs GRAH-syahs ah*

thank-you gracias *GRAH-syahs*

that (conj.) que *keh*; **(adj.)** aquel *ah-KEHL*, ese *EH-seh*, aquella *ah-KEH-yah*, esa *EH-sah*

the el *ehl*, los *lohs*, la *lah*, las *lahs*

theater el teatro *teh-AH-troh*

their su *soo*

there ahí *ah-EE*, allí *ah-YEE*, allá *ah-YAH*; **there is (are)** hay *AH-ee*

thermometer el termómetro *tehr-MOH-meh-troh*

these estos *EHS-tohs*, estas *EHS-tahs*

they ellos *EH-yohs*, ellas *EH-yahs*

thick espeso *ehs-PEH-soh*, denso *DEHN-soh*, grueso *GRWEH-soh*

thief el ladrón *lah-DROHN*

thigh el muslo *MOOS-loh*

thing la cosa *KOH-sah*

think (v.) pensar *pehn-SAHR*

third tercero *tehr-SEH-roh*

thirsty (to be) tener sed *teh-NEHR sehd*

thirteen trece *TREH-seh*

thirty treinta *TREYN-tah*

this este *EHS-teh*, esta *EHS-tah*

those esos *EH-sohs*, aquellos *ah-KEH-yohs*, esas *EH-sahs*, aquellas *ah-KEH-yahs*

thousand mil *meel*

thread el hilo *EE-loh*

three tres *trehs*; **. . . times** tres veces *trehs BEH-sehs*

throat la garganta *gahr-GAHN-tah*

through por *pohr*, a través de *a trah-BEHS de*

thumb el pulgar *pool-GAHR*

thunder el trueno *TRWEH-noh*; **to thunder** tronar (ue) *troh-NAHR*

Thursday el jueves *HWEH-behs*

ticket el billete *bee-YEH-teh*; **. . . window** la ventanilla *behn-tah-NEE-yah*

tie (neck) la corbata *kohr-BAH-tah*

tighten (car, brakes) apretar *ah-preh-TAHR*

till hasta (que) *ahs-tah-KEH*

time el tiempo *TYEHM-poh*, la hora *OH-rah*; **on . . .** a tiempo *ah-TYEHM-poh*; **at what . . . ?** ¿a qué hora? *ah-keh-OH-rah*

timetable el horario *oh-RAH-ryoh*

tint (hair) (v.) teñir *tehn-YEER*

tip (gratuity) la propina *proh-PEE-nah*

tire (car) la llanta *YAHN-tah*, el neumático *neh-oo-MAH-tee-koh*

tired (to be) cansado (estar) *kahn-SAH-doh (ehs-TAHR)*

tissue paper el papel de seda *pah-PEHL deh SEH-dah*

to a *ah*, por *pohr*, para *PAH-rah*

toast (bread) la tostada *tohs-TAH-dah*; **(drink)** el brindis *BREEN-dees*

tobacco el tabaco *tah-BAH-koh*

today hoy *oy*

toe el dedo del pie *DEH-doh dehl PYEH*

together juntos *HOON-tohs*

toilet el retrete *reh-TREH-teh*; **toilet paper** el papel higiénico *pah-PEHL ee-HYEH-nee-koh*

token (bus or phone) la ficha *FEE-chah*

tomato el tomate *toh-MAH-teh*

tomorrow mañana *mahn-YAH-nah*

tongue la lengua *LEHN-gwah*

tonic (hair) el tónico para el pelo *TOH-nee-koh pah-rah ehl PEH-loh*

tonight esta noche *ehs-tah NOH-cheh*

too (also) también *tahm-BYEHN*; **. . . bad!** ¡es lástima! *ehs LAHS-tee-mah*; **. . . much** demasiado *deh-mah-SYAH-doh*

tooth el diente *DYEHN-teh*, la muela *MWEH-lah*

toothache el dolor de muelas *doh-LOHR deh MWEH-lahs*

toothbrush el cepillo de dientes *seh-PEE-yoh deh DYEHN-tehs*

toothpaste la pasta dentífrica *PAHS-tah dehn-TEE-free-kah*

top la cima *SEE-mah*

touch (v.) tocar *toh-KAHR*

tough duro *DOO-roh*

tourist el (la) turista *too-REES-tah*

tow (car) (v.) remolcar *reh-mohl-KAHR*

toward hacia *AH-syah*

towel la toalla *toh-AH-yah*

town el pueblo *PWEH-bloh*, la población *poh-blah-SYOHN*

track (R.R.) los rieles *RYEH-lehs*

traffic light la luz de parada *loos deh pah-RAH-dah*, la luz de tráfico *loos deh TRAH-fee-koh*, el semáforo de circulación *seh-MAH-foh-roh deh seer-koo-lah-syohn*

train el tren *trehn*

transfer (ticket) el transbordo *trahns-BOHR-doh*; **to transfer** transbordar *trahns-bohr-DAHR*

translate (v.) traducir *trah-doo-SEER*

travel (v.) viajar *byah-HAHR;*
 travel insurance el seguro de viaje *seh-GOO-roh deh BYAH-heh*

traveler el viajero *byah-HEH-roh;*
 traveler's check el cheque de viajeros *CHEH-keh deh byah-HEH-rohs*

tree el árbol *AHR-bohl*

trip voyage el viaje *BYAH-heh*

trolley car el tranvía *trahn-BEE-ah*

trouble (to be in) tener dificultades *teh-NEHR dee-fee-kool-TAH-dehs,* estar en un apuro *ehs-TAHR ehn oon ah-POO-roh*

trousers los pantalones *pahn-tah-LOH-nehs*

truck el camión *kah-MYOHN*

true verdadero *behr-dah-DEH-roh*

trunk compartment (car) el portaequipaje *pohr-tah-eh-kee-PAH-heh,* el baúl *bah-OOL*

try on (v.) probarse *proh-BAHR-seh*

try to (v.) tratar de (+ infinitive) *trah-TAHR deh*

tube (inner) la cámara de aire *KAH-mah-rah deh AH-ee-reh*

Tuesday el martes *MAHR-tehs*

Turkish turco *TOOR-koh*

turn (n.) la vuelta *BWEHL-tah;* **to turn** doblar *doh-BLAHR,* volver *bohl-BEHR*

tuxedo el smoking *SMOH-keeng*

twelve doce *DOH-seh*

twenty veinte *BEYN-teh*

twice dos veces *dohs BEH-sehs*

twin beds las camas gemelas *KAH-mahs heh-MEH-lahs*

two dos *dohs*

U

ugly feo *FEH-oh*

umbrella el paraguas *pah-RAH-gwahs*

uncle el tío *TEE-oh*

uncomfortable incómodo *een-KOH-moh-doh*

under debajo de *deh-BAH-hoh deh,* bajo *BAH-hoh*

undershirt la camiseta *kah-mee-SEH-tah*

understand comprender *kohm-prehn-DEHR,* entender *ehn-tehn-DEHR*

underwear la ropa interior *ROH-pah een-teh-RYOHR*

university la universidad *oo-nee-behr-see-DAHD*

until hasta *AHS-tah*

up arriba *ahr-REE-bah*

upon sobre *SOH-breh,* encima de *ehn-SEE-mah-deh*

upper alto *AHL-toh*

upstairs arriba *ahr-REE-bah*

U.S.A. los Estados Unidos de América *ehs-TAH-dohs oo-NEE-dohs deh ah-MEH-ree-kah* [abbreviate EE.UU.]

use (purpose) el uso *OO-soh,* el empleo *ehm-PLEH-oh;* **to use** usar *oo-SAHR,* emplear *ehm-pleh-AHR*

V

valise la maleta *mah-LEH-tah*

veal la ternera *tehr-NEH-rah*

vegetables las legumbres *leh-GOOM-brehs;* **green . . .** las verduras *behr-DOO-rahs*

velvet el terciopelo *tehr-syoh-PEH-loh*

very muy *mooy*

vest el chaleco *chah-LEH-koh*

veterinarian el veterinario *beh-teh-ree-NAH-ryoh*

view la vista *BEES-tah*

vinegar el vinagre *bee-NAH-greh*

visit (sojourn) la visita *bee-SEE-tah*; **to visit** visitar *bee-see-TAHR*, hacer una visita *ah-SEHR oo-nah bee-SEE-tah*

visitor el visitante *bee-see-TAHN-teh*

W

waist la cintura *seen-TOO-rah*, el talle *TAH-yeh*

wait (for) (v.) esperar *ehs-peh-RAHR*

waiter el camarero *kah-mah-REH-roh*; **head ...** el jefe de comedor *HEH-feh de koh-meh-DOHR*

waiting room la sala de espera *SAH-lah deh ehs-PEH-rah*

waitress la camarera *kah-mah-REH-rah*

wake up (v.) despertarse *dehs-pehr-TAHR-seh*

walk (take a) (v.) dar un paseo *dahr oon pah-SEH-oh*

wall el muro *MOO-roh*, la pared *pah-REHD*

wallet la cartera (de bolsillo) *kahr-TEH-rah (deh bohl-SEE-yoh)*

want (v.) querer *keh-REHR*

warm caliente *kah-LYEHN-teh*

was era *EH-rah*, estaba *ehs-TAH-bah*

wash (v.) lavarse *lah-BAHR-seh*

washroom el lavabo *lah-BAH-boh*

watch (clock) el reloj *reh-LOH*; **to watch** mirar *mee-RAHR*; **... out!** ¡cuidado! *kwee-DAH-doh*

water el agua (f.) *AH-gwah*

watermelon la sandía *sahn-DEE-ah*

way (path, mode) la vía *BEE-ah*, la manera *mah-NEH-rah*, el modo *MOH-doh*; **by ... of** (por) vía (de) *(pohr) BEE-ah (deh)*, pasando por *pah-SAHN-doh pohr*; **one ...** dirección única *dee-rehk-SYOHN OO-nee-kah*; **this ...** por aquí *pohr ah-KEE*; **which ...?** ¿por dónde? *pohr DOHN-deh*; **wrong ...** rumbo equivocado *ROOM-boh eh-kee-boh-KAH-doh*

we nosotros *noh-SOH-trohs*

weak débil *DEH-beel*

wear (v.) llevar *yeh-BAHR*

weather el tiempo *TYEHM-poh*

Wednesday el miércoles *MYEHR-koh-lehs*

week la semana *seh-MAH-nah*

weigh (v.) pesar *peh-SAHR*

weight el peso *PEH-soh*

welcome (you're) de nada *deh NAH-dah*

well bien *byehn*; **well-done (steak)** bien hecho *byehn EH-choh*

west el oeste *oh-EHS-teh*

wet mojado *moh-HAH-doh*; **wet paint** recién pintado *reh-SYEHN peen-TAH-doh*

what qué *keh*

wheel la rueda *RWEH-dah*; **steering ...** el volante *boh-LAHN-teh*

when cuando *KWAHN-doh*

where donde *DOHN-deh*

which cual *kwahl*

whiskey el whiskey *WEES-kee*

white blanco *BLAHN-koh*

who quien *kyehn*, quienes (pl.) *KYEH-nehs*

whom a quien *ah kyehn*, a quienes (pl.) *ah KYEHN-ehs*

whose de quién *deh kyehn*, de quiénes (pl.) *deh KYEHN-ehs*

why por qué *pohr KEH*

wide ancho *AHN-choh*

width la anchura *ahn-CHOO-rah*

wife la señora *sehn-YOH-rah*, la esposa *ehs-POH-sah*

wind el viento *BYEHN-toh*

window la ventana *behn-TAH-nah*; **display . . .** el escaparate *ehs-kah-pah-RAH-teh*; **(train, post office, bank)** la ventanilla *behn-tah-NEE-yah*

windshield el parabrisas *pah-rah-BREE-sahs*

windy ventoso *behn-TOH-soh*; **it is . . .** hace viento *ah-seh BYEHN-toh*

wine el vino *bee-noh*; **. . . list** la lista de vinos *LEES-tah deh BEE-nohs*

winter el invierno *een-BYEHR-noh*

wiper (windshield) el limpiaparabrisas *LEEM-pyah-pah-rah-BREE-sahs*

wire (high-tension) el cable de alta tensión *KAH-bleh deh AHL-tah tehn-SYOHN*; **hold the . . .** no se retire *noh seh reh-TEE-reh*

wish (v.) querer *keh-REHR*, desear *deh-seh-AHR*

wishes (best) saludos *sah-LOO-dohs*

with con *kohn*

without sin *seen*

woman la mujer *moo-HEHR*

wood la madera *mah-DEH-rah*

wool la lana *LAH-nah*

word la palabra *pah-LAH-brah*

work el trabajo *trah-BAH-hoh*; **(creative work)** la obra *OH-brah*; **to work** trabajar *trah-bah-HAHR*

worry (v.) preocuparse *preh-oh-koo-PAHR-seh*; **don't . . .** no se preocupe *noh seh preh-oh-KOO-peh*

worse peor *peh-OHR*

worst el peor *peh-OHR*

worth (to be) valer *bah-LEHR*

wound (injury) la herida *eh-REE-dah*

wounded herido *eh-REE-doh*

wrap up (v.) envolver *ehn-bohl-BEHR*

wrapping paper el papel de envolver *pah-PEHL deh ehn-bohl-BEHR*

wrench (tool) la llave inglesa (de tuercas) *YAH-beh een-GLEH-sah (deh TWEHR-kahs)*

wrist la muñeca *moon-YEH-kah*; **wrist watch** el reloj de pulsera *reh-LOH-deh pool-seh-rah*

write (v.) escribir *ehs-kree-BEER*

writing paper el papel de cartas *pah-PEHL deh KAHR-tahs*, el papel de escribir *deh ehs-kree-BEER*

wrong (to be) equivocarse *eh-kee-boh-KAHR-seh*, no tener razón *noh teh-NEHR rah-SOHN*

X

X-ray la radiografía *rah-dyoh-grah-FEE-ah*, los rayos X *lohs rahl-yohs EH-kees*

Y

year el año *AHN-yoh*

yellow amarillo *ah-mah-REE-yoh*

yes sí *see*

yesterday ayer *ah-YEHR*

yet todavía *toh-dah-BEE-ah*; **not . . .** todavía no *toh-dah-BEE-ah noh*

you   usted *oo-STEHD*, ustedes *oo-STEH-dehs*, tú *too*

young   joven *HOH-behn*

your   su, sus *soo, soos*, de usted *deh oo-STEHD*, de ustedes *deh oo-STEH-dehs*

youth hostel   albergue juvenil *ahl-behr-gheh hoo-ben-EEL*

Yugoslav   yugoeslavo *yoo-goh-eh-SLAH-boh*

Z

zipper   la cremallera *kreh-mah-YEH-rah*, el cierre relámpago *syehr-reh reh-LAHM-pah-goh*

zoo   el jardín zoológico *hahr-DEEN soh-oh-LOH-hee-koh*

SPANISH-ENGLISH DICTIONARY

(In accordance with the Spanish alphabet, ch, ll, ñ, and rr are treated as separate letters; therefore ch follows c, ll follows l, ñ follows n, rr follows r.) Also, only masculine forms of adjectives are given here.

A

a to, at, in, on, upon

abajo down, downstairs

abierto open

¡abran paso! make way!

abrelatas m. can opener

abrigo m. overcoat

abril April

abrir to open

acabado over, finished

acabar to finish; **acabar de** to have just (done something)

aceite m. oil; . . . **de oliva** olive oil; . . . **de ricino** castor oil

aceituna f. olive

acera f. sidewalk

acero m. steel

acetona f. nail-polish remover

aclarar to clear up (weather)

acordarse to remember

acostarse to lie down, to go to bed

acuerdo m. agreement; **estar de acuerdo** to agree

acumulador m. battery

adelante ahead, forward, onward; **¡adelante!** come in!

adiós good-by, farewell

aduana f. customs, customs house

afuera out, outside

agosto August

agradable pleasant

agradecido grateful

agrio sour

agua m. water; . . . **corriente** running water; . . . **de Colonia** Cologne; . . . **mineral** mineral water

aguardar to expect, to wait for

aguja f. needle

agujero m. hole

ahí there

ahora now; . . . **mismo** right now

ajo m. garlic

ajustar to adjust

albaricoque m. apricot

albornoz m. bathrobe

alcachofa f. artichoke

alcoba f. bedroom

alegrarse to be glad, to rejoice

alegre glad, merry

alemán m. German

alfiler m. pin

alfombra f. rug

algo something, anything; **¿algo más?** anything else?

algodón m. cotton

alguien someone, somebody, anyone, anybody

algún, alguno some, any; **algunas veces** sometimes

alicates m. pl. pliers

almacén m. department store, warehouse

almendra f. almond

almidón m. starch

almidonar to starch

almohada f. pillow

almorzar to lunch

almuerzo m. lunch

alquilar to rent

alquiler m. rent (payment)

alrededor de around, about; **(los) alrededores** environs, outskirts

alto tall

¡alto! halt! stop!

allá there, over there

allí there, right there

amargo bitter

amarillo yellow

americana f. coat

amigo m. friend

ampliación f. enlargement

amueblado furnished

ancho wide

anchura f. width

andén m. platform

angosto narrow

anillo m. ring

anteojos m. pl. eyeglasses

antes de before

antipático unpleasant, not likable (person)

año m. year

apearse to get off

apellido m. family name, surname

apio m. celery

aprender to learn

apretar to tighten brakes (car)

apuro m. trouble, difficulty

aquel that

aquí here

árabe Arab

árbol m. tree

arena f. sand

arete m. earring

armario m. closet

arrançue m. starter (car)

arreglar to fix, to repair

arriba up, above

arroz m. rice

asado m. roast

asar to roast

ascensor m. elevator

asegurar to insure

así so, thus

asiento m. seat (on conveyance); **. . . reservado** reserved seat

asoleado sunny

asomarse a to lean out

atrás back, backward, behind

aturdido (estar) to feel dizzy

austríaco Austrian

avellana f. hazelnut

avería f. breakdown (car)

avión f. airplane

aviso m. notice, sign, warning

ayer yesterday

ayudar to help

ayuntamiento m. city hall

azafata f. stewardess (plane)

azúcar m. sugar

azul blue

B

bailar to dance

baile m. dance (ball)

bajada f. down grade

bajar to go down, to come down

bajo low

bañarse to bathe, to take a bath

baraja f.   deck of cards

barato   cheap

barba f.   chin

barco m.   boat

barrera f.   gate, barrier

barrio m.   district

¡basta!   enough!, cut it out!; **bastante**   enough (plenty)

bata f.   robe, dressing gown

baúl m.   trunk

beber   to drink

bebida f.   drink

belga   Belgian

bello   beautiful

bencina f.   lighter fluid

besar   to kiss

beso m.   kiss

biblioteca f.   library

bien   well; . . . **hecho**   well done

billete m.   ticket, bill (banknote); . . . **de ida y vuelta**   round-trip ticket

blanco   white

blando   soft

boca f.   mouth

bocacalle f.   intersection

bocado m.   mouthful, bite; **tomar un . . .**   to have or get a bite

bocina f.   car horn

bolsa f.   purse

bolsillo m.   pocket

bollito m.   roll

bombilla f.   electric bulb

bonito   pretty

boquilla f.   cigarette holder

bordo: a . . .   on board; **¡a bordo!**   all aboard!

borla f.   powder puff

borracho   drunk

bote m.   boat; **. . . salvavidas** m.   lifeboat

botón m.   button

botones m.   bellboy, bellhop

bragas f. pl.   panties

brasileño   Brazilian

brazo m.   arm

brillar   to shine

brindis m.   toast (drink)

brocha de afeitar f.   shaving brush

bueno   good

bufanda f.   scarf

bujía f.   sparkplug, candle

bulto m.   package

buque m.   ship, boat

buscar   to look for, to search

buzón m.   letterbox, mailbox

C

caballero m.   gentleman

caballo m.   horse

cabello m.   hair

cabeza f.   head

cabina f.   phone booth

cables de alta tensión m. pl.   high-tension wires

cada   each; **. . . uno**   each one

cadena f.   chain

cadera f.   hip

caer   to fall

café m.   coffee, café; **. . . solo**   black coffee

caja f.   box, case; **pague en la . . .**   pay the cashier

caja fuerte f.   safe (strongbox)

cajero m.   teller, cashier

cajón m.   drawer

caliente   warm, hot

calor m.   heat, warmth; **hace . . .**   it's warm, hot

calzoncillos m. pl.   shorts (underwear)

calle f.   street

cama f.   bed

cámara de aire f.   inner tube

cámara fotográfica f.   camera

camarera f.   waitress, maid

camarero m.   waiter, valet; . . . **de cubierta** m.   deck steward

camarón m.   shrimp

camarote m.   stateroom

camas gemelas f. pl.   twin beds

cambiar   to change, to exchange

cambio m.   change

camino   road; . . . **equivocado** wrong way

camión m.   truck

camisa f.   shirt

camiseta f.   undershirt

camisón m.   nightgown

campo m.   countryside

canción f.   song

cansado (estar)   to be tired

cantar   to sing

cantina f.   saloon

capó m.   hood (car), bonnet

cara f.   face

caro   expensive

¡caramba!   darn it!

carne f.   meat, flesh; . . . **de cerdo** f.   pork; . . . **de cordero** f. lamb; . . . **de vaca** f.   beef

carta f.   letter, playing card

cartera (de bolsillo) f.   pocketbook (wallet)

carretera f.   auto highway

casa f.   house, home; **en** . . .   at home; . . . **de correos** f.   post office; . . . **de huéspedes** f. boardinghouse

casi   almost

caso   case

castaña f.   chestnut

castaño   brown

castillo m.   castle

catarro m.   cold (respiratory)

catorce   fourteen

caucho m.   rubber

cebolla f.   onion

ceja f.   eyebrow

cena f.   supper

cenicero m.   ash tray

cepillar   to brush

cepillo m.   brush; . . . **de dientes** toothbrush; . . . **de ropa** clothes brush

cerca de   near, close

cerdo m.   pig, hog; **carne de** . . . pork

cereza f.   cherry

cerilla f.   match

certificado   registered (mail)

cerveza f.   beer

cerrado   closed

cerradura f.   lock

cerrajero m.   locksmith

cerrar   to close, to shut

cesta f.   basket

(For words starting with ch, look after the Cs; CH is counted as a separate letter in the Spanish alphabet.)

cielo m.   sky, heaven

cien, ciento   hundred

cierre relámpago m.   zipper

cima f.   top

cincuenta   fifty

cine m.   movie house, movie show

cinta f.   ribbon

cintura f.   waist

cinturón m.   belt

ciruela f.   plum; . . . **pasa** f. prune

cirujano m.   surgeon

ciudad f.   city

claro   light (color), clear; **¡claro!** of course!

cobrar   to collect, to cash

cocido cooked; meat and vegetable stew

cocina f. kitchen

cocinar to cook

coche m. coach, auto, R.R. car;
. . .**-cama** m. sleeping car;
. . .**-comedor** m. dining car;
. . .**-fumador** m. smoking car

cochero m. coachman

codo m. elbow

coger to catch, take

colchón m. mattress

cojinete m. bearing (car)

col f. cabbage

colgador m. coat hanger

color de canela tan

colorete rouge

collar m. necklace

combinación f. slip (garment)

comenzar to begin, to start

comer to eat

comida f. meal; . . . **a precio fijo**, . . . **corrida (or completa)** f. table d'hôte, price-fixed meal

comisaría f. police station

como as, like

cómo how

cómodo comfortable

compañía f. company

componer to fix

composturas f. pl. repairs

compota f. preserve; stewed fruit

compra f. purchase (item)

comprar to buy, to purchase

comprender to understand

con with; . . . **mucho gusto** gladly

conducir to drive

conferencia interurbana f. long-distance phone call

conocer to know, to make acquaintance of

conseguir to get, to obtain

contar to count, to tell

contar con to depend on, to count on

contestación f. answer, to reply

contestar to answer, to reply

contra against

contraventana f. shutter

contusión f. bruise

copia f. print (photo)

copos de jabón soap flakes

corazón m. heart

corbata f. necktie

cortar to cut

corte de pelo m. haircut

cortés polite

cortesía f. politeness, courtesy

corto short

correa f. strap; . . . **de ventilador** f. fan belt

correo m. mail, post office; . . . **aéreo** m. air mail; . . . **urgente** m. special delivery

correr to run

corriente de aire m. draft (current of air)

cosa f. thing

costilla f. rib

creer to believe

crema f. cream; . . . **de afeitar** f. shaving cream

cremallera f. zipper

cruce m. crossroad

cuadra f. block (city)

cuadrado m. square (shape)

cuadro m. picture

cuál which?, which one?

cualquier, cualquiera any; **en cualquier caso, de cualquier modo** in any case

cuándo when?

cuánto how much?; . . . **tiempo** how long?

cuántos how many?

cuarenta forty

cuarto room, quarter; . . . **de baño** m. bathroom; . . . **tocador** m. powder room

cuatro four

cubierta f. deck (ship)

cuchara f. spoon

cucharada f. spoonful

cucharadita f. teaspoonful

cucharilla f. teaspoon

cuchillo m. knife

cuello m. neck, collar

cuenta f. bill (restaurant)

cuentagotas m. dropper (eye)

cuerda f. rope, cord, string

cuero m. leather, hide

cuerpo m. body

cuidado m. care; **con** . . . carefully; **tener** . . . to be careful; **¡cuidado!** be careful! watch out! attention!

cura m. priest

chal m. shawl

chaleco m. vest

chanclos m. pl. rubbers

checo Czech

cheque m. check (bank); . . . **de viajero** m. traveler's check

chileno Chilean

chino Chinese

chirrido m. squeak (noun)

chorizo m. sausage

chuleta f. chop, cutlet

D

danés Danish

dar to give; . . . **a** to face; . . . **las gracias a** to thank; . . . **un paseo** to take a walk

darse prisa to hurry

de of, from

debajo de under, beneath

deber to have to, to owe

débil weak

décimo tenth

decir to say, to tell

dedo m. finger

dejar to let, to permit, to leave behind

demasiado too much

dentadura f. denture

dentro inside, within

depósito m. tank

derecho right (opposite of left); **todo** . . . straight ahead

derechos de aduana m. pl. customs duties

desayunarse to have breakfast

desayuno m. breakfast

descansar to rest

descolorante hair bleach

descuento m. discount

desde since; . . . **luego** of course

desear to wish

desembarcar to land (from ship)

desodorante m. deodorant

despacio slowly

despejarse to clear up (sky)

despertador m. alarm clock

despertarse to wake up

después (de) after, afterward, later

destinatario m. addressee (on packages or letters)

destornillador m. screwdriver

desviación f. detour

detrás de back of, behind

devolver to return, to give back

día m. day; **por** . . . by the day; **buenos días** good morning, good day

diablo m. devil; **¡qué diablo!** what the devil!

diecinueve nineteen

dieciocho eighteen

dieciséis sixteen

diecisiete seventeen

diente m. tooth

diez ten

difícil difficult, hard

diluviar to pour (rain)

dinero m. money; . . . **contante** m. cash

dirección f. address, direction; . . . **única** f. one-way traffic

dirigir to direct

disco m. phonograph record

disparate m. nonsense

dispensar to excuse, to pardon; **dispénseme Ud.** pardon (excuse) me

distancia f. distance; **¿a qué distancia?** how far?

doblar to turn, to fold

doce twelve

docena dozen

dolor m. pain, ache; . . . **de cabeza** m. headache; . . . **de estómago** m. stomachache; . . . **de garganta** m. sore throat; . . . **de muelas** m. toothache

domingo m. Sunday

donde where

dormir to sleep

dormitorio m. bedroom

dos two; . . . **veces** twice

ducha f. shower

dulce sweet; **dulces** m. pl. candy

durar to last

durazno m. peach

duro hard, tough

E

elástico m. rubber band

ellas they (f.)

ellos they (m.)

embrague m. car clutch

emparedado m. sandwich

empastar to fill a tooth

empaste m. filling (tooth)

empezar to begin, to start

emplear to use

empleo m. use (purpose)

empujar to push

en on, in, at; . . . **casa** at home; . . . **casa de** at the home of; . . . **seguida** at once, immediately, right away

encaje m. lace

encendedor m. cigarette lighter

encender to light

encendido m. car ignition

encías f. pl. gums

encima (de) above, over, upon

encontrar to find, to meet

encrucijada f. crossroad

encurtidos m. pl. pickles

enchufe m. electric outlet

enero m. January

enfermedad f. illness

enfermera f. nurse

enfermo ill

engranaje m. gears (car)

engrasar to grease, to lubricate (car)

enhorabuena f. congratulations

enjuague m. mouthwash

ensalada f. salad

enseñar to teach, to show

entender to understand

entrar to enter, come in

entre between, among

entrega f.   delivery

entregar   to deliver, to hand over

entremés m.   appetizer, hors d'oeuvre

enviar   to send

envolver   to wrap

equipaje m.   baggage

equivocarse   to be mistaken

esa, ese, eso   that; **a eso de**   at about, approximately (a certain hour)

esas, esos   those

escalera f.   stairs

escalofrío m.   chill

escaparate m.   display window

escape m.   exhaust (car), leak

escarpado   steep

escoger   to choose, to select

escribir   to write

escuchar   to listen to

escuela f.   school

escupir   to spit; **prohibido . . .** spitting forbidden

esmalte m.   nail polish

espalda f.   back (of body)

español   Spanish

esparadrapo m.   adhesive tape, bandage

espejo m.   mirror

esperar   to hope, to expect, to wait for

espeso   thick

espinacas f. pl.   spinach

esposa f.   wife

esposo m.   husband

esta, este, esto   this

está bien   all right, okay

estación f.   season; **. . . de ferro-carril** f.   railroad station

estacionar   to park; **se prohibe estacionarse**   no parking

Estados Unidos de América m. pl.   U.S.A.

estanco m.   cigar store

estar   to be; **. . . de pie**   to be standing; **. . . de vuelta**   to be back

estas, estos   these

este   east; this

estancia f.   stay

estofado m.   stew

estómago m.   stomach; **dolor de . . .** m.   stomachache

estrecho   narrow, straight

estrella f.   star

esquina f.   street corner

etiqueta f.   label, etiquette; **traje de . . .** m.   evening dress

evitar   to avoid

extranjero m.   foreign, foreigner

F

facturar   to check (baggage)

faja f.   girdle

falda f.   skirt

faro m.   headlight

farol m.   street lamp; **. . . delan-tero** m.   headlight; **. . . trasero (de cola)** m.   tail light

favor m.   favor; **por . . .**   please; **haga el . . .**   please

febrero m.   February

fecha f.   date; **. . . de hoy**   to-day's date

¡Felices Pascuas!   Merry Christmas!

felicitaciones f. pl.   congratulations

feliz   happy; **¡. . . Año Nuevo!** Happy New Year!; **¡. . . Navi-dad!**   Merry Christmas!

feo   ugly

ferrocarril m. railroad

fiambre m. cold cuts

ficha f. token (for bus or phone)

fiebre f. fever

fieltro m. felt

fila f. row (theater)

fin m. end

flor f. flower

fonda para estudiantes f. youth hostel

fósforo m. match

francés French

frenos m. pl. brakes

frente m. front, forehead

fresa f. strawberry

fresco fresh, cool

frijol colorado m. kidney bean

frío m. cold; **hacer . . .** to be cold (weather); **tener . . .** to be cold (person)

frito fried

fuego m. fire

fuente f. fountain

fuera out, outside

fuerte strong

fumador m. smoker, smoking car

fumar to smoke

función f. performance

funda f. pillowcase

furgón m. baggage car

G

gabán m. overcoat

gafas f. pl. eyeglasses

gana f. desire; **tener ganas de** to feel like

ganado m. cattle

gancho m. hook

ganga f. bargain sale

ganso m. goose

garganta f. throat; **dolor de . . . m.** sore throat

gasa f. gauze

gastar to spend (money)

gasto m. expense, expenditure; **. . . mínimo** cover charge

gato m. cat, car jack

gemelos m. pl. twins, cuff links, binoculars

gente f. people

gerente m. manager

ginebra f. gin

giro postal m. money order

goma de recambio f. spare tire

gorra f. cap

gorro de baño m. bathing cap

gracias f. pl. thanks, thank-you

grande big, large, great

granizar to hail (weather)

granizo m. hail (weather)

griego Greek

grifo m. tap, faucet

gris gray

grueso thick, stout

guante m. glove

guardar to keep

guardabarros m. fender

guía m., f. guide; guidebook

guiar to drive

guisado m. stew

guisante m. pea

gustar to like, to be pleasing

gusto m. taste, pleasure; **con mucho . . .** gladly

H

habichuela f. string bean

habitación f. room; **. . . para dos personas f.** double room; **. . . individual f.** single room

hablar to speak, to talk

hace ago

hacer to do, to make, to pack (baggage); . . . **cola** to stand in line

hacerse to become

hacia toward

haga el favor please

hallar to find

hasta until, even; . . . **mañana** see you tomorrow; . . . **la vista** good-by, till we meet again

hay there is, there are

hebreo Hebrew

hecho a mano handmade

helado m. ice cream

herida f. wound

herido wounded

herir to wound, to hurt

hermana f. sister

hermano m. brother

hermoso beautiful

hervido boiled

hielo m. ice

hierro m. iron (metal)

hígado m. liver

higo m. fig

hierba f. grass

hilo m. thread, string

hinchado swollen

hinchar to swell

hoja de afeitar f. razor blade

hombre m. man

hombro m. shoulder

hongo m. mushroom

hora f. hour, time; ¿**qué . . . es?** what time is it?; **por . . .** by the hour

horario m. timetable

horno m. oven; **al . . .** baked

horquilla f. hairpin

hoy today

hueso m. bone

huevo m. egg; . . . **duro m.** hard-cooked egg

húngaro Hungarian

I

idioma m. language

iglesia f. church

imperdible safety pin

impermeable raincoat

importar to be important, to import; **no importa** it doesn't matter

impuesto m. tax

incómodo uncomfortable

indicar to indicate

infierno m. hell

informes m. pl. information

inglés English

interruptor m. electric switch

invierno m. winter

ir to go; . . . **a casa** to go home; . . . **de compras (de tiendas)** to go shopping

irse to go away, to leave, to depart, to get out

izquierdo left (opposite of right)

J

jabón m. soap; **copos de . . . m. pl.** soap flakes

jamás never

jamón m. ham

jaqueca f. headache

jarabe m. syrup; . . . **para la tos m.** cough syrup

jardín m. garden; . . . **zoológico m.** zoo

jarro m. pitcher

jefe m.   chief, leader, head; . . . **de camareros** m.   headwaiter; . . . **de estación** m.   stationmaster

jira f.   picnic

joven   young, young person

joya f.   jewel

joyería f.   jewelry, jewelry shop

joyero m.   jeweler

judío   Jewish

juego m.   game

jueves m.   Thursday

jugar   to play (game)

jugo m.   juice

julio m.   July

junio m.   June

L

labio m.   lip; **lápiz de labios** m.   lipstick

lado m.   side; **por otro** . . .   on the other hand

ladrón m.   thief, robber

lámpara f.   lamp

langosta f.   spiny lobster

lápiz m.   pencil; . . . **de labios** m.   lipstick

largo   long; **el** . . . m.   length

lástima f.   pity; **¡es** . . . !   too bad; **¡qué** . . . !   what a pity!

lastimar   to hurt, to injure, to bruise

lata f.   can (noun)

lavabo m.   sink, washroom, lavatory; . . . **de señoras** m.   ladies' room; . . . **de caballeros** m.   men's room

lavandera f.   laundress

lavandería f.   laundry

lavar   to wash (something)

lavarse   to wash oneself

laxante m.   laxative

leche f.   milk

lechuga f.   lettuce

leer   to read

legumbres f. pl.   vegetables

lejos   far, distant, far away

lengua f.   tongue; language

lentamente   slowly

lento   slow

letra f.   bank draft

letrero m.   sign, poster, placard

levantar   to lift

levantarse   to get up, to stand up, to rise

libre   free

librería f.   bookstore

libro m.   book

liga f.   garter; . . . **de goma** f.   rubber band

ligero   light (adj.)

lima de uñas f.   nail file

limpiar   to clean

limpieza a seco f.   dry-cleaning

limpio   clean

lindo   pretty

línea aérea f.   airline

lino m.   linen

linterna eléctrica f.   flashlight

lista   list; . . . **de correos** f.   general delivery; . . . **de platos** f.   menu; . . . **de vinos** f.   wine list

litera f.   berth; . . . **alta** (. . . **de arriba**) f.   upper berth; . . . **baja** f.   lower berth

(Words starting with LL follow after those with Ls. Spanish regards *LL* as a separate letter of the alphabet.)

loco   crazy

lograr   to obtain, to get to

luego   then, afterward; **desde** . . .   of course; **hasta** . . .   see you later

lugar m.   place, spot, site

luna f.   moon

lunes m. Monday

luz f. light (n.); **. . . de parada f.** stop light; **. . . de tráfico (. . . de tránsito) f.** traffic light

llamada f. telephone call; **. . . local f.** local phone call; **. . . a larga distancia, conferencia f.** long-distance phone call

llamar to call, to knock, to ring; **. . . por teléfono** to phone

llamarse to be named, to be called; **¿cómo se llama Ud.?** what is your name?

llanta f. car tire

llave f. key; **. . . inglesa (. . . de tuerca) f.** wrench

llegada f. arrival

llegar to arrive

llenar to fill, to fill out; **¡llénelo Ud.!** fill her up!

lleno full

llevar to carry, to wear, to take a person or thing somewhere

llover to rain

lluvia f. rain

M

madera f. wood

madre f. mother

maíz m. corn

mal bad, badly; **estar . . .** to be ill

maleta f. suitcase, valise, bag

mandar to send, to order, to command

mandarina f. tangerine

manga f. sleeve

mano f. hand; **de segunda . . .** secondhand

manteca f. lard, fat, butter

mantel m. tablecloth

mantequilla f. butter

manzana f. apple, block (of houses)

mañana f. morning, tomorrow; **por la . . .** in the morning; **hasta . . .** (so long) until tomorrow; **pasado . . .** the day after tomorrow

mapa m. map; **. . . de carreteras (de automovilista) m.** road map

maquinilla f. hair clippers; **. . . de afeitar f.** safety razor

mar m. sea

mareado seasick

mareo m. seasickness

marido m. husband

mariscos m. pl. seafood

martes m. Tuesday

martillo m. hammer

marzo m. March

más more

masaje m. massage

mayo m. May

medianoche f. midnight

medias f. pl. stockings

médico m., (adj.) doctor; medical

medidas f. pl. measurements, measures

medio (adj.) half; **. . . crudo** medium rare

mediodía m. noon, south

mejilla f. cheek

mejillón m. mussel

mejor better, best

mejores saludos m. pl. best wishes

melocotón m. peach

menos less, least, fewer; **al (por lo) . . .** at least

mente f. mind

menudo small, minute; **a . . .** often

mercado m. market

mes m.   month

mesa f.   table, plateau

meter   to put in, insert

miedo m.   fear; **tener . . .**   to be afraid, to fear

miércoles m.   Wednesday

mil   thousand; **. . . millones**   billion

mirar   to look, to look at

misa cantada (mayor) f.   high mass

mismo   same; **ahora . . .**   right now; **hoy . . .**   this very day

mitad f.   half (n.)

moda f.   fashion, style

modo m.   way, mode, manner

mojado   wet

mojarse   to get wet

molestar   to bother, to annoy; **no se moleste**   don't bother, don't trouble yourself

moneda f.   coin; **. . . corriente** f.   currency; **. . . suelta** f.   change

morada f.   stay

morado   purple

moreno   brunette, dark-complexioned

mosquitero m.   mosquito netting

mostaza f.   mustard

mostrar   to show

mozo m.   porter, waiter

muchacha f.   girl

muchacho m.   boy

mucho   much, a great deal of, a lot of

muchos   many, lots of

muelle m.   pier, dock, wharf

muerte f.   death

muerto   dead

mujer f.   woman, wife

multa f.   fine (n.)

muñeca f.   wrist, doll

muro m.   (outside) wall

museo m.   museum

muslo m.   thigh

muy   very

N

nacer   to be born

nada   nothing; **de . . .**   you're welcome, don't mention it; **. . . más**   nothing else

nadar   to swim

nadie   no one, nobody

naranja f.   orange

nariz f.   nose

navaja de afeitar f.   razor

Navidad f.   Christmas

necesitar   to need

neumático de repuesto m.   spare tire

nevar   to snow

niebla f.   fog

nieve f.   snow

ninguno   none

niño m.   child

no se retire   hold the wire

noche f.   night; **buenas noches**   good evening, good night

nombre m.   name

norte m.   north

noruego   Norwegian

nos   us, ourselves

nosotros   we, us

novela f.   novel

noveno   ninth

noventa   ninety

nube f.   cloud

nublado   cloudy

nuestro   our, ours

nueve   nine

nuevo   new; **de . . .**   again, anew

nuez f. walnut
número m. number
nunca never

O

occidente m. western world
octavo eighth
ocupado busy, taken
ocurrir to happen
ochenta eighty
ocho eight
oeste m. west
oficina office; **. . . de cambio f.**
exchange office; **. . . de informes f.** information bureau;
. . . de objetos perdidos f.
lost-and-found
oído m. ear (internal); **dolor de
. . . m.** earache
oír to hear
ojo m. eye
olvidar, olvidarse de to forget
once eleven
óptico m. optician
oreja f. ear (external)
oro m. gold
ostra f., ostión m. oyster
otoño m. autumn, fall
otra vez again
otro other, another

P

padre m. father
pagar to pay, to cash
página f. page
país m. country (nation)
paja f. straw
pájaro m. bird

palabra f. word
pan m. bread
panecillo m. roll
pantalones m. pl. trousers, pants
pañales m. pl. diapers
paño m. cloth
pañuelo m. handkerchief
papa f. potato
papel m. paper; **. . . de cartas
(de escribir) m.** writing paper;
. . . de envolver m. wrapping
paper; **. . . de seda m.** tissue
paper; **. . . higiénico m.** toilet
paper
papelería f. stationery store
paquete m. packet, package, parcel; **. . . postal m.** parcel post
par m. pair
para for purpose or destination; **es
para Ud.** it's for you
parabrisas m. windshield
parachoques m. car bumper
parada f. stop; **. . . de señal f.**
signal stop; **. . . intermedia f.**
stop-over; **. . . ordinaria f.**
scheduled bus stop
paraguas m. umbrella
parar to stop, to stall (car)
pardo brown
parecer to seem, to appear
pared m. inner wall
párpado m. eyelid
partida f. game
parrilla f. grill; **a la . . .** broiled
pasado past, last; **el mes . . .**
last month
pasajero m. passenger
pasar to pass, to happen, to spend
(time)
pasear, pasearse to take a walk,
ride; **¡pase Ud!** come! come in!
paseo m. ride, walk; **. . . en
coche m.** drive

paso a nivel m.   railroad crossing

pastel m.   pie

pastilla f.   tablet, cake (of soap)

pato m.   duck

peatón m.   pedestrian

pecho m.   chest

pedazo m.   piece

pedernal m.   flint

pedir   to ask for; . . . **prestado** to borrow

peinar   to comb, to set hair

peine m.   comb

película f.   film; . . . **de color** f. color film

peligro m.   danger

peligroso   dangerous

pelo m.   hair

pelota f.   (bouncing) ball

peluquería f.   barbershop

peluquero m.   barber

pendiente m.   earring

pensar   to think, to intend

pensión completa f.   American plan

peor   worse, worst

pepino m.   cucumber

pequeño   small, little

pera f.   pear

perder   to lose, to miss (a train or boat)

¡perdón!   pardon me!

perdonar   to pardon, to excuse

perfumería f.   perfume shop

periódico m.   newspaper

permiso m.   pass, permit

permitir   to permit, to allow

perno m.   bolt (car)

pero   but

perro m.   dog

persa   Persian

pertenecer   to belong

pesado   heavy

pesar   to weigh

pescado m.   fish (when caught)

peso m.   weight, monetary unit

pestaña f.   eyelash

pez m.   fish (in water)

pie m.   foot; **a . . .**   on foot

piel f.   skin, fur, leather

pierna f.   leg (of body)

pieza f.   play (theater)

piezas de respuesto f. pl.   spare parts

píldora f.   pill

pimienta f.   black pepper

pimientos m. pl.   peppers

pinacoteca f.   art gallery

pinchazo m.   puncture (tire)

piña f.   pineapple

piscina f.   swimming pool

piso m.   apartment, suite, floor

pista f.   plane runway

pitillera f.   cigarette case

pitillo m.   cigarette

placer m.   pleasure

plancha f.   flat iron

planchar   to iron, to press

planilla f.   form, document

plata f.   silver

plátano m.   plantain, banana

platillo m.   saucer

plato m.   plate, course (meal); . . . **del día** m.   today's special

playa f.   beach

plaza f.   square (n.); . . . **de toros** bull ring

pluma f.   pen; . . . **fuente** f. fountain pen

poblado m.   village

pobre   poor

poco   little; **un . . .**   a little; . . . **asado (hecho)**   rare (steak)

pocos few, a few

poder to be able

polvo m. powder; **. . . de talco m.** talcum powder

polvos para la cara m. pl. face powder

pollo m. chicken

poner to put, to place

ponerse to put on, to become

por for (exchange), by; **pagar . . .** to pay for; **. . . aquí** this way; **. . . día** by the day; **¿. . . dónde?** which way?

porque because

¿por qué? why?

portaequipajes m. trunk (car)

porte m. postage

portero m. doorman, janitor

poseer to possess, to own

postre m. dessert

precio m. price, cost

pregunta f. question, inquiry

preguntar to ask, to inquire

preocuparse to worry; **no se preocupe** don't worry

presentar to introduce, to present

prestar to lend

primavera f. spring (season)

primera cura f. first aid

primero first

prisa f. hurry, haste; **darse . . .** to hurry

probarse to try on

prohibido prohibited, forbidden

prohibir to forbid; **se prohibe la entrada** no admittance; **se prohibe el paso** no thoroughfare

prometer to promise

pronto quick, quickly, soon

propina f. tip (gratuity)

provisionalmente temporarily

próximo next; **el año . . .** next year

puede ser perhaps, maybe

puente m. bridge

puerta f. door

puerto m. port, harbor

pulgar m. thumb

pulsera f. bracelet; **reloj de . . .** wrist watch

pulverizar to spray

puro pure, cigar

Q

que that, which, who

qué what?, how?

quebrado broken

quedarse to remain, to stay, to be left; **. . . con** to keep

queja f. complaint

quejarse to complain

quemadura f. burn

quemar to burn

querer to wish, to want, to desire, to love; **. . . decir** to mean

queso m. cheese

quién (pl.) quiénes who?, which?; **¿quién sabe?** who knows?, perhaps, maybe

quijada f. jaw

quince fifteen

quinto fifth

quitarse to take off

quitasol m. parasol

quizá maybe

quizás perhaps

R

rábano m. radish

rabino m. rabbi

radiografía f.   X-ray

raíz f.   root

raya f.   part (of hair); **hacer la . . .** to part hair

razón f.   reason, right; **tener . . .** to be right; **no tener . . .** to be wrong

real   royal, real

recado m.   message

recalentar   to overheat (motor)

receta f.   prescription, recipe

recibir   to receive

recibo m.   receipt

recién pintado   fresh paint, freshly painted

recobrar   to recover, to get back

recomendar   to recommend

reconocer   to recognize

recordar   to remember

recuerdos m. pl.   regards

rechazar   to refuse, to reject

red f.   net, train rack

redecilla f.   hair net

redondo   round

refresco m.   soft drink

regalo m.   gift, present

rehusar   to refuse

reírse   to laugh

rejilla f.   rack (in R.R. coach)

relámpago m.   lightning

reloj m.   watch, clock; **. . . de pulsera** m.   wrist watch

remendar   to mend

remitente m.   sender, shipper (mail)

remolacha f.   beet

remolcar   to tow

repente   sudden; **de . . .** suddenly

repentino   sudden

repetir   to repeat

reponerse   to recover health

requemado   overdone

resfriado   cold (respiratory)

resorte m.   spring (mechanical)

respirar   to breathe

responder   to answer

respuesta f.   answer

resultar   to result, to turn out to be, to prove to be

retrete m.   rest room, washroom, toilet

revelar   to develop (film)

revisor m.   conductor

revista f.   magazine

rico   rich

rieles m. pl.   R.R. tracks

río m.   river

robar   to rob, to steal

rociar   to spray

rodilla f.   knee

rojo   red

rollo m.   roll (of film)

romper   to break

ropa f.   clothes; **. . . blanca** f.   linen; **. . . interior** f.   underwear

rosado   pink

roto   broken

rueda f.   wheel

ruido m.   noise

ruidoso   noisy

rumano   Rumanian

ruso   Russian

S

sábana f.   bedsheet

sábado m.   Saturday

saber   to know a fact, to know how

sabroso   tasty

sacacorchos m.   corkscrew

sacar   to take out, to extract

saco m.   coat

sal f.   salt

sala f.   living room, hall; . . . de equipajes f. checkroom, baggage room; . . . de espera f. waiting room

salado   salty

salchicha f.   sausage

salchichón m.   salami

sales aromáticas f. pl.   smelling salts

salida f.   exit

salir   to leave, to depart, to go out

salón   lounge; . . . de belleza m. beauty parlor; . . . (de entrada) m. lobby

salsa f.   sauce, gravy

salud f.   health; ¡a su salud! to your health!

saludo m.   greetings

saludos m. pl.   greetings, regards; muchos . . . best wishes

salvavidas m.   life preserver

sandalia f.   sandal

sandía f.   watermelon

sangre f.   blood

sanidad f.   health

santuario m.   shrine

sastre m.   tailor

sazonado   seasoned

se   self, himself, herself, itself, themselves

seco   dry; limpieza en . . . f. dry-cleaning

sed f.   thirst; tener . . . to be thirsty

seda f.   silk; papel de . . . m. tissue paper

seguir   to follow, continue; . . . la derecha (izquierda) keep right (left)

segundo   second

seguro   sure, insurance; . . . de viaje m. travel insurance

seis   six

sellar   to seal

sello m.   postage stamp, seal

semana f.   week

semáforo de circulación m.   traffic light

sentar   to fit; to seat

sentarse   to sit down

sentir   to be sorry

sentirse   to feel (in health)

señor m.   Mr., sir, gentleman

señora f.   Mrs., lady, madam

señorita f.   Miss, young lady

séptimo   seventh

ser   to be

servicio m.   service

servilleta f.   napkin

servir   to serve

servirse (+ infinitive)   please (do something); ¡sírvase hablar más despacio! please speak more slowly!

servirse   to help, serve oneself; haga el favor de . . . please help yourself

sesenta   sixty

setenta   seventy

sexto   sixth

si   if

sí   yes

siempre   always

siete   seven

significar   to signify, to mean

silla f.   chair; . . . de cubierta f. deck chair

sillón m.   armchair

simpático   pleasant, likable

sin   without

sinagoga f.   synagogue

sitio m.   place, spot

smoking m.   tuxedo

sobre   on, upon; . . . todo above all, especially

sobrecargo m. purser

sobretodo m. overcoat

sol m. sun

solamente only, solely

solo alone, only, sole; **café . . . m.** black coffee

sombra f. shade; **a la . . .** in the shade

sombrería f. hat shop

sombrero m. hat

sortija f. ring

sostén m. bra, brassiere

su, sus his, her, its, their, your

suave mild, soft

subir to go up, to climb

suceder to happen

sucio dirty, soiled

sud m. south

sueco Swedish

suela f. sole (shoe)

suelo m. floor, ground, soil

suelto (adj.), m. loose; small change

sueño m. sleep, dream; **tener . . .** to be sleepy

suerte f. luck; **¡buena . . . !** good luck

suizo Swiss

sujeto a derechos de aduana dutiable

supuesto supposed; **por supuesto** of course, naturally

sur m. south

suyo his, hers, yours, theirs, one's, its

T

taberna f. tavern, saloon

tacones de goma m. pl. rubber heels

tafetán adhesivo m. adhesive tape, bandage

talón m. baggage check, heel of foot

tal vez perhaps, maybe

talle m. waist

tamaño m. size

también also, too

tapa f. lift (of shoe)

taquilla f. theater box office, ticket office

tarde late; **la . . .** afternoon; **¡Buenas tardes!** Good afternoon!

tarifa f. fare, rate; **. . . nocturna f.** night rate; **. . . por hora f.** hourly rate

tarjeta postal f. postcard

taza f. cup

té m. tea

techo m. roof, ceiling

tela f. cloth

telefonista m., f. telephone operator

temporalmente temporarily

temprano early

tenazas f. pl. pliers

tenedor m. fork

tener to have, to possess; **. . . noticias de** to hear from; **. . . prisa** to be in a hurry; **. . . que** to have to

teñir to tint

tercero third

terciopelo m. velvet

ternera f. veal

tía f. aunt

tiempo m. weather, time

tienda f. store, shop

tierra f. land, earth

tijeras f. pl. scissors

timbre m. bell

tinta f. ink

tintorería f. dry cleaners

tío m. uncle

tirantes m. pl.   suspenders
toalla f.   towel
tobillo m.   ankle
tocar   to play an instrument
tocino m.   bacon
todavía   still, yet; . . . **no**   not yet
todo   all, everything, every, each; . . . **el mundo**   everybody, everyone
todos   everybody, everyone, all
tomacorriente m.   electric outlet
tomar   to take
tontería f.   nonsense
torcedura f.   sprain
toro m.   bull
toronja f.   grapefruit
toros m. pl.   bulls, bullfight
torta f.   cake
tortilla f.   omelet, cornmeal cake
tos f.   cough
toser   to cough
tostada f.   toast
trabajar   to work
traducir   to translate
traer   to bring
traje m.   suit (of clothes); . . . **de baño** m.   bathing suit; . . . **de etiqueta** m.   evening clothes
transbordar   to transfer
transbordo   transfer (pass)
tranquilo   quiet
tranvía m.   trolley, streetcar
trece   thirteen
treinta   thirty
trepar   to climb
tres   three; . . . **veces**   three times
tronar   to thunder
trueno m.   thunder
tuerca f.   nut (mechanical)
turco   Turkish
turismo m.   tourism

U

un, una   a, an, one; **una vez**   once
uno   one, someone, people
uña f.   nail (finger or toe)
usar   to use
uso m.   use (purpose)
usted (Ud., Vd.)   you
ustedes (Uds., Vds.)   you (pl.)
uvas f. pl.   grapes

V

vacío   empty
valer   to be worth
válido   valid, good for
variedades f. pl.   vaudeville
varios   several
vaso m.   drinking glass
¡váyase!   scram! go away!
veinte   twenty
velocidad máxima f.   speed limit
venda f.   bandage
vendar   to bandage
vender   to sell
veneno m.   poison
venir   to come
venta f.   sale
ventana f.   window
ventanilla f.   train, ticket window; . . . **de los certificados** f.   registry window
ventilador m.   fan (car or electric)
ver   to see
verano m.   summer
verdad f.   truth
verdaderamente   really, truly
verdadero   true
verde   green

verduras f. pl.   green vegetables
vestido m.   dress
vestirse   to get dressed
vez f.   time (occasion); **una . . .** once; **en . . . de**   instead of, in place of
viajar   to travel
viaje m.   voyage, trip, journey; **¡buen viaje!**   bon voyage! have a pleasant trip!
viajero m.   traveler
vida f.   life
vidrio m.   glass (material)
viejo   old
viento m.   wind; **hace (hay) . . .** it's windy
viernes m.   Friday
vino m.   wine
vista f.   view
vitrina f.   showcase
vivir   to live
volante m.   steering wheel

volver   to return, turn
vuelo m.   flight
vuelta f.   turn

Y

y   and
ya   already
yo   I
yodo m.   iodine
yugoeslavo   Yugoslav

Z

zanahoria f.   carrot
zapatería f.   shoe shop, store
zapatillas f. pl.   slippers
zapato m.   shoe
zarpar   to sail
zarzuela f.   musical comedy
zumo m.   juice

INDEX

READY REFERENCE KEY

Here are some phrases and words from the book that you are likely to use most often. For a more extensive list of phrases, refer to the appropriate chapter within the book.

SIMPLE WORDS AND PHRASES

Do you speak English?	**¿Habla usted inglés?** *ah-blah oos-TEHD een-GLAYS*
Do you understand?	**¿Comprende usted?** *kohm-PREHN-day oos-TEHD*
I don't speak Spanish.	**No hablo español.** *noh AH-bloh ehs-pah-NYOHL*
I don't understand.	**No comprendo.** *noh kohm-PREHN-doh*
Please speak slowly.	**Hable despacio, por favor.** *HA-blay dehs-PAH-see-oh pohr fah-BOHR*
Please repeat.	**Repita, por favor.** *ray-PEE-TAH pohr fah-BOHR*

BEING POLITE

Please.	**Por favor.** *pohr fah-BOHR*
Thank you very much.	**Muchas gracias.** *MOO-chahs GRAH-see-ahs*
Excuse me.	**Perdón.** *pehr-DOHN* or **con permiso** *kohn pehr-MEE-soh*
Good morning.	**Buenos días.** *bway-nohs DEE-ahs*
Good afternoon.	**Buenas tardes.** *bway-nahs TAHR-dehs*
Good evening.	**Buenas noches.** *bway-nahs NOH-chehs*

NEEDS AND WANTS

I need ____.	**Necesito ____.** *neh-seh-SEE-toh*
We need ____.	**Necesitamos ____.** *neh-seh-see-TAH-mohs*

I wish to ____.	**Quiero** ____. *kee-YEHR-oh*
I want ____.	**Quiero** ____. *kee-YEHR-oh*
I'm looking for ____.	**Busco** ____. *BOOS-koh*
We'd both like ____.	**Quisieramos** ____. *kee-SYEHR-ah-mohs*
Please bring me ____.	**Traigame, por favor** ____. *TRAH-ee-gah-may pohr fah-BOHR*
Please send up ____.	**Haga el favor de mandarnos** ____. *HA-gah ehl fah-BOHR day mahn-DAHR-nohs*

TIMES

What time is it?	**¿Qué hora es?** *kay OH-rah ehs*
What day is today?	**¿Qué día es hoy?** *kay DEE-ah ehs oy*
It's noon.	**Es mediodia.** *ehs meh-dee-oh-DEE-ah*
It's 3:00, etc.	**Son las tres,** etc. *sohn lahs trehs*
A.M.	**de la mañana** *day lah man-YAH-nah*
P.M.	**de la tarde** *day lah TAHR-day* or **de la noche** *day lah NOH-chay*

Today is ____.	**Hoy es** ____.	*oy ehs*
yesterday	**ayer**	*ah-YEHR*
tomorrow	**mañana**	*mahn-YAH-nah*
day after tomorrow	**pasado mañana**	*pah-SAH-doh mahn-YAH-nah*
tonight	**esta noche**	*EHS-tah noh-chay*
last night	**anoche**	*ahn-OH-chay*
this week	**esta semana**	*EHS-tah seh-MAH-nah*
last week	**la semana pasada**	*lah seh-MAH-nah pah-SAH-dah*

next week	**la semana próxima**	*lah seh-MAH-nah PROHK-see-mah*
it's early	**es temprano**	*ehs temp-RAH-noh*
it's late	**es tarde**	*ehs TAHR-day*

COMPARATIVES/ADJECTIVES

good/better	**bueno/mejor**	*bweh-noh/may-HOHR*
small/smaller	**pequeño/ más pequeño**	*peh-KAYN-yoh/ mahs peh-KAYN-yoh*
large/larger	**grande/ más grande**	*GRAHN-day/ mahs GRAHN-day*
short	**corto**	*KOHR-toh*
long	**largo**	*LAHR-goh*
fast	**rápido**	*RAH-pee-doh*
slow	**despacio**	*dehs-PAH-see-oh*
cheap	**barato**	*bah-RAH-toh*
expensive	**costoso**	*koh-STOH-soh*
easy	**fácil**	*FAH-seel*
difficult	**difícil**	*dee-FEE-seel*
more	**más**	*mahs*
less	**menos**	*may-nohs*
too much	**demasiado**	*day-mahs-ee-AH-doh*
enough	**bastante**	*bahs-TAHN-tay*

DIRECTIONS

I'm lost.	**Me he perdido.**	*may heh pehr-DEE-doh*
We're lost.	**Nos hemos perdido.**	*nohs HEH-mohs pehr-DEE-doh*
I am looking for ＿＿＿.	**Busco ＿＿＿.**	*BOOS-koh*

Where is ____?	¿Dónde está ____?	*DOHN-day eh-STAH*
to the left	**a la izquierda**	*ah lah ess-kee-EHR-dah*
to the right	**a la derecha**	*ah lah dehr-EH-chah*
straight ahead	**derecho**	*deh-REH-choh*
How far away is ____?	¿A qué distancia está ____?	*ah kay dees-TAHN-see-ah esh-tah*
Can you show it to me on the map?	¿Puede indicármelo en el mapa?	*PWEH-day een-dee-KAHR-may-loh ehn ehl MAH-pah*

SHOPPING

bakery	**panadería**
bookstore	**librería**
butcher shop	**carnicería**
candy store	**confitería**
cheese store	**quesería**
clothing store	**ropería**
dairy	**lechería**
department store	**el bazar** (Spain), **el almacén** (Latin America)
furniture store	**mueblería**
greengrocer	**verdulería**
grocery (Carib.) wine store (Sp.)	**bodega**
hardware store	**ferretería**
jewelry store	**joyería**
market	**mercado**
shoe store	**zapatería**
supermarket	**supermercado**

barber	**barbería, peluquería**
beauty salon	**salón de belleza**
couturier	**costurería**
dry cleaner	**tintorería**
laundry, cleaner	**lavandería (en seco)**
tailor	**sastrería**
watchmaker	**relojería**

SOME COMMON SIGNS

Abajo/Arriba	Down/Up
Abierto/Cerrado	Open/Closed
Caballeros/Señoras (Damas)	Men's Room/Ladies Room
Caliente (C)/Frío (F)	Hot/Cold
Entrada/Salida	Entrance/Exit
Empuje/Tire	Push/Pull
Libre/Ocupado	Vacant/Occupied
Alto	Stop
Ascensor	Elevator (Lift)
Caja	Cashier
No Tocar	Don't Touch
¡Pase!	Walk
Peligro	Danger
Prohibido el Paso	No Entrance
Prohibido Fumar	No Smoking
Servicios	Toilets
Venta	Sale